A Nature Guide To Northwest North Carolina

Stewart Skeate

2005

Parkway Publishers, Inc.
Boone, North Carolina

Available from:
Parkway Publishers, Inc.
P. O. Box 3678
Boone, North Carolina 28607
Telephone/Facsimile: (828) 265-3993

www.parkwaypublishers.com

Library of Congress Cataloging in Publication Data

Skeate, Stewart T., 1952-
A nature guide to northwest North Carolina / by Stewart Skeate.
p. cm.
Includes bibliographical references and index.
ISBN 1-887905-96-0
1. Natural history—North Carolina—Guidebooks. 2. North Carolina—Guidebooks. I.
Title.

QH105.N8S59 2004
578'.09756'8—dc22
2004012052

Editing, Layout and Book Design: Julie Shissler
Cover and Graphic Design: Aaron Burleson

Table of Contents

FOREWORD
page *vii*

INTRODUCTION
Page 1

GEOLOGY
Page 5

CLIMATE and WEATHER
Page 11

SEASONALITY
Page 14

ECOLOGICAL COMMUNITIES
Page 20

NORTHERN HARDWOOD AND COVE FORESTS
Page 21

MIXED OAK FOREST
Page 36

DRY RIDGE FOREST
Page 42

PIONEER FOREST
Page 46

SPRUCE-FIR FOREST
Page 48

HEATH
Page 52

ROCKY OUTCROPS
Page 55

MOUNTAIN BOGS
Page 60

GRASSY BALDS
Page 109

OLD FIELD
Page 112

BIRDS
Page 120

MAMMALS
Page 134

REPTILES
Page 145

AMPHIBIANS
Page 150

FISHES
Page 158

LOCALES
Page 163

EPILOGUE
Page 183

SUGGESTED FIELD GUIDES AND REFERENCES
Page 185

ACKNOWLEDGEMENTS

This project was but a dormant seed until a conversation with Rao Aluri, Miles Tager, and John Higby provided the necessary stimulus for its germination and growth. I thank Rao Aluri of Parkway Publishers for his encouragement in the development of this book. Many thanks to editor Julie Shissler, as we have worked on draft after draft.

It was a pleasure to work with technical wizard Aaron Burleson, and I appreciate his patience with the book's finicky photographer (me). Chris Larson, our talented Lees-McRae College alumnus, is responsible for the maps.

Gene Spears, Loren Raymond, Curtis Smalling, and John Higby reviewed a number of the chapters, and their suggestions and corrections greatly improved the text.

Nonetheless, I take full credit for any mistakes that may be present. Finally, I thank Grandfather Mountain, Inc. and the North Carolina Nature Conservancy for their friendly cooperation over the years in allowing me access to their holdings.

this book is dedicated to

Bayard Brattstrom,
who introduced me to the world of natural history,

and to my naturalist students,
who are discovering this world today.

FOREWORD

During my travels I have learned to depend on regional guides. Either before or upon arriving at my destination, I try to find a book that describes the natural history of the area that I am visiting. Books that describe the different habitats found in an area and what plants and animals are likely to be found are especially useful. This is what I have tried to produce in this book, a general guide to the natural communities, plants, and animals of northwestern North Carolina.

When I arrived in northwest North Carolina in 1985 to teach biology at Lees-McRae College in Avery County, it was a wonder to live in one of the greatest ecosystems, the Southern Appalachians, in the world. I found myself surrounded by thousands of acres of natural areas, waiting exploration. I also found that I was woefully ignorant of what surrounded me. Slowly, year by year I have worked to try to understand the incredible diversity and complex communities of our area. I am still learning. I have learned from colleagues, students, numerous field guides, and from just getting out in the mountains and poking around. I was especially fortunate to find as a home an old farm in western Watauga County. Nature is no farther than our back porch and is often inside our house as well. Many of my most rewarding nature observations have come in my "backyard". I have also been fortunate to have a job that results in many hours outdoors with eager young naturalists with curious minds and sharp eyes. Indeed these students have taught their teacher a great deal.

The purpose of this book is not to replace the many fine field guides that are available for plant and animal identification. Instead it is my hope that this book will supplement these guides and may be used to get a better understanding of this region for those looking to gain more information about the natural history of our area. While most field guides focus on identification of particular plant or animal groups, I have instead tried to give an overall description of the different local communities and the plants and animals one may encounter in their journeys through these different habitats. I have limited the animals to the vertebrates, including fish, amphibians, reptiles, birds, and mammals. This should not be interpreted that invertebrates and especially insects are any less important or interesting, but as there are so many of them, doing justice to this group would expand this book considerably.

References to particular locations will be made throughout the guide so that the reader may visit these places and hopefully this guide will improve their understanding of the communities in these locales. I have also included a list of specific locales with short descriptions that may be useful. Many of these locales are easily accessible from a parking area, while others may involve enjoyable day-hikes or overnight trips. I have also listed a number of reference books and field guides that I have found useful for our region. For each book I have included a general description and its strengths.

Nature for many people is something to be enjoyed and treasured. By understanding more about our natural surroundings, our interest and curiosity only increases. Familiarity with nature can only add to the enjoyment of spending time outdoors. Hopefully this guide will add to your understanding of the natural history of this special area and thus increase your appreciation of the wonders of the Southern Appalachians.

"Label each notable tree, not with pieces of tin or wood nailed to the bark, but with pieces of thought and understanding nailed to your mind."

Aldo Leopold

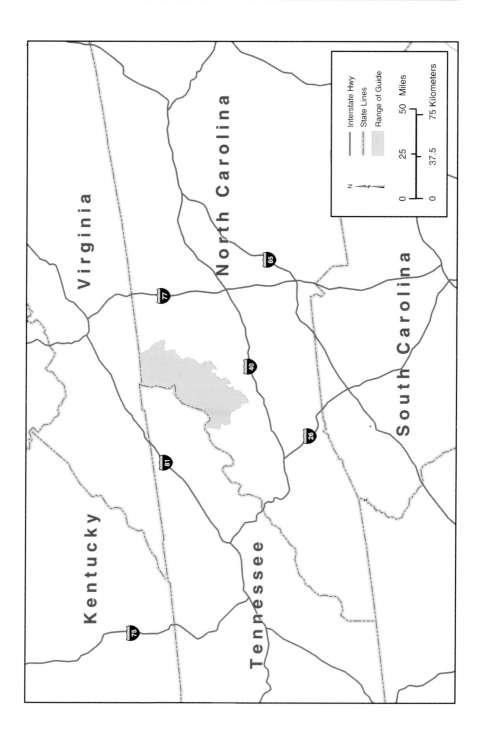

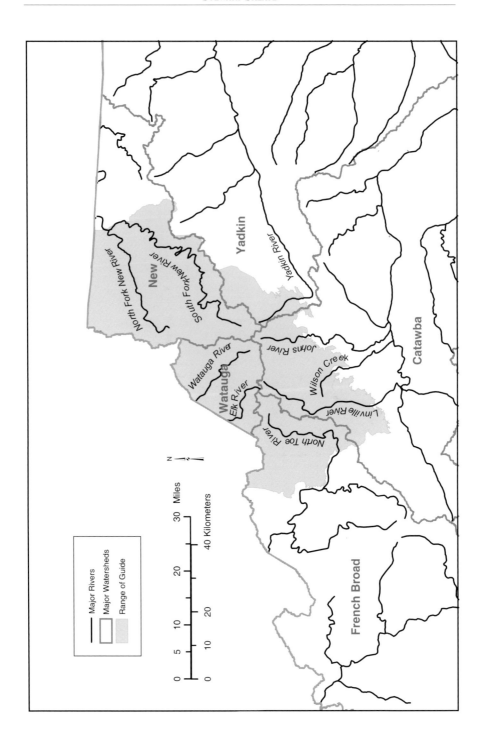

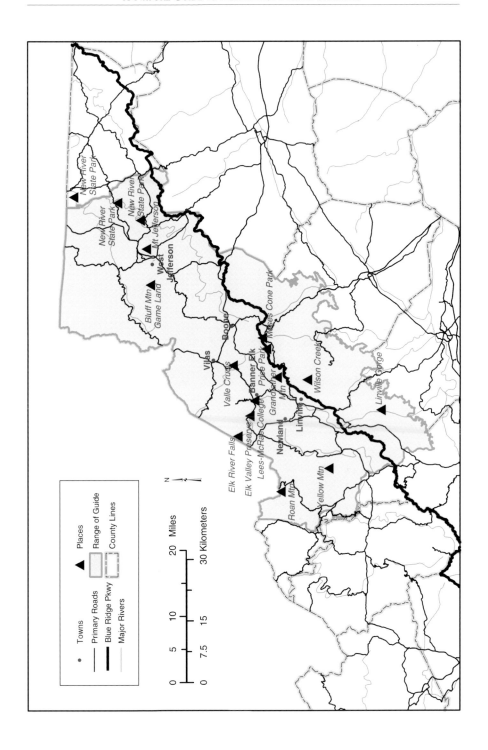

New River State Park

New River State Park

New River State Park

Mt Jefferson

West Jefferson

Bluff Mtn Game Land

Boone

Moses Cone Park

Vilas

Valle Crucis

Banner Elk

Price Park

Grandfather Mtn

Wilson Creek

Linville Gorge

Elk River Falls

Elk Valley Preserve

Lees-McRae College

Newland

Linville

Yellow Mtn

Roan Mtn

N

Towns
Primary Roads
Blue Ridge Pkwy
Major Rivers

Places
Range of Guide
County Lines

Miles
0   5   10   20
0 7.5 15   30 Kilometers

INTRODUCTION

As one drives on the Blue Ridge Parkway during summer in northwestern North Carolina the surrounding forest appears as waves in a sea of green. This vast forest is part of the great Eastern Deciduous Forest of eastern North America that stretches from Canada to northern Florida. However if you get out of your car and hike along different trails it soon becomes apparent that the forest differs from place to place. In one area, Yellow Birch may be a common tree while in another area Chestnut Oak is common, but Yellow Birch is absent. One area may have dense thickets of rhododendron, while another area may have an open understory with the forest floor covered with herbaceous plants. These changes in forest type may be abrupt, occurring over short distances as topography or elevation changes. With time you begin to recognize distinct communities, each with its own characteristic trees, shrubs, herbs, and animals.

Changes in altitude, topography, and orientation produce different physical and climatic conditions that are responsible for this fascinating variety of communities. Cool sheltered coves, dry south-facing slopes, and fog-covered high elevation ridgelines each have distinctive conditions that result in different communities. These communities host an astonishing diversity of plants, making the Southern Appalachians one of the most species rich regions in North America. This great diversity is due to a number of factors, including a moderate climate, substantial rainfall, diverse topography, range of altitude, rich and diverse soils, and geographic location.

Historical factors have been especially important, as it is likely that the ancient Southern Appalachians have been forested for over 100 million years. Many plants in our forests have relatives in such distant locales as Asia and Europe, indicating physical connections in the ancient past. The combination of diverse topography and changing climate over long time periods is highly conducive to the formation of new species as populations become isolated from one another and develop new traits.

The absence of glaciers during the last glacial period that ended about 12,000 years ago has also contributed to the overall diversity of the region. It is believed that during this last glacial period the Southern Appalachians served as a "refugium" for many northern species. While it is possible that the higher peaks may have been covered in ice, the lower valleys were ice-free and vegetated. Northern species, including hardwoods and conifers, moved south from the glaciated north and became a part of these southern forest communities. At the end of this glaciation, as the forests moved north again, many of these northern species remained in our area, as evidenced by the high-elevation Spruce-Fir community. At the same time southern species spread through the area resulting in the combination of northern and southern species that we see today.

It is important to understand that the forests and communities that we see today are different in many ways from those of pre-colonization days. Most of the "virgin" or old growth forest that once covered this area is gone, as much of the area was logged in the late 1800's and early 1900's. Thus most of our forests are second growth or secondary forest. Some areas escaped the axe, including tracts of the Linville Gorge and small fragments elsewhere. Forests have also been cleared for farmland, creating a mosaic of field and forest that make up our rural areas. Introduced plant and animal species have also become part of many communities, especially disturbed and man-made communities such as fields and ponds.

Thus the communities in our area are truly dynamic, changing in many ways, whether it is a pioneer forest moving into a climax state or a fallow field that is being invaded by shrubs and trees. Ecological succession is an ongoing process and plays an important part in the diversity and structure of many of our communities.

The Southern Appalachians typically refers to the part of the Appalachian range from West Virginia south to northern Georgia. As would be expected in so large an area, there are many floral differences between the northern and southern parts of the Southern Appalachians. This also holds true for many species of animals, especially among the salamanders, many of which have small, restricted distributions.

Northwestern North Carolina

The geographical focus of this guide is Avery, Watauga, and Ashe Counties and parts of northeastern Mitchell, northeastern McDowell, northwestern Caldwell, and northwestern Burke Counties. For the most part this region is highly mountainous, Avery County having the highest slope of any county in the state. This area is rich in natural areas and it is not surprising that the region is extremely popular for ecotourism. The Blue Ridge Mountains dominate the area, attaining their greatest elevations in this region with Grandfather Mountain rising to 5,964 feet, the tallest peak in the Blue Ridge. The stretch of the Blue Ridge Parkway through our area is especially scenic and diverse, offering excellent opportunities for nature study. Thousands of acres of the Pisgah National Forest are found in this area, including the Linville Gorge Wilderness Area and the Wilson Creek area. This area also boasts the impressive Roan Mountain massif. Roan Mountain at 6,286 feet, is the highest peak of the Unaka Mountains, and is home to the unique high elevation Grassy Balds and Spruce-Fir Forest communities.

This region contains thousands of streams and creeks that form the headwaters of a number of large river basins. River basins are large drainage systems whose shapes are determined by geographical and geological features. As creeks descend down mountainsides they empty into rivers that continue downhill through valleys. These winding rivers wriggle like snakes out of our mountains in almost every direction. The North Toe River in Avery County and Mitchell County forms the northeast beginning of the French Broad River Basin. The Linville River of Avery County and Burke County forms the beginning of the Catawba River Basin. The headwaters of the Yadkin River in Caldwell County and Watauga County form the beginning of the Yadkin–Peedee River Basin. The New River in Watauga County and Ashe County begins the New River Basin. The Watauga River and the Elk River in Avery County and Watauga County begin the Watauga River Basin. The Catawba and Yadkin-Peedee River Basins run eastward to the Atlantic Ocean, while the French Broad, New, and Watauga River Basins run west towards the Mississippi and the Gulf of Mexico.

The eastward and westward water movements originate along the Eastern Continental Divide. In northwestern North Carolina the Continental Divide runs through the Blue Ridge Mountains, including the ridgeline of Grandfather Mountain. The Continental Divide separates the eastern and western watersheds and rivers, where waters on the eastern side run to the

Atlantic, while waters on the western slopes run to the Mississippi and the Gulf of Mexico.

Nature, of course, does not pay heed to man-made geographical boundaries, and the natural areas just across the North Carolina line in Tennessee are equally spectacular. Although this guide focuses on locales in northwestern North Carolina, many of the same ecological communities, plants, and animals are also found in northeastern Tennessee.

GEOLOGY

The geological history of the Southern Appalachians is a long and complex one. This is not surprising as the formation of these mountains involved a series of orogenic (mountain building) events beginning in the Precambrian Era over 1200 million years ago and continuing into the late Paleozoic Era 300 million years ago. Geographers and geologists divide the Appalachians into areas called "provinces". Geographers base their "physiographic" provinces on topography, whereas geologists use the ages and types of rocks to determine "geological" provinces. The provinces trend northeast to southwest and trend parallel to one another.

The physiographic Southern Appalachian Mountains are made up of the Ridge and Valley Province on the west; the Blue Ridge Province in the middle, bordering the Piedmont Province to the east. The Blue Ridge Province extends from southern Pennsylvania to northern Georgia, a distance of some 550 miles. In central Virginia, the Blue Ridge Province is narrow; however, as it reaches North Carolina and Eastern Tennessee, it broadens to some 60 miles across and contains the highest mountains of the entire Appalachian chain. In our area, the Unaka Mountains along the North Carolina and Tennessee line form the high northwestern margin of the Blue Ridge Province, whereas the Blue Ridge Mountains form the eastern margin.

The formation of the Blue Ridge Province reached its culmination during the Alleghanian Orogeny, during the late Carboniferous and Permian periods about 325 to 250 million years ago. At this time Africa collided with southeastern North America, producing the huge set of thrust sheets extending from Alabama-Tennessee-southwestern Virginia on the west to the Pine

Mountain-Charlotte-High Point areas on the east. These thrust sheets were pushed westward over older "basement" rocks. In places, thrust sheet domes were formed where underlying rock folded as the thrust sheets moved across. It was these tectonic movements that created the wrinkled and folded appearance of our mountains, thus producing the distinctive series of ridges and valleys. The Southern Appalachian Mountains of the early Mesozoic Era were a more extensive and higher-elevation mountain chain than what we see today. With the cessation of mountain building about 280 million years ago, however, the erosion process has slowly worn the mountains down. The rocks of the Appalachians were transformed by weathering and erosion into sediment that moved into streams, rivers, and onto the Coastal Plain, with some eventually deposited in the Gulf of Mexico and the Atlantic Ocean. These sediments have helped form the coastal plains of the Carolinas, Georgia, and the Gulf Coast. Eventually the Southern Appalachians will wear slowly away to a piedmont-like topography, so this is an especially good time to visit them.

The powers of erosion are great in this area, as high rainfall, freezing temperatures, and steep slopes are highly conducive to physical erosion. Rocks are also susceptible to chemical weathering, as water combines with chemicals in the atmosphere and in the soil to produce a weak acid that dissolves rocks. Certain rock types such as gneiss react to these acids more than other types, such as metaquartz arenite, and are broken down faster. In some places erosion has exposed a "window" of younger rocks beneath the thrust sheets. During mountain formation, large sheets of rock slid over adjacent sheets. Thus, younger rocks were trapped below the older, lower layers of the covering sheet. Millions of years of erosion eventually wore away these upper layers, exposing these younger rocks in "windows" into the lower rock layers. One of the best known of these windows is the Grandfather Mountain Window, where younger, but still Precambrian rock, can be seen below the older overthrust rocks of the Blue Ridge Belt.

Rock types

The rocks of the Southern Appalachians fall into three basic rock groups based on how they are formed. Igneous rocks are formed from molten rock. Below the earth's surface this molten rock material is called magma, while on the surface it is called lava. Common igneous rocks include basalt and granite. Basalt, a black or gray rock, is typically formed from lava flows and is widespread and abundant. Granite, characterized by a granular texture and a light color, has feldspar and quartz as its two most abundant minerals.

Sedimentary rocks are formed by the accumulation and cementation of fragments of rocks and minerals. Sedimentary rocks tend to be distinctly layered, and the rocks are divided into individual strata or beds. Sedimentary rocks include conglomerate, sandstone, siltstone, limestone, dolostone, and mudstone. Conglomerate, sandstone, and siltstone are formed from cemented gravel, sand, and mud, respectively. It is in sedimentary rock that fossils are most commonly deposited and found. However, as most of the sedimentary rock in the Blue Ridge and Piedmont of the Southern Appalachians was deposited as sediment prior to the explosion of multicellular life around 560 million years ago, fossils are rare in our area.

Metamorphic rocks are sedimentary or igneous rocks that have undergone changes in composition and texture due to heat, pressure, or some chemical effect. Common metamorphic rocks include gneiss, metasandstone, amphibolite, schist, and phyllite. Gneiss is one of the most plentiful of the metamorphic rocks. It is typically coarse-grained with a variety of minerals, including feldspar, quartz, and mica. It is formed from many different rocks including granite, shale, rhyolite, and slate. Some of the oldest rocks in the Blue Ridge are gneisses that date to some 1,800 to 1,000 million years old. A formation of gneiss in this area is the Cranberry Gneiss, a rock unit characterized by light and dark gray to light-pink layers that locally contain layers of epidote-biotite schist and intruded and metamorphosed amphibolitic metagabbro. Examples of Cranberry Gneiss may be seen along the Appalachian Trail near its crossing of Highway 19E.

Metaquartz arenite, a type of metasandstone, is formed by the metamorphism of quartz sandstone, amphibolite by the metamorphism of basalt or gabbro, and rarely siliceous dolomite, schist by the metamorphism of shale and rhyolite, and phyllite by a lesser degree of metamorphism of shale. Metamorphic rocks such as gneiss, schists, and amphibolites have also been important in soil formation. In the Southern Appalachians, igneous and metamorphic rocks are the most common rocks, as most of the sedimentary rocks have been metamorphosed over the long periods of time during the geological events that have occurred.

Of the many minerals that are found in our local rocks, quartz is possibly the most noticeable and outstanding. Quartz or silicon dioxide forms crystals of relatively high hardness. It is usually white in color, but can be found in various shades ranging from almost clear to pink. It is not uncommon to find veins of quartz running through other rocks, and large masses of quartz in place such as on the northwest slope of Grandfather Mountain have been mined. Quartz is also an important rock-forming mineral and is found in many rocks, including sandstone, granite, metaquartz arenite, amphibolite, schist, and gneiss.

Grandfather Mountain, the highest peak in the Blue Ridge Mountain chain, is composed predominately of metasandstone and metaconglomerate that have resisted erosion. Metaquartz arenite, the most common type of metasandstone on Grandfather, is a very hard rock, formed by the metamorphism of quartz sandstone. Metaquartz arenite may be fine-grained or almost granular. Minerals include quartz, feldspar, and muscovite mica. Occasionally unweathered metaquartz arenite is colorful due to the pink feldspar or green muscovite mica minerals in the rock. Exposed metaquartz arenite may be seen in Banner Elk at the intersection of NC 184 and Hickory Nut Gap Road, CR 1342.

In addition to metaquartz arenite, phyllite, marble, metarhyolite, metabasalt, and metaconglomerate are found in the Grandfather Mountain Formation. Phyllite is a fine-grained, blue-gray rock that is often folded, whereas metabasalt is metamorphosed basaltic lava rock. The basalt originally occurred as volcanic flows. Highly folded phyllite may also be seen on NC 184, 0.6 miles north from the intersection with NC 105. Metabasalt outcrops are found on NC 184 south of Hickory Nut Gap Road, just past the old hospital. Metabasalt may also be seen exposed on the road cuts on NC 105 at the northeast end of the Watauga River Bridge 4.7 miles from Boone.

A particularly striking rock is metaconglomerate, a mix of pebbles of quartz, feldspar, phyllite, granite, and sandstone that has been metamorphosed. Metaconglomerate rocks were formed when flooding streams carried rocks, sand, and boulders down the steep slopes to form gravel deposits. Eventually these deposits consolidated into rock and were later metamorphosed. An especially impressive mass of metaconglomerate may be found near the top of the Profile Trail on Grandfather Mountain. Metaconglomerate is also common along the Elk River behind the Lees-McRae College Campus.

Metaquartz arenite is prevalent in the peaks of Linville Gorge. This resistant rock forms the rocky outcrops and steep cliffs of mountains such as Table Rock and Hawksbill, while the rocks at the bottom of the gorge are granitic gneisses. Granitic gneiss and metaquartz can also be seen at the Linville Falls. The upper falls runs over granitic gneiss, while the lower falls runs over metaquartz arenite. This is an example of the edge of the Grandfather Mountain Window, where the upper rocks of gneiss lie directly over the younger metaquartz arenite rocks. A thrust fault separates the granitic gneiss from the metaquartz arenite. This fault occurs at the base of the upper falls on the west side of the river 100 yards upstream from the upper falls overlook. The Linville River above the falls is considered in maturity due to the presence of a flood plain and gently rolling valley walls. Below the falls, the river with steep valley walls reflects a stream in a youthful stage of erosion.

Amphibolite is a common rock in Watauga and Ashe Counties and makes up the mountains that form the chain that includes Rich Mountain, Snake Mountain, Elk Knob, Three-Top Mountain, and Mount Jefferson. Amphibolite is a metamorphic rock that contains hornblende, feldspar, and in some cases, quartz. Common accessory minerals include garnet and epidote. Amphibolite may be seen on many of the road cuts on Meat Camp Road off of NC 194 in Watauga County, including the cuts at Liberty Baptist Church and at Proffits Grove Missionary Baptist Church.

Blue Ridge Escarpment

The physiographic border of the Blue Ridge Province and its neighbor to the east, the Piedmont Province is the sloping Blue Ridge Escarpment. The Blue Ridge Parkway closely follows the top of the escarpment, separating the two provinces from Alleghany County to Yancey County. Driving on NC 181 from Morganton to Jonas Ridge, one will pass from the Piedmont into the Blue Ridge, with an elevation rise from 1200 feet to 4000 feet. This is also the case as one drives west up NC 321 from Lenoir into Boone or west on NC 421 from Wilkesboro into Boone. The town of Blowing Rock is located on the edge of the Blue Ridge Escarpment. The town is named after a large rocky outcrop of Blowing Rock gneiss. This type of gneiss contains large white feldspar crystals in a matrix of mica.

The large difference in average elevations between the Blue Ridge and Piedmont sides of the escarpment is surprising, as the rocks on both sides are mostly of the same type. The sharp drop-off has likely been created by rapid erosion by east flowing streams on the southeast side of the Blue Ridge Mountains. An excellent overall view of Blue Ridge may be obtained from the top of Grandfather Mountain. Looking to the north and west, the Blue Ridge Mountains appear, including Hanging Rock, Beech Mountain, Big Yellow Mountain, and Hump Mountain. To the southwest is Linville Gorge, including Hawksbill and Table Rock. To the south and east, the Blue Ridge Escarpment drops some 4,000 feet to the Piedmont Province.

CLIMATE and WEATHER

The cool and wet climate of the Southern Appalachians has played an important role in determining what plants and thus ecological communities occur in our area. These conditions allow many northern species to thrive at our lower latitudes, while southern species are often limited to the lower elevations. Latitude, elevation, and topography combine to produce the weather and climate of an area. Thus while at the same latitude of 36° as Duck on the Outer Banks and Burlington in the Piedmont, the mountain village of Banner Elk shows a dramatically different climate due to the influence of elevation and topography.

Summers are generally mild in the high country, while winters may be cold and harsh. With each 1,000 feet rise in elevation, mean temperatures drop some 3.5°F. January and February are typically the coldest months, while July and August are the warmest months. Banner Elk (elevation 3,750 ft) has monthly temperature averages of 30.7°F in January and 66.1°F in July with an average annual temperature of 49.5°F. Low elevation temperature ranges in summer run between 51°F and 86°F and between −7°F and 54°F in winter. High elevation temperatures on Grandfather Mountain range between 55°F and 70°F in summer and −14°F and 36°F in winter. Temperatures tend to be colder in the northern mountains of North Carolina compared to the southern mountains due to the higher latitude and the higher elevations in the valleys.

The principal sources of moisture for our area are the Gulf of Mexico and the Atlantic Ocean. As air leaves the Gulf into the interior of the continent it is deflected so that the moisture-laden winds move southwesterly by the time they reach the western edge of the Blue Ridge Mountains. Air from the Atlantic loses most of its moisture as it ascends the eastern slopes of the mountains. This combination produces high rainfall throughout much of the area. During winter the direction of the wind is predominately from the west.

Generally rainfall increases with increasing altitude. As moisture-laden air moves up a mountain it cools and condenses as rain or fog. Banner Elk at an elevation of about 3,800 feet receives about 50 inches of rain per year, while the nearby weather station at 5,280 feet on Grandfather Mountain receives about 63 inches per year. High-elevation precipitation levels are elevated by moisture from fog condensation. The ridgeline of Grandfather Mountain averages 129 fog days per year. Precipitation is highest between June and August and also January and March, with September and October being the driest months. An exception to this tendency of dry autumns occurs when hurricanes make their way to the Southern Appalachians. In September of 2004, hurricanes Frances and Ivan slammed into northwest North Carolina, causing severe flooding and resulting in a monthly record rainfall of 27.3 inches and a daily record of 11.3 inches on September 8 at Grandfather Mountain.

Snow, wind, and ice are important climatic features of the high country. It is not unusual for the first snows to appear in November and spring snows in April are also not uncommon. Grandfather Mountain averages about 57 inches of snow per year, while Banner Elk averages 47 inches. Snow levels may vary dramatically from year to year and even month to month. Watauga County received 57 inches of snow in March of 1960, a state record. Heavy snowfalls are usually the result of a combination of moist air from the Gulf of Mexico, a deep trough in the upper level jet stream, and cold air from Canada. These snowstorms often occur in the spring as in March of 1993 when three feet of snow (six feet at the higher elevations) fell over two days paralyzing the high country for a week. Snowfall amounts often vary locally with the western slopes of the mountains generally receiving more snow than the eastern slopes as most winter storms move from west to east over the mountains.

Wind speeds rise with increasing elevation. High elevations experience winds of up to 62 miles per hour for 20 to 25 days per year. Winds on high summits can reach over 125 miles per hour. A record 195.5 miles per hour wind speed was recorded on Grandfather Mountain on 18 April 1997.

Also of importance are ice storms that occur periodically. Ice storms are the result of atmospheric inversions, where below freezing temperatures at the surface lie beneath above freezing temperatures in the atmosphere, thus producing precipitation in the form of freezing rain and sleet. The branches of trees and shrubs become covered with ice, often causing breakage of limbs and tree falls. Ice storms play an important role in "opening" gaps in our forests.

Local climate differences are an important factor in the diversity of plant communities in our area. Physical characteristics such as topography and slope orientation produce pronounced variations in temperature and precipitation over short distances. Daytime heating causes the rising of air up a mountain slope, producing a "valley breeze". This process reverses at night and cold, dense air or a "mountain breeze" from the higher elevations moves down the slope to the valley bottom. Thus occurs the paradox of colder nighttime and morning temperatures occurring at the lower elevation valleys compared to the slopes. Banner Elk and the surrounding valley show this cold air drainage as evidenced by its lower temperatures and common frosts in the spring and fall.

South facing slopes, receiving more sunlight have higher evaporation levels and tend to be hotter and drier than the cooler and wetter north facing slopes. This slope effect results in the different plant communities found on south and north facing slopes respectively. It is especially evident in winter as snow on north facing slopes persists for longer periods of time. Slope effect is more pronounced at the lower elevations. Mountain ridges below 4,000 feet tend to be dry, while higher elevation ridges above 5,000 feet tend to be cool and moist. Thus the crests of the peaks of Linville Gorge support dry plant communities, while the peaks of Grandfather Mountain support moist plant communities. Sheltered coves that lie between the ridges also show cooler temperatures in winter and summer due to cold air drainage. These coves support a heavy growth of vegetation and include our most diverse communities. This is visually evident in the winter months when looking at mountains from a distance. The indented coves are a darker brown, indicating more vegetation, than the lighter, surrounding ridges.

Differences in local rainfall and moisture is further complicated by the "rain shadow" effect. As moisture laden winds move up the windward side of a mountain it cools and precipitation results. Once this dry air passes over peak or ridge, it descends and warms and dries the leeward side of the mountain.

Although long-term climate patterns are generally predictable, day-to-day weather conditions are much less so and often confound residents and tourists alike. Thus a 55°F high winter day followed by a 10°F high day is not uncommon. Year-to-year differences may also be striking. The summer of 2002 was one of severe drought, while the following summer of 2003 was one of the wettest on record. Nonetheless while people may have problems adjusting to our quirky climate and weather, our natural communities are amazingly well adapted to whatever Mother Nature throws at them.

SEASONALITY

The Southern Appalachians are well known for their changing seasons. Within each season there are also continual changes or events occurring on a predictable basis. The timing of these events such as flowering, fruiting, leafing, and dropping leaves is referred to as *phenology*. It is difficult to understand our ecological communities without witnessing first-hand these seasonal changes. These changes, which have such a profound effect on the local flora and fauna make this region one of the most interesting in the world. The physical and biotic transformation of our communities from winter to spring is truly amazing and a much welcome event for our winter weary residents. But no less remarkable are the changes occurring during the spring, summer, and fall months as plants pass through a progression of leafing, flowering, fruiting and leaf dropping. Many of these changes may not be obvious to the casual observer, but for those who seek discovery the rewards will be great.

Flowering

Many plants, especially the herbs, are not especially obvious until they flower. Suddenly a nondescript plant is transformed by the appearance of its unique flower. The beauty of these flowers attracts many people into our forests and fields and adds much to our appreciation of nature. However the timing of the visits will determine what flowers we see. There are plants in flower in the area from March to late October. An individual plant species however will typically flower only for several weeks. Thus Serviceberry (*Amelanchier arborea*), one of our earliest flowering trees, will flower for several weeks in April. Witch-

Hazel *(Hamamelis virginiana)*, meanwhile, does not begin flowering until September and will continue flowering through October. Certain species have long extended flowering periods. Ox-eye Daisy *(Chrysanthemum leucanthemum)* for instance may be found in flower from June through October.

Altitude plays an important part in determining when a plant will flower. A plant at 2,000 feet may begin flowering at least two weeks earlier than the same species at 4,000 feet. Catawba Rhododendrons *(Rhododendron catawbiense)* flower in early May along the rocky ridges of Linville Gorge at 3,500 feet but does not flower until mid June in the Heath Balds of Roan Mountain at 6,000 feet. Thus it is difficult to pinpoint the flowering period for any species unless the altitude is specified.

There are number of times during the spring, summer, and fall when peaks of flowering occur. In the forests, many species put out their flowers from mid April to early May when the forest trees have yet to leaf out or have leafed out but the canopy is still open. These plants take advantage of this sunny environment to attract insect pollinators to their flowers. This is especially true for many of the herbaceous plants, including the trilliums, irises and violets. The number of herbs in flower reaches a peak in early May and by the end of the month many forest species have finished flowering. For the wildflower enthusiast, April and May are a fine time for a walk in the woods.

A number of trees also flower early in the spring. Red Maple *(Acer rubrum)* is one of the earliest, flowering in early April at the mid-elevations. Red Maple produces many flowers, however, as their pollen is wind-dispersed the flowers are small and inconspicuous. Serviceberry *(Amelanchier arborea)* also flowers at this time, however its white flowers are quite obvious. Following Serviceberry, Fire Cherry *(Prunus pennsylvanica)* produces an abundance of fragrant white flowers in April. Fraser Magnolia *(Magnolia fraseri)*, Cucumber Magnolia *(Magnolia acuminata)*, Black Cherry *(Prunus serotina)*, Yellow Buckeye *(Aesculus flava)*, Yellow Birch *(Betula alleghaniensis)*, Striped Maple *(Acer pennsylvanicum)*, and Mountain Holly *(Ilex montana)* all flower in May.

While the number of forest plants in flower declines in late June, July, and early August, many of the mid-summer bloomers are very impressive. This is especially true for some of the shrub species. Flame Azalea *(Rhododendron calendulaceum)* and Mountain Laurel *(Kalmia latifolia)* produce their showy blooms in late May and early June and Rosebay Rhododendron *(Rhododendron maximum)* can produce spectacular flower displays in July. The mass flowering of Catawba Rhododendron *(Rhododendron catawbiense)* in mid-June on Roan

Mountain should not be missed. Large clumps of Wild Hydrangea (*Hydrangea arborescens*) produce a fragrant and attractive flowering display in June and July.

As summer progresses there is a shift of flowering plants from the forest to the more open areas. By the end of the summer, there is an abundance of species in flower in open areas, including old fields, forest edges and roadsides. Dozens of species bloom, dominated by members of the daisy family, Asteraceae (see Old Field section). This pulse of wildflowers continues through September and into October. There is also an increase of flowering species in the forests at this time. White Snakeroot (*Eupatorium rugosum*), Curtis' Goldenrod *(Solidago curtisii)* and White Wood Aster *(Aster divaricatus)* add color to the forest in the fall.

The changing face of our forests and fields during the spring, summer, and fall months due to this sequence of flowering makes every visit different and exciting, revealing new plants and beautiful flowers.

Fruiting

The end product of flowering is fruit production. The types of fruits produced by our plants vary greatly as evidenced by the explosive seed pods of the jewelweeds, the wind-dispersed winged seeds of Tuliptree (*Liriodendron tulipifera*) and Red Maple, the clinging burs of Common Burdock (*Arctium minus*), the hard nuts of Yellow Buckeye and the oaks (*Quercus spp.*) and the sweet juicy fruits of the blueberries *(Vaccinium spp.)* and blackberries (*Rubus spp.*). As plants must flower before they produce their fruit, most plants do not start producing fruits until at least June. Wild Strawberry *(Fragaria virginiana)* and Serviceberry both flower early in the spring and start producing ripe fruit early in June.

The majority of the plants take most of the summer to produce their fruits. Late summer and fall are the peak times of fruit production, especially for the fleshy, bird-dispersed fruits. It is at this time that large numbers of birds are migrating south. Sugar-rich fruits offer migrating birds an easy meal and many plants take advantage of birds to disperse their seeds at this time.

Many of these plants produce striking fruiting displays to attract birds. These include the elderberries *(Sambucus spp.)*, Mountain Ash *(Sorbus americana),* and the dogwoods *(Cornus spp.)*. Hobblebush (*Viburnum lantanoides*) produces a display of fruit with both red and black fruits, the black being ripe and the red unripe. White Baneberry (*Actea pacypoda*) produces an unusual fruit, white with a black dot, thus the name "doll's-eye". Take note that while this fruit is eaten by birds it is toxic to people. Indeed this is the case for a number of fleshy, bird-dispersed fruits, which are usually bitter to the taste.

Other bird-dispersed fruits include False Solomon's Seal (*Smilacina racemosa*), Solomon's Seal *(Polygonatum biflorum)*, Indian Cucumber Root (*Medeola virginiana*), Mountain Holly (*Ilex montana*), Fraser Magnolia (*Magnolia fraseri*), Cucumber Magnolia *(Magnolia acuminata)*, Pokeweed (*Phytolacca americana*), Blue Cohosh *(Caulophyllum thalictroides)*, Fire Cherry *(Prunus pennsylvanica)*, Bluebead Lily *(Clintonia borealis)*, Speckled Wood Lily (*Clintonia umbellulata*), Wild Sarsaparilla (*Aralia nudicaulis*), Partridge Berry (*Mitchella repens*), Possumhaw (*Viburnum nudum*), and Maple-leaf Viburnum (*Viburnum acerifolium).*

Other species, such as the blackberries and blueberries are referred to as "mammal-bird" fruits as they are sweet and fed on by both mammals (including hungry hikers) and birds.

It may be surprising that one of our most important seed dispersal agents is the ant. It is estimated that approximately 30% of the herbaceous plants in the deciduous forests of eastern North America have their seeds dispersed by ants. These include the trilliums (*Trillium spp.*), violets (*Viola spp.*), irises (*Iris spp.*), Bloodroot (*Sanguinaria canadensis*), Dutchman's Breeches (*Dicentra cucullaria*), Spring Beauty (*Claytonia spp.*), and Pale Corydalis (*Corydalis sempervirens).* The seeds of these plants typically have a nutritious attachment called an *elaisome* that attract ants. The ants take the seeds to their nests, devour the fatty elaisomes, and then discard the seeds into their garbage dumps where the seeds germinate and grow in the rich nest soil.

Leafing

In our area the forests have leaves for almost half of the year and are leafless the other half. The transformation of the forest from the brown, open forest to the closed, green forest begins in March. Many of the trees take on a red or purple tinge at this time as their leaf and flower buds begin to swell. The trees begin to put out their leaves in April at the lower elevations, but it is not until the first two weeks in May that trees at the mid-elevations are leafing out. Not all trees leaf out at the same time. Yellow Buckeye is one of the first trees to leaf out, while Black Locust (*Robinia pseudoacacia*) and the oaks leaf out last. Some trees such as Serviceberry and Red Maple flower before they leaf out. By mid-May all the trees are in leaf and deep shade returns to the forests.

Leaf color change and the subsequent leaf fall begins in early October. The timing of this event is important in that many people visit the mountains to see the brilliant fall colors. The timing of color change as well as the intensity of the color is dependent on a number of factors including the amount of rainfall, temperature, and especially the occurrence of a hard frost. A warm, dry fall often produces a subdued fall color, while a cool fall with a hard frost may produce a spectacular color display. The cold temperatures stimulate the trees to pull out the green chlorophyll pigment from their leaves, revealing red, orange, and yellow pigments that produce such vibrant colors. Under warmer, drier conditions this process occurs more gradually and the colors may not be as pronounced. Color may also vary dramatically from location to location, where open valleys that are "frost pockets" often have more colorful displays.

Fall is a stressful time for a leaf. The aging leaf must continue to photosynthesize and send its products to those tissues that survive the winter. Also the leaf must salvage as much of its nitrogen as possible as it begins to break down. At the same time, seasonal stresses such as cold temperatures and bright light make life difficult for the aging leaf. Studies suggest that leaves produce red pigments or anthocyanins at this time to help keep the leaf functioning until its end. Anthocyanins have been shown to protect leaves from light overdose, from freezing, and they may have antioxidizing powers. Leaves bathed in strong sunlight and cold temperatures tend to turn red, while shaded, protected leaves that don't develop anthocyanins turn yellow. The yellow pigments are always in the leaf and are only exposed when the green chlorophyll pigment disappears. This explains why there may be red and yellow leaves on the same tree.

The rich spectrum of fall colors is due to the variety of colors shown by the different species. Sourwood (*Oxydendron arboreum*), Northern Red Oak (*Quercus rubra*), Scarlet Oak (*Quercus coccinea*), Black Gum (*Nyssa sylvatica*), Mountain Ash *(Sorbus americana)*, Sassafras (*Sassafras albidum*), Red Maple (*Acer rubrum*), and Sugar Maple (*Acer saccharum)* all show brilliant red fall leaves, although the maples may also be orange or yellow. American Basswood (*Tilia americana*), Yellow Birch *(Betula alleghaniensis)*, Sweet Birch (*Betula lenta)*, Tuliptree *(Liriodendron tulipifera)*, Striped Maple (*Acer pennsylvanicum)*, Cucumber Magnolia (*Magonlia acuminata)*, Fire Cherry (*Prunus pennsylvanica)*,

Black Cherry *(Prunus serotina),* and Witch Hazel *(Hammelis virginiana)* show yellow fall leaves. Chestnut Oak *(Quercus montana),* American Beech *(Fagus grandifolia),* Fraser Magnolia *(Magnolia fraseri),* and White Ash *(Fraxinus americanus)* produce brown fall leaves. This combination of reds, oranges, yellows, browns, and greens produces one of nature's greatest shows.

Typically the fall colors peak at the mid-elevations around the second week of October, although this may vary by a week in either direction. By November, most trees have lost their leaves except for the few evergreen species including Eastern Hemlock *(Tsuga canadensis),* White Pine *(Pinus strobus),* and the rhododendrons. One exception among the deciduous trees is the American Beech, which often retains its curled brown leaves for several months into the fall. For the next six months the landscape transforms to an open mixed woodland of brown and gray deciduous trees and evergreens.

ECOLOGICAL COMMUNITIES

Ecological communities include all the living organisms interacting in a particular area. Communities are often defined by the dominant type of vegetation present, such as Mixed Oak Forest. They may also be labeled according to other factors such as moisture or outstanding geological features. Regardless of the name given to the community, the plants within the community form the living framework or habitat that determines what animals will be present. In this section, therefore, the focus is on the common plants of the respective communities. In later sections, the relationship of the different animals to these ecological communities will be explored.

Botanists working for the North Carolina Natural Heritage Program have described at least 15 different distinct ecological communities that occur in our area. I have used a number of their community types and have combined several into broader categories in an attempt to simplify the classification of the different types. The scientific name of each plant species is included. Many plants have several common names thus the use of scientific names may be important in locating different species in the various guides. Also as a number of species have been reclassified, I have tried to include both the new and old scientific names by adding the old name in brackets. This is done to facilitate identifying these species in field guides, where the older scientific names are generally used.

NORTHERN HARDWOOD and COVE FORESTS

The Northern Hardwood Forest is a common habitat in our area. Its name comes from the similarity of this community with forests in the Northern Appalachians. Nonetheless, the Northern Hardwood Forest of the Southern Appalachians is clearly distinct from its northern cousin, due to the different plants, animals, and history of the two regions. This community typically occurs above 4,000 feet on north facing slopes, although it may extend to lower elevations in sheltered coves and valleys. These valley forests are often referred to as Cove Forests. Aside from location, the flora and fauna of Northern Hardwood and Cove Forests are often very similar.

The cool temperatures and high rainfall of these communities result in moist conditions, highly conducive to plant growth. It is in these lush forests that plant diversity is at its highest. The presence of streams at the bottom of most coves adds greatly to overall diversity as well. As these forests are considered "climax" forests (the final stage of community succession), they may contain trees well over one hundred years in age. As large trees die or are blown over by strong winds, gaps occur in the forest, allowing forest regeneration and colonization of new species. These gaps play a vital role in the diversity and ecology of these forest communities.

Northern Hardwood and Cove Forests show a highly "layered" structure. The top layer of vegetation is the canopy consisting of the tallest trees in the community. The next layer is the subcanopy, consisting of shorter trees or trees that have not yet reached the canopy. The shrub layer follows and then the herbaceous layer. Finally the ground layer typically consists of ground-hugging species like mosses and liverworts.

Trees

Yellow Birch *(Betula alleghaniensis)* with its distinctive yellowish papery bark is a common member of this community, especially above 3,000 feet. Along shaded streams it is often the dominant tree and is usually the last deciduous tree found at elevations over 5,000 feet. This tree with its wintergreen scented twigs may attain great size and girth. An old, gnarly Yellow Birch is an impressive sight. Yellow Birch can be found as low as 2,000 feet along creeks such as Lost Cove Creek in the Pisgah National Forest, but conditions need to be cool and wet for them to appear at these lower elevations.

The other common Birch is Sweet Birch *(Betula lenta)* also known as Black Birch or "Mahogany" by the early settlers. Its reddish brown bark does not peel and its twigs have a strong wintergreen smell. Sweet Birch is widespread in our forests and often inhabits drier habitats than the Yellow Birch.

American Beech *(Fagus grandifolia)* also prefers these cooler forests. At elevations over 4,000 feet Beech may become very common and on certain mountains such as Yellow Mountain they form a dense, dwarf beech forest. An interesting plant associated with American Beech is Beech Drops *(Epifagus virginiana)*. This small herb is parasitic on the roots of the beech. It has branching, grayish-purple stems with scale-like leaves without chlorophyll. Its small lobed flowers are found along the stems. Another parasitic plant, One-flowered Cancer Root *(Orobanche uniflora)*, like its relative Beech Drops, is only evident when flowering in spring, producing several slender flower stalks with tubular white flowers.

Yellow Buckeye *(Aesculus flava [octandra])* is typically the first tree to leaf out in the spring and drop its leaves in the fall. This tree with its distinctive large capsules containing several large brown seeds may also attain great size. The Tanawha Trail on the Blue Ridge Parkway between Ship Rock and Wilson Creek has some impressive specimens.

Four species of Maples are found in these forests, however, only two, Sugar Maple *(Acer saccharum)* and Red Maple *(Acer rubrum)* achieve a large size. Sugar Maple has an Appalachian distribution, extending up the mountain chain into Canada, forming the "sugar bush" of the north woods. Sugar Maple never attains this type of dominance in our woods, however in certain places, especially at the higher elevations, it is a common tree. While Sugar Maple is restricted to moist forests, Red Maple is widespread. It is found in every deciduous forest type from dry to moist forest and from low to high elevations. Indeed Red Maple has the greatest north-south distribution of any tree species in eastern North America, occurring from Canada to Florida. As Sugar Maples and Red Maples age their bark becomes very shaggy, unlike the smooth gray bark of the younger trees.

White Ash (*Fraxinus americana*) with its compound leaf and straight trunk can also attain great height and size. Its bark has a pattern of crisscrossing lines, producing a somewhat reptilian scale pattern. American Basswood (*Tilia americana*), with its large heart shaped leaves typically grows with several trunks coming out in a group. It commonly grows in coves along streams.

Three species of magnolia are found locally, Fraser Magnolia (*Magnolia fraseri*), Cucumber Magnolia (*Magnolia acuminata*), and Umbrella Magnolia (*Magnolia tripetala*). Unlike their evergreen southern cousin, Southern Magnolia, our magnolias are deciduous. Fraser Magnolia has leaves with "dog ears", while Cucumber Magnolia and Umbrella Magnolia's leaf bases connect directly to the stem. The leaf base of Cucumber Magnolia is wedge shaped, while the Umbrella's base is tapered. Also the leaves of the Umbrella are clustered near the end of twigs (thus its name), while the Cucumber's leaves are spaced along the twigs. Cucumber Magnolia gets its name from its cone-like fruit. Magnolia "cones" contain seeds with red, fleshy coats. In the fall these cones open up, exposing the red seeds for bird consumption. Magnolias produce large showy white or greenish-yellow flowers. Interestingly, the flowers of Fraser Magnolia are quite fragrant while Umbrella and Cucumber flowers are rather stinky.

Black Cherry (*Prunus serotina*) with its dark, scaly bark is common in these forests. Black Cherry shows a straight growth form often attaining impressive girths and heights. The leaves, twigs, and seeds of cherries contain hydrocyanic acid, giving an acrid odor to crushed leaves and broken twigs. Its small black fruits are bitter, although fruit-eating birds don't seem to care.

The tree that symbolizes the coming of spring to many mountain folk is Serviceberry (*Amelanchier arborea*). A small tree, Serviceberry produces a welcome display of white flowers in April, before the other trees have leafed out. Once the other trees leaf out, Serviceberry is lost from sight until early summer, when its large crop of sweet red fruits are devoured by birds and hungry hikers.

Tuliptree (*Liriodendron tulipifera*), also known as Yellow Poplar, is another common tree. Due to its fast and straight growth, it often towers above the other trees. Its large cup shaped yellow, green and orange flowers produce a stunning display in early May, while in the fall its wind-dispersed winged seeds rain down. Northern Red Oak *(Quercus rubra)* is the most common oak found in these forests, although not nearly to the extent it is in the drier Mixed Oak Forests. Flowering Dogwood (*Cornus florida*) occurs as a small subcanopy tree, although it is rare above 4,000 feet.

The one evergreen tree found in significant numbers is Eastern Hemlock (*Tsuga canadensis*). This hemlock can be found in most forest types, however it is often common along streams in moist, shady coves. Occasionally Eastern Hemlock may become the dominant tree in an area. These "Canada Hemlock Forests" are rare due to our past history of logging, however an outstanding stand of old growth hemlock still exists on the Lees-McRae College campus on a north-facing slope along the Elk River. Tree core samples have shown that some trees have ages of over 500 years. This forest shows impressive stratification with a high canopy of Eastern Hemlock, a middle canopy of Yellow Birch, Black Cherry, Sugar Maple, Red Maple and Fraser Magnolia, a subcanopy of Mountain Holly and young trees, and a dense shrub layer of Rosebay Rhododendron.

A serious concern to our hemlock populations is the recent arrival of the Hemlock Wooly Adelgid (*Adelges tsugae*). This insect, a native of Asia, has spread down the Appalachians and was first observed in our area in 2002. Trees with the adelgid show white cotton-like clusters on the branches and needles. Heavy infestations can kill adult trees. Researchers are currently experimenting with predatory insects to control this introduced pest. Another insect that attacks hemlocks, the Elongate Hemlock Scale, has also been recently reported in our area. The potential impact of these insects on hemlocks and on our forest ecology could be devastating.

Shrubs

The shrub layer of these forests may be dominated by the shade tolerant Rosebay Rhododendron *(Rhododendron maximum)*, forming dense thickets or "laurel hells". These thickets are especially common along streams. The flowering display of Rosebay Rhododendron with its light pink flowers in June and July can be spectacular. These heavy flowering episodes typically occur every other year. Wild Hydrangea (*Hydrangea arborescens*) with its opposite, ovate, toothed leaves and large heads of fragrant white flowers often grows in thick clusters in cool ravines and along creeks. Hobblebush (*Viburnum lantanoides [alnifolium]*) is found above 4,500 feet and can be recognized by its large ovate opposite leaves. In the fall these leaves turn maroon and the plant presents a striking fruit display of red and black drupes.

Striped Maple (*Acer pennsylvanicum*), Mountain Maple *(Acer spicatum)*, Alternate-leaf Dogwood *(Cornus alternifolia)*, and Mountain Holly (*Ilex montana*) typically do not exceed shrub height. Striped Maple and Mountain Maple both have toothed, three lobed leaves and can best be differentiated by the greenish trunk and white stripes of the Striped Maple. While Striped Maple can be found in most forests at all elevations, Mountain Maple prefers forests above 4,000 feet.

Mountain Holly, unlike the evergreen American Holly, is deciduous without any leaf spines. It also does not typically grow in a tree form, but sends up several thin trunks, growing in a cluster. In the fall after its leaves drop, it produces a fine display of red berries. American Holly (*Ilex opaca*) is found typically at the lower elevations, especially along streams.

Alternate-leaf Dogwood (*Cornus alternifolia*) is an erect shrub that is often easy to overlook. It has leaves with prominent veins that curve towards the apex of the blade. Although its leaves are alternate, they are typically clustered at the twig tips. When in doubt whether a shrub is a dogwood or not, give it the "*Cornus*"test. Take a leaf and pull it slowly apart. As the leaf rips, the veins will appear as thin threads if it is a true dogwood. The fruit of Alternate-leaf Dogwood is quite different from its cousin, Flowering Dogwood. They appear in prominent clusters and are blue black. Pepperbush (*Clethra acuminata*) can also be found in these forests, although it occurs in drier forests also. This shrub can be recognized by its reddish, peeling bark.

Vines

The main vine of these forests is Dutchman's Pipe (*Aristolochia macrophylla*). Its brown, woody vines can be seen spiraling around tree branches often forming impressive formations. Its large heart shaped leaves often make it difficult to spot its brownish-purple, pipe shaped flowers that appear in May. The forest floor may also be covered with young plants twining up shrubs on their way to the canopy. This vine is the primary food plant for the larvae of the Pipevine Swallowtail Butterfly (*Battus philenor*). This large black butterfly lays its eggs on Dutchman's Pipe and the hungry caterpillars devour the leaves. The eggs of this butterfly can be seen on the stalk of Dutchman's Pipe flower in Plate 59.

Herbs

The herb layer in these forests is typically rich and includes many northern species. In the early spring, before the trees have leafed out, large beds of individual species may dominate the forest floor. Trout Lily or Yellow Adder's Tongue (*Erythronium umbilicatum),* Mayapple *(Podophyllum peltatum),* Fringed Phacelia *(Phacelia fimbriata),* Spring Beauty (*Claytonia virginica* and *Claytonia caroliniana)*, and violets (*Viola spp.)* carpet the forest in April and early May. Over 20 species of violet occur in our area, including blue, yellow and white flowered species. Some such as the Common Blue Violet (*Viola sororia[papilionacea])*, Sweet White Violet (*Viola blanda),* and Round-leaved Violet (*Viola rotundifolia)* have basal leaves only. The Common Blue Violet can be especially abundant. Other violets such as the Halbard-leaved Violet *(Viola hastata)* and Canada Violet *(Viola canadensis)* have stem leaves. For those ready to tackle the identification of the many violet species, most of our local species are described in Newcomb's Wildflower Guide.

One of the earliest of the spring wildflowers, appearing in April, is Bloodroot *(Sanguinaria canadensis)* a member of the poppy family. While this plant often grows in small colonies, each individual plant has but one flower and one lobed, heart-shaped leaf. The blood-red root of this plant is a powerful alkaloid and was used by American Indians for a wide variety of ailments and also as a love potion. Bloodroot is most common below 3,500 feet.

The greatest number of herbs have their flowering peak in April and May. These include numerous members of the lily family such as Wake Robin (*Trillium erectum),* Painted Trillium (*Trillium undulatum),* False Solomon's Seal (*Smilacina racemosa),* Solomon's Seal (*Polygonatum biflorum),* Rosy Twisted Stalk (*Streptopus roseus),* Yellow Mandarin (*Disporum lanuginosum),* Bluebead Lily (*Clintonia borealis),* Speckled Wood Lily (*Clintonia umbellulata),* Canada Mayflower (*Maianthemum canadense),* Lily of the Valley (*Convallaria montana),* Large-flowered Bellwort (*Uvularia grandiflora),* Indian Cucumber Root (*Medeola virginiana),* and Wild Leek (*Allium tricoccum).*

Wake Robin and Painted Trillium are the two common trilliums in our area. They are easily separated when flowering by the red flower of the former and the white flower of the latter. After they flower they can be distinguished by the purple fruit of the Wake Robin and the bright red fruit of the Painted Trillium. Interestingly, trillium seeds are dispersed by ants. The ants carry the seeds back to their colonies, feed on a nutritious package of food attached to each seed, and then discard the seed to germinate near their colony. Large-flowered Trillium (*Trillium grandiflorum*) with its large white flowers occurs sporadically in our area, but where it does occur it forms large spectacular colonies.

False Solomon's Seal (also known as Solomon's Plume), Solomon's Seal, Rosy Twisted Stalk and Yellow Mandarin all have similar appearances and can be confusing. False Solomon's Seal and Solomon's Seal both have a single stem, however, the former has a terminal flower cluster, while the latter has pairs of tubular white flowers dropping below the leaves at each axil. Yellow Mandarin and Rosy Twisted Stalk typically have branched stems. Yellow Mandarin has nodding, green, bell-shaped flowers while the rarer Twisted Stalk has a zigzag stem with purple-pink flowers. In the fall, Yellow Mandarin displays bright orange berries.

The two species of *Clintonia*, Bluebead Lily and Speckled Wood Lily, also have very similar leaves and are difficult to separate without their flowers. Bluebead Lily has nodding, yellow flowers, while Speckled Wood Lily has small erect white flowers. These two species often grow in colonies with individual plants typically having three thick, large, oval, basal leaves. In the fall Bluebead Lilies have striking blue berries, while the Speckled Wood Lilies have smaller black fruits.

Canada Mayflower (also known as False Lily of the Valley) is a common herb, often forming dense beds. It is a small herb with usually just two alternate leaves. Lily of the Valley is less common, although where it is found it can also form dense beds. The Flat Rock Trail on the Blue Ridge Parkway has such a bed as does the Table Rock Trail in the Linville Gorge. Large-flowered Bellwort is easy to spot due to its large drooping bright yellow flower.

Wild Leek or Ramp is well known in this area for its pungent bulb, which is eaten. This native onion sends up its long elliptical leaves early in the spring. These leaves have reddish bases and have a distinctive onion smell. The leaves are usually gone by the time its long flower stalk with clusters of white flowers appears. Although not as pungent as its bulbs and leaves, even the flowers have a strong onion smell.

Other common spring herbs include White Baneberry (*Actaea pachypoda*), Wood Anemone (*Anemone quinquefolia*), Jack in the Pulpit *(Arisaema triphyllum)*, Dutchman's Breeches (*Dicentra cucullaria*), Squirrel Corn *(Dicentra canadensis)*, Cutleaf Toothwort (*Dentaria laciniata*), Crested Dwarf Iris (*Iris cristata*), Wild Stonecrop (*Sedum ternatum*), Heart–leaved Alexanders (*Zizia aptera)*, Golden Alexanders (*Zizia aurea*), and Sweet Cicely *(Osmorhiza claytoni)*.

White Baneberry is most noticeable in the fall when it produces a striking display of white berries with red stalks with black dots on each berry. These berries are responsible for its other name, Doll's Eye. These berries are reported to be poisonous, although the berries appear to be bird-dispersed.

A common, though cryptic herb is the easily recognized Jack-in-the-Pulpit. Because of its green leaves and flowers it is often passed by. The flower spathe may be striped with purple, thus making these individuals more conspicuous. In the fall clusters of its bright red fruits stand out on the forest floor. This herb is unusual in that it displays sequential sexual hermaphroditism, starting life out as a male plant and then switching to a female plant as it gets larger.

Indian Physic or Bowman's Root (*Gillenia trifoliata*) flowers from May to July, producing flowers with five, long, twisted petals. Tea from this plant has been used as a laxative and an emetic. Indian Physic often grows in dense colonies along woodland edges and is especially common along the Blue Ridge Parkway.

An unusual plant of woodlands is the fungi-like Indian Pipe (*Monotropa uniflora*). This saprophytic plant (feeds on decaying matter) has distinctive white, waxy stems with solitary nodding flowers.

Along the cool, wet streamsides, Foamflower (*Tiarella cordifolia*), Mountain Meadow Rue (*Thalictrum clavatum*), Mountain Lettuce (*Saxifraga micranthidifolia*), Brook Saxifrage (*Boykinia aconitifolia*), Waterleaf (*Hydrophyllum virginianum*), Broad-leaved Waterleaf (*Hydrophyllum canadense*), Black Snakeroot (*Cimicifuga racemosa*), Pink Turtlehead (*Chelone lyonii*), Blue Cohosh (*Caulophyllum thalictroides*), Miterwort (*Mitella diphylla*), Yellowroot (*Xanthorhiza simplicissima*), Small Enchanter's Nightshade (*Circaea alpina*), Cowbane (*Oxypolis rigidior*), Water Hemlock (*Circuta maculata*), and Filmy Angelica (*Angelica triquinata*) flourish.

In open areas along streams and rivers Thyme-leaved Bluets (*Houstonia serpyllifolia*) and Forget-me-nots (*Mysotis scorpioides*) may form extensive beds. At the lower elevations, Cardinal Flower (*Lobelia cardinalis*) is found along open creeks such as Wilson Creek and Lost Cove Creek. In late summer their striking, 2-lipped, scarlet flowers are difficult to miss.

In the shaded cove forests be on the lookout for Wood Nettle (*Laportea canadensis*). Chances are that you will "feel" this plant before you notice it as stinging hairs on its stems and leaves produce an itching sensation. This herb has alternate, ovate, toothed leaves and often grows in large patches along creeks. Its small greenish flowers grow in clusters from the leaf axils in July and August. A more obvious herb of wet areas is Umbrella Leaf (*Diphylleia cymosa*). Usually growing in colonies with umbrella-like toothed leaves up to 2 foot wide and with stems up to 4 feet high, it is hard to miss. A cluster of white flowers above the leaves is seen throughout June, while in the fall a showy display of blue berries attached to red stems attracts migrating birds.

An unusual plant of streamsides is Dodder or Witch's Hair (*Cuscuta gronovii*). This rootless, leafless plant is comprised of orange strings that twine around other herbs. This plant is parasitic, using small suckers to suck out nutrients from its host. Dense clusters of small white flowers appear in July and August.

Orchids

Finding an orchid in flower is an exciting and for some almost a religious experience. As some 25 species of orchid are found in our area, this region is a mecca for orchid lovers. Although orchids may be found in a variety of habitats, including bogs and meadows, many species prefer the moist, rich hardwood forests. These include the Showy Orchis *(Galearis [Orchis] spectabilis)*, Large Round-leaved Orchid (*Platanthera [Habenaria] orbiculata*), Green Wood Orchid (*Platantherea [Habenaria] clavellata*), Large Purple Fringed Orchid (*Platanthera [Habenaria] grandiflora*), Green Fringed Orchid (*Plantanthera [Habenaria] lacera*)Cranefly Orchis (*Tipularia discolor*), and Puttyroot (*Aplectrum hyemale*). Typically most orchids are not common and it is often a challenge to locate them. This is the case for Appalachian Twayblade (*Listera smallii*), named for its two basal leaves that appear midway up the stem. This rare orchid is at home in the dense rhododendron thickets.

Possibly the most common woodland orchid is Downy Rattlesnake Plantain (*Goodyera pubescens*). This orchid is best known not for its delicate stalk of small, white flowers, but for its basal rosette of striking net-veined leaves. These orchids typically grow in colonies in most of our forests. Another orchid that typically grows in colonies is the Pink Lady's Slipper (*Cypripedium acaule*). This large showy orchid is often found in woodlands dominated by pines, especially White Pine *(Pinus strobus)*. For those with the "orchid bug", Newcomb's Wildflower Guide covers almost all of the orchids native to our area and is an excellent source for their identification.

Ferns

Where the forest floor is open, ferns may be abundant. Hay-Scented Ferns (*Dennstaedtia punctilobula*) may carpet large patches of the forest floor due to its habit of spreading by its rhizomes. Unlike other ferns that grow as a single cluster, its leaves grow singly or in small groups. The Hay-Scented Fern is found in moist and drier mixed oak forests as well as in open areas. Fragile Fern (*Cystopteris protrusa*) prefers moist locales, especially in shaded boulder fields and rocky ledges. Evergreen or Fancy Woodfern (*Dryopteris intermedia*) also likes it wet, often being found along shaded creeks. The leaves of this fern persist into the fall and early winter, although new leaves sprout in the spring. Another "evergreen" fern is the Christmas Fern (*Polystichum acrostichoides*). This common fern has dark green, leathery leaves that emerge in a circular fashion from a central rootstock. Its leaflets have a distinctive "ear" at their base. It gets its name due to the persistence of its green leaves during the Christmas season. Other common ferns include the Southern Lady Fern (*Athyrium filix-femina*) and the Marginal Shield Fern (*Dryopteris marginalis*). Rock Cap Fern or Rock Polypody (*Polypodium virginianum*) is found growing on boulders or at the base of trees. In the fall the Grape Ferns (*Botrychium spp.*) appear. The grape ferns are an enigmatic group of ferns often referred to as the "succulent" ferns. These primitive ferns are fleshy and do not produce a fiddlehead. Instead the young sprout comes through in a bent form. In the fall just as most other herbaceous plants are dying back, the grape ferns appear above the leaf litter, sending up two stalks. One stalk is bears the triangular leaf, while the taller stalk bears the reproductive spores. These ferns persist into the winter.

Club Mosses

Distant cousins to the ferns are the Club Mosses (*Lycopodium spp.*). These small, evergreen denizens of the forest floor are the survivors of an ancient group of trees that once dominated the Carboniferous forests three hundred million years ago. Today they grow either in an upright or creeping form and their resemblance to evergreens has resulted in their being called ground pines or running cedar. Indeed, their many common names are a constant source of confusion as a single species may be called Ground Pine, Running Pine or Running Cedar. Clubmosses are small plants, seldom reaching a foot in height with small, simple, pointed, stemless leaves arranged around the stem. Although club mosses reproduce by spores, their ability to spread from their rootstocks often results in dense mats on the forest floor. Some clubmosses such as Shining Clubmoss (*Lycopodium lucidulum*) produce erect single stems that often branch up the stem. Ground Cedar (*Lycopodium tristachyum*), meanwhile, has an erect tree-like form with fan-shaped branches. Its spores are borne on candelabra like structures rising above the leaves. Finally the branched stems of Running Pine (*Lycopodium complanatum*) typically creep or crawl along the ground.

Late Summer and FallWildflowers

By the end of July most of the "spring herbs" have all but vanished and are replaced by several common and often abundant wildflowers. Two species of jewelweed, Pale Jewelweed (*Impatiens pallida*) and Spotted Jewelweed (*Impatiens capensis*) appear together in forests and along forest edges. Their other name of Touch-me-nots refers to their exploding seed pods. Many jewelweed flowers are victimized by "nectar thieves", bees that chew through the side of their tubular flower so they can get at the nectar. Look for holes on the sides of these flowers as evidence of past crimes.

Bee Balm (*Monarda didyma*) also forms beds producing a stunning display of whorls of red tubular flowers. A member of the mint family, Bee Balm has pleasantly aromatic leaves. Bee-Balm flowers are especially popular with foraging Ruby-throated Hummingbirds. While Bee Balm is typically found in moist areas, its close relative Wild Bergamot (*Monarda fistulosa*) is found in drier woods, edges, and meadows. Occasionally one will find these two growing near each other and a purple flowered hybrid, sometimes labeled *Monarda media*, appears. Another aromatic mint that flowers in August is Horse Balm (*Collinsonia canadensis*). The large toothed leaves of this waist-high herb have a strong citronella odor when crushed.

In moist openings and forest edges, showy clusters of Green-headed Coneflowers (*Rudbeckia laciniata*), Turk's Cap Lily (*Lilium superbum*), Tall Bellflower (*Campanula americana*), and Greater Coreopsis (*Coreopsis major*) begin to flower in mid-July. Green-headed Coneflowers with their drooping rays and prominent disks can reach heights of over 6 feet. Turk's Cap Lilies grow up to 8 feet and may be loaded with nodding, orange, spotted flowers. Tall Bellflower's blue flower is actually not bell-like, but more star-like with a distinctive long, curving style. Greater Coreopsis with their large yellow 7 or less rayed flowers have whorls of 6 leaflets along the stem.

By August the turtleheads are in flower, typically along creeks and in moist ravines. These aptly named flowers have small openings at their ends that allow pollinators to squeeze into the body of the flower. Pink Turtlehead (*Chelone lyonii*) is more common in our area than White Turtlehead (*Chelone glabra*). Filmy Angelica (*Angelica triquinata*) also thrives along the cool, wet streams. This member of the parsley family often grows waist-high and has large umbels of greenish flowers. Another late-summer wildflower is Broad-leaved Bunchflower (*Melanthium hybridum*). This striking lily can be found in flower along the Profile Trail on Grandfather Mountain in August. Several Gentians appear in our area, the two most common being Bottle Gentian (*Gentiana clausa*) and Stiff Gentian (*Gentiana quinquefolia*). Both flower in the fall and have blue, bottle shaped flowers. The flowers of Bottle Gentian are tightly closed, while those of Stiff Gentian are open at the top with five pointed lobes evident.

Several fall composites become obvious in August and September. White Snakeroot (*Eupatorium rugosum*), with its showy head of white flowers, appears in August and may be scattered throughout the forest floor. Fall asters include White Wood Aster (*Aster divaricatus*) and Heart-leaved Aster (*Aster cordifolius*). Purple Joe-Pye Weed (*Eupatorium purpureum*) looks similar to its relative Hollow Joe-Pye Weed (*Eupatorium fistulosum*), but has a solid stem, lighter purple flowers, and prefers moist woods. While most goldenrods are found in open habitats, the Zigzag Goldenrod (*Solidago flexicaulis*) is found within these forests. The yellow clusters of flowers of this goldenrod are found in the leaf axils or in a terminal cluster. The terminal end of the stem has an obvious zigzag growth form.

Riparian Forests

The term riparian refers to the habitats bordering a river. Along the Elk River, Watauga River, and Linville River long stretches have forested banks. Typically these forests are moist in nature. Yellow Birch is usually abundant in riparian forests, especially at mid to high elevations. Eastern Hemlock also thrives in this environment and impressive specimens may be found along the Linville River in the Linville Gorge. Also the ubiquitous Rosebay Rhododendron thrives in these shady, cool locations, forming dense thickets along the riverbanks.

Several species of trees and shrubs seem to be limited to these riparian habitats. Sycamores (*Platanus occidentalis*) are easily recognized by their habit of shedding their outer bark, revealing the gray-white underbark. Also their large, lobed, toothed leaves and ball-shaped fruits are distinctive. Another riverside dweller is American Hornbeam or Ironwood (*Carpinus caroliniana*). This small tree is most easily recognized by its gray, sinewy trunk that resembles muscles. While both of these trees occur away from water in other parts of their range, in our area they seem to be restricted to riparian habitats.

Several shrubs seem to be limited to riparian habitats. Tag Alder (*Alnus serrulata*) forms thickets along rivers and streams at the lower elevations. It has dark green, toothed, ovate leaves and distinctive clusters of woody fruit cones that persist even after its nutlets are released. Dog Hobble (*Leucothoe fontanesiana [axillaris]*) also grows in dense colonies. This low-growing evergreen has dark green, narrowly ovate, pointed leaves. It produces dense racemes of white, bell-shaped flowers that turn into persistent dry capsules. Ninebark (*Physocarpus opulifolius*) is a loosely branched shrub, often growing right on the water's edge. It gets its name from its peeling bark. This member of the rose family produces rounded clusters of small white flowers in early summer that are extremely popular with insect pollinators. Swamp Azalea (*Rhododendron viscosum*) also known as Clammy Honeysuckle has sticky leaves and white flowers that appear in mid-summer.

Boulderfield Forests

Scattered throughout the middle and high elevations are patches of forest where the ground is dominated by different sized, moss-covered boulders. These boulderfield forests are believed to be relicts of periglacial action in the Pleistocene. These areas have little soil possibly due to water drainage. This rocky environment appears to limit the number of species that can survive here. Yellow Birch is usually common, probably due to its ability to send out its snaky lateral roots over rock surfaces. Yellow Buckeye is also common here, often attaining a large size. At higher elevations, Red Spruce (*Picea rubens*) may appear.

Common shrubs include three species of gooseberry, Skunk Gooseberry (*Ribes glandulosum*), Roundleaf Gooseberry (*Ribes rotundifolium*), and Dogberry (*Ribes cynosbati*). Gooseberries are typically small shrubs, sometimes with prickles, with lobed, toothed leaves. The leaves of Skunk

Gooseberry have a strong odor when crushed. While the berries of Skunk Gooseberry and Dogberry have prickles, the berry of Roundleaf Gooseberry is smooth. Striped Maple is common here also, typically growing no taller than a shrub.

The open canopy of the boulderfield forest produces well-lit gaps. The higher light levels and moist conditions favor dense patches of herbs, including Bee Balm, Green-headed Coneflower, and Jewelweed. Ferns that appear on the boulders include Rock Polypody (*Polypodium virginianum*) and Brittle Fern *(Cystopteris protrusa)*. Nice examples of the boulderfield forest may be found on Grandfather Mountain along the Profile and Tanawha trails.

High Elevation Deciduous Forests

The Northern Hardwood Forest extends to over 5,000 feet where it is replaced on the higher peaks by the Spruce-Fir Forest. These high elevation deciduous forests have a lower diversity as many tree species drop out as altitude increases. Some deciduous trees that occur in these high elevation deciduous forests include Yellow Birch, American Beech, Yellow Buckeye, Hawthorne (*Crataegus spp.)*, Northern Red Oak, Sugar Maple, and Mountain Ash (*Sorbus americana)*. In some areas stunted forms of American Beech form dense thickets or dwarf forests.

At these high elevations, Rosebay Rhododendron becomes uncommon so the herb layer is open and well developed. In May dense carpets of flowering Spring Beauty may cover the ground and Golden Ragwort (*Senecio aureus*) with its attractive yellow flower clusters may also be common. Other herbs may include False Hellebore (*Veratrum viride*), Small-flowered Hellebore (*Veratrum parviflorum)*, Tassel Rue (*Trauvetteria carolinensis*), Black Snakeroot *(Cimicifuga racemosa)*, Mayapple (*Podophyllum peltatum)*, and Wood Sorrel (*Oxalis montana)*.

An outstanding example of this high elevation deciduous forest is found on Yellow Mountain. Ancient Yellow Birch and Northern Red Oak are scattered in this open woodland setting with stands of dwarf American Beech running along the edge of the forest. Grandfather Mountain also has some fine high elevation forests, easily accessible from the Profile Trail and the Daniel Boone Scout Trail. For the long distance hiker, the Appalachian Trail from the 19E trailhead to Roan Mountain passes through several tracts of this forest type as it climbs up to Hump Mountain.

Profile Trail

For the total Northern Hardwood and Cove Forest experience, I recommend Grandfather Mountain's Profile Trail. This trail begins along a creek, with an abundance of spring wildflowers growing along the stream bank. The trail then meanders up the mountain passing through dense forest and crossing several streams, where moisture-loving herbs abound. After about .5 miles look out for a large bed of Fraser's Sedge (*Cymophyllus fraseri*) on the bank. This rare, unusual sedge with its broad leaves is only found in scattered locations in the Southern Appalachians. In May it produces showy white flowers at the end of stalks, producing a nice flowering display. The trail eventually passes through a woodland glade, where the shrub layer is absent resulting in a rich herb layer. Be careful however as one of the common herbs is Wood Nettle. Eventually the trail moves into the transition zone of deciduous forest and Spruce-Fir Forest. Many impressive ancient Yellow Buckeye, Sugar Maple and Yellow Birch are found in this rocky area and the herb layer is well developed. Finally at 2.7 miles the trail ends at the Calloway Trail and the Spruce-Fir Forest replaces the deciduous forest. Notice how the deciduous trees become smaller and less common as the evergreen forest takes over, until just the occasional Yellow Birch is found.

MIXED OAK FOREST

This forest type has been historically referred to as the Oak-Chestnut Forest, based on the shared dominance of the American Chestnut *(Castanea dentata)* and the various oak species. Unfortunately the introduced chestnut blight, a fungus, has decimated this magnificent tree. Amazingly, however, root sprouts continue to come up from the rot resistant stumps of diseased trees. Once these sprouts reach tree size however, the bark is afflicted with the blight and the tree dies back again. Occasionally you will run across a tree-sized chestnut that is fruiting. Hopefully, these may be blight resistant trees. Look for these chestnut root sprouts with their characteristic curved teeth leaves within the shrub layer. In the fall these sprouts are easier to spot as the leaves turn a rich brown.

Above 4,000 feet Mixed Oak Forests typically occur in drier locations, often on south facing slopes. Below 4,000 feet it is the dominant forest type, occurring from the dry ridge tops to the moist valleys and rich coves. Five species of oak can be found in the Mixed Oak Forest community, Northern Red, White, Black, Scarlet and Chestnut. Northern Red Oak *(Quercus rubra)* with its sharp toothed leaves is usually the dominant oak of the group, however, in drier habitats Chestnut Oak *(Quercus montana [prinus])* becomes dominant. Chestnut Oak can be recognized by its deep bark furrows and its large, broadly rounded toothed leaves. This tree can attain a large size and impressive specimens can be found throughout Linville Gorge.

Black Oak *(Quercus velutina)* has leaves similar to Red Oak but are glossy above, while Red Oak leaves are dull. Black Oaks also have hairy buds and bowl-shaped acorn cups, while the Red Oak has hairless buds and saucer-like acorn cups. Black Oak bark also lacks the light, shiny ridges of the Northern Red Oak. White Oak (*Quercus alba*) is less common than Northern Red Oak and Chestnut Oak. White Oak leaves are similar to Northern Red Oak, except that the lobes are rounded without bristle tips. The bark is also quite different, being light gray with shallow furrows.

Closely associated with oaks is the unusual Squawroot (*Conopholis americana*). This plant is a root parasite of oaks, its presence betrayed only by clusters of yellow, cigar-shaped "cones" that irrupt from the leaf litter in May. These cones are stems that bear scale-like leaves and small yellowish 2-lipped flowers above each scaly bract. The flowers develop into round capsule fruits giving these stalks the appearance of a corncob, thus another of its names, "bear-corn".

During mast years, oaks synchronize their fruiting and the forest floor becomes covered with acorns. Acorns with holes in them are the doings of Black Oak Acorn Weevils (*Curculio rectus*). The female weevil bores a small hole through an acorn, lays an egg in the hole and then seals the opening with a fecal pellet. The larva feeds and pupates inside the acorn and then exits through the hole.

A large mast crop is a boon to local wildlife, including squirrels, deer, bear and turkey. Interestingly, squirrels will *scatterhoard* (bury acorns separately as compared to caching them in a bunch) Northern Red Oak acorns but not White Oak. The reason for this is that White Oak acorns begin to germinate in the fall sending out the young root while Northern Red Oak acorns do not begin to germinate until the following spring. While germinating in the fall, White Oak acorns do not send out their shoots until spring. As for the acorns infested with weevils, the squirrels eat both the acorns and the tasty weevil larvae.

Other trees found in the Mixed Oak Forest include White Pine *(Pinus strobus)*, Fraser Magnolia *(Magnolia fraseri)*, Tuliptree *(Liriodendron tulipifera)*, Red Maple *(Acer rubrum)*, Striped Maple *(Acer pennsylvanicum)*, and Sweet Birch *(Betula lenta)*. Four species of hickory are found in our area, Bitternut Hickory *(Carya cordiformis)*, Mockernut Hickory *(Carya tomentosa)*, Shagbark Hickory *(Carya ovata)*, and Pignut Hickory *(Carya glabra)*. While hickories are common trees of the Carolina Piedmont, this is not the case in our area. Hickories are uncommon above 4,000 feet, being found typically at the lower elevations.

Shrubs

The shrub layer in the Mixed Oak Forest is usually open with a mix of Rosebay Rhododendron *(Rhododendron maximum)*, Mountain Laurel *(Kalmia latifolia)*, Witch Hazel *(Hamamelis virginiana),* and Flame Azalea (*Rhododendron calendulaceum)*. It is in this community that Flame Azalea is found in its greatest numbers. When not in flower this deciduous shrub is inconspicuous, however, in May when the azaleas are in flower, the forest becomes transformed with their attractive flowers. Their flowers are unusual in that their color ranges from a deep orange to a light yellow.

Witch Hazel is a common shrub, found in both Mixed Oak and Northern Hardwood Forests. Witch Hazel typically grows as a large shrub with a cluster of crooked trunks each about an arm's diameter. Its leaves are ovate (egg-shaped) with coarse, wavy teeth. Witch Hazel is unusual in that it flowers late in the fall, taking advantage of night moths for pollination. The flowers are also unusual looking with four long yellow petals that are curled and twisted. The fruit, a woody capsule, also looks unusual. The fruit takes a year to mature and the following fall it explodes open, expelling its two seeds like miniature rockets. The open pods persist on the plant into the winter. It is the branches of the Witch Hazel that are preferred as divining rods for locating subterranean water sources.

Maple-leaf Viburnum *(Viburnum acerifolium)* is easy to overlook as its leaves have a strong resemblance to Red Maple. Its leaves, however, are three-lobed and opposite and it usually grows in colonies. Maple-leaf Viburnum produces flat clusters of small white flowers and bluish black drupes (fleshy fruits with a single pit) in the fall.

Herbs

The herb layer is often well developed in the Mixed Oak Forest. Wild Sarsparilla *(Aralia nudicaulis)*, Spikenard *(Aralia racemosa),* Bluebead Lily *(Clintonia borealis)*, False Solomon's Seal *(Smilacina racemosa)*, Solomon's Seal *(Polygonatum biflorum)*, Wake Robin *(Trillium erectum)*, Fly Poison *(Amianthium muscaetoxicum)*, Jack-in-the-Pulpit *(Arisaema triphyllum)*, Galax *(Galax urceolata [aphylla])*, Large Houstonia *(Houstonia purpurea)*, Whorled Loosestrife *(Lysimachia quadrifolia)*, Cow Wheat *(Melampyrum lineare),* and Wild Bergamot *(Monarda fistulosa)* may all be found here.

Wild Sarsparilla with its umbrella-like leaves divided into 5 leaflets is often confused with its prized relative, Ginseng (*Panax quinquefolius*). Wild Sarsparilla has three flower clusters, while Ginseng has only one flower cluster. The fruits of Wild Sarsparilla are dark purple, while Ginseng's are bright red. Wild Sarsparilla is usually found in drier forests while Ginseng occurs in rich, moist forests. It is the roots of these two herbs that are in demand, Wild Sarsparilla for a tasty drink, while Ginseng is a medicinal herb.

Spikenard is a much larger plant, with compound leaves that may reach 2 feet in length and a large inflorescence of small white flowers. Spikenard looks similar to Devil's Walking Stick (*Aralia spinosa*), although the latter is a woody shrub with thorns around its stem. Both Spikenard and Devil's Walking Stick are found in rich woods.

Fly Poison, so named due to its toxic roots and leaves, has thin grass-like leaves and is easy to overlook until it flowers in June. It then sends up an attractive raceme of small white flowers that tower above the leaves. Indian Cucumber Root (*Medeola virginiana*) is also common, producing drooping flowers in May and June that migrate to the top of the plant in late summer producing a showy purple fruit for bird consumption. Mountain Bellwort (*Uvularia puberula [pudica]*) has drooping, pale yellow, bell-shaped flowers. In July, Carolina Lily (*Lilium michauxii*) blooms. This southern lily looks similar to the Turk's Cap Lily (*Lilium superbum*), but is shorter, with fewer flowers that have extremely recurved petals.

Fire Pink (*Silene virginica*) with its brilliant crimson (not pink) flowers stands out during the spring and summer months. Fire Pink prefers rocky hillsides and banks, adapting well to wooded roadsides. The road banks on Highway 194, between Valle Crucis and Banner Elk, produces nice displays of this wildflower during the summer. In late May and early June the slopes of some oak forests may have large patches of Small's Penstemon (*Penstemon smallii*). The pink and white flower of this attractive beardtongue has two lobes above and three lobes below.

Several herbs of the Mixed Oak Forest have distinctive leaves that stand out. Rattlesnake Weed (*Hieracium venosum*) has purple-veined basal leaves, while Spotted Wintergreen (*Chimaphila maculata*) has leathery dark green leaves with a prominent white stripe down the middle. Partridge Berry (*Mitchella repens*) often forms trailing beds on the forest floor. Its small, round, evergreen leaves may have white veins. Partridge Berry produces paired, white flowers with four petals. These flower pairs develop into a single red, fleshy berry that persists into the winter. The four species of Heartleaf Ginger (*Hexastylis arifolia, H. heterophylla, H. shuttleworthii, and H. virginica*) all produce leathery, evergreen, dark green, heart-shaped leaves that when crushed have the unmistakable smell of ginger. To find the ginger's jug-like flowers, carefully clear away the leaf litter under the leaves. These "buried" flowers use ground-dwelling insects such as beetles for pollination.

Several wildflowers appear in late summer and fall. Appalachian False Foxglove *(Aureolaria laevigata [Gerardia laevigata])* stands out with its display of yellow, funnel-shaped flowers beginning in July. Its round yellow flower buds are also quite noticeable. This herb is partially parasitic on the roots of oaks. Lion's Foot (*Prenanthes serpentaria*) has nodding, greenish-white, tubular flowers. Its lower leaves are bluntly lobed and have a paw-like appearance. Panicled Hawkweed (*Hieracium paniculatum*) has slender, branching stems and yellow, dandelion-like flowers. Southern Harebell (*Campanula divaricata*) produces nodding, bell-shaped light blue flowers. Beginning in August, White Wood Aster *(Aster divaricatus),* Curtis' Aster (*Aster curtisii),* and Curtis' Goldenrod (*Solidago curtisii*) give added color to this forest.

Vines

Several kinds of vines are found in Mixed Oak Forests. The main woody species is Summer Grape (*Vitis aestivalis*). This high-climbing vine has a shaggy, reddish-brown bark and large, three lobed, toothed leaves. In late summer it produces clusters of tart, black grapes. Other vines found in more open forests include Catbrier (*Smilax spp.*), Virginia Creeper (*Parthenocissus quinquefolia),* and Poison Ivy (*Toxicodendron radicans*). Catbrier or Greenbrier (*Smilax glauca* and *Smilax rotundifolia*) has distinctive green, thorny stems and leathery, evergreen leaves. Virginia Creeper (*Parthenocissus quinquefolia*), a member of the grape family, has its leaves divided into five toothed leaflets. Poison Ivy (*Toxicodendron radicans*) with its distinctive three leaflets produces a hairy, woody vine that grows up a tree trunk, although it often may grow herb-like on the forest floor. Poison Ivy is more common at lower elevations and in disturbed areas.

Local Mixed Oak Forests

The Mixed Oak Forest is widespread in our area. This forest extends from low to middle elevations and from dry ridge (see below) to sheltered coves. A nice of example of this forest is on the Moses Cone Estate on the Blue Ridge Parkway. The miles of carriage trails wind through a beautiful Mixed Oak Forest. The Flat Rock Trail on the Blue Ridge Parkway is also a good introduction to the Mixed Oak community. Oak forests dominate the Wilson Creek area of the Pisgah National Forest and the Linville Gorge Wilderness. An excellent trail to see the changes of a Mixed Oak Forest from Dry Ridge to a moist Mixed Oak Forest is the Conley Cove Trail, located on Kistler Highway in the Linville Gorge Wilderness. This trail is especially appealing in May and early June as Small's Penstemon, Fire Pink, Spiderwort (*Tradescantia subaspera*), and other wildflowers put on a nice flowering show.

DRY RIDGE FOREST

Trees

The Dry Ridge Forest is really a type of Mixed Oak Forest, occurring along the mountain ridges below 4,000 feet. The drier condition on the ridges produces a somewhat different plant association than on the slopes and coves below. Here Chestnut Oak is dominant, although on some dry ridges, Scarlet Oak *(Quercus coccinea)* with its deeply divided bristle-tipped lobes and reddish inner bark may be common. In the autumn this oak stands out as its foliage turns a brilliant scarlet.

Pines are well represented in this community. Pitch Pine *(Pinus rigida)* with its bundles of three stiff needles is the common pine here. This pine can often be distinguished by the presence of small twigs with needles sprouting out of the trunk of the tree. Virginia Pine *(Pinus virginianus)* is also found in this habitat. It can be separated easily from Pitch Pine in that its twisted needles are in bundles of two. The cones of Pitch Pine and Virginia Pine remain attached at maturity. White pine *(Pinus strobus)* with 5 slender needles per bundle is also found here. White Pine is the largest of the pines with some individuals reaching 100 feet. The cones of White Pine are long and slender, falling off the tree at maturity, often littering the ground.

Beginning in the summer of 2000, numerous dead pines began to appear in northwestern North Carolina and especially in the Dry Ridge Forest community. This was the work of the Southern Pine Borer *(Dendroctonus frontalis)*, a native beetle. The genus name, *Dendroctonus,* means "tree killers" and they have lived up to their name as evidenced by the many dead trees along the ridges and slopes of our mountains. These beetles are capable of incredible population growth. They can grow from egg to adult in 30-40 days and one generation may result in a 10-fold increase in numbers. Evidence of this beetle becomes obvious when the bark falls off of the dead trees revealing a network of surface tunnels chewed out by the beetle larvae.

Other trees in the Dry Ridge Forest community may include Eastern Hemlock (*Tsuga canadensis*), Carolina Hemlock *(Tsuga caroliniana)*, Red Maple (*Acer rubrum*), White Oak (*Quercus alba*), Sassafras *(Sassafras albidum)*, Sourwood (*Oxydendron arboreum*), and Black Gum *(Nyssa sylvatica)*. Carolina Hemlock, unlike its larger cousin, Eastern Hemlock, is not common or widespread. It can be distinguished from Eastern Hemlock by its needles. In Carolina Hemlock the needles are longer and occur at various angles around the twig, while in Eastern Hemlock the needles appear mostly in a horizontal plane. The cones of Carolina Hemlock are also larger, typically around an inch long. It is not uncommon to find these two hemlocks growing next to each other. Carolina Hemlock may be found along the ridges of Linville Gorge.

Sassafras rarely attains great height, usually being shrub-sized. Sassafras may be easily identified by its aromatic leaves that come in three shapes, unlobed, two-lobed (looks like a mitten), and three lobed. Sourwood has distinctive deeply furrowed bark and drooping clusters of fragrant white flowers. Sourwood gets its name by the bitter taste of its leaves. In the fall its narrow, finely-toothed leaves turn a brilliant scarlet adding spectacular color to this community. Black Gum has simple, entire leaves that also turn a brilliant red in the fall.

Shrubs

The shrub layer is well developed in this forest. It is here that Mountain Laurel may reach its greatest density. Mountain Laurel flowers in late May and early June, producing a wonderful display of pink. Rosebay Rhododendron is also common, as is its relative the Catawba Rhododendron (*Rhododendron catawbiense*). The Catawba Rhododendron is distinguished from the Rosebay by shorter, more oval leaves and deep purple flowers. Unlike the Rosebay it is shade intolerant and prefers more open areas.

Other shrubs include Mountain Fetterbush (*Leucothoe recurva*), a deciduous member of the blueberry family (Ericaceae) with dry fruit capsules, and Sweetleaf (*Symplocos tinctoria*). The leaves of the latter have a sweet apple-like taste. Blueberry bushes are common in this community. Due to their habit of hybridizing, it is often difficult to identify individual species. Blueberry bushes can be separated into high and low growing forms. The higher forms in this community include Northern Highbush Blueberry (*Vaccinium corymbosum*), Highbush Blueberry (*Vaccinium constablaei*), and Deerberry (*Vaccinium stamineum*). While the fruits of the Northern Highbush Blueberry and Highbush Blueberry are quite tasty, Deerberry fruits are usually inedible. Early Lowbush Blueberry (*Vaccinium pallidum [vaccillans]*) and Black Huckleberry (*Gaylussacia baccata*) are also present and form low growing thickets.

Several prostrate shrubs of the blueberry family are also found on the forest floor. Wintergreen (*Gaultheria procumbens*) has leathery, evergreen, rounded, glossy leaves and a distinctive wintergreen smell when crushed. This oil of wintergreen (methyl salicylate) is also found in birch bark. In late summer, this common mini-shrub produces a small red berry that also has the wintergreen flavor. Trailing Arbutus (*Epigaea repens*) with its evergreen, oblong, wrinkled leaves can be found creeping along the forest floor. In May it produces fragrant, 5-petalled, light pink flowers.

Herbs

The herb layer here is not as well developed as in the moister forests. Galax (*Galax urceolata [aphylla]*) with its large heart-shaped evergreen leaves often forms extensive beds in this community. The roots of Galax are responsible for producing a strong musky odor that many people find offensive, although I have grown fond of it. In June, Galax produces nice flowering displays as the colony sends up spikes of small white flowers. In the winter, the green leaves change color to a deep maroon.

In May and June flowering displays of Turkey Beard (*Xerophyllum asphodeloides*) appear in this forest. A tall (up to 5 feet) flower stalk with a white cluster of flowers emerges from a rosette of long needlelike leaves. Turkey Beard can be found along the ridges and rocky outcrops of Linville Gorge, including Table Rock. Ground Pine (*Lycopodium spp.*) may also be common on the forest floor.

Fire

The Dry Ridge Forest is a fire-adapted community as evidenced by the Linville Gorge fire in November of 2000. Approximately 10,000 acres of Dry Ridge Forest and Mixed Oak Forest burned along the eastern edge of the gorge on Linville Mountain. Much of the damage was to the shrub layer, although a number of trees were killed. The following year, however, many shrubs and trees sent up new growth from their roots, taking advantage of the nutrients released from the fire. The forest floor has also been opened up for herbs and young trees to become established. A visit to Linville Gorge is an excellent way to see the effects of fire on a community.

Another example of a Dry Ridge Forest may be found in the Pisgah National Forest east of Grandfather Mountain. The Little Lost Cove Cliff Trail traverses excellent dry ridge habitat, as does Timber Ridge above Lost Cove Creek.

PIONEER FORESTS

As local farming declined over the last half of the 20th century, many pastures and fields have gone through a series of changes or succession. Initially the pasture becomes an "old field" as many herbaceous plants become established. Eventually trees begin to invade the field. These include Black Locust (*Robinia pseudoacacia*) and Fire Cherry (*Prunus pennsylvanica*). Black Locust becomes highly visible in early June when it produces showy and fragrant hanging clusters of white pea-shaped flowers. Its thick, gray bark is distinctive with deep furrows forming long ridges running up the tree. Black Locust is the last tree to leaf out in the spring, producing pinnately compound leaves with small rounded leaflets. Its twigs bear sharp spines. Black Locust is known for its hard, rot resistant wood that is prized for fence posts and firewood. It is also highly prized by the Locust Borer Beetle (*Megacyllene robiniae*). The female of this striking black and yellow beetle cuts into the bark and deposits single eggs inside. The larvae bore through the bark and feed on the sapwood of the tree, forming twisting grooves through the wood. After pupation the adults emerge in late summer when they can be found gorging on goldenrod nectar and pollen.

Fire Cherry, also known as Pin Cherry, has an interesting distribution, ranging up the Appalachians to Canada and then west to British Columbia and south through the Rocky Mountains. In the west it is also called Fire Cherry as its seedlings often come up after forest fires. In our area it typically occurs above 3,000 feet in forest gaps, in young second growth forests, and along forest edges. This cherry is easy to pick out with its shiny, smooth reddish brown bark with crossbars. In late August it produces large crops of sour, red cherries that are cherished by many birds, thus another name, Bird Cherry. This popularity with birds, especially robins and catbirds, helps disperse cherry seeds to other open habitats. Unlike the Black Cherry, Fire Cherry is not long-lived. It is fast growing, but after some 20 years it usually dies.

Fire Cherry is often victimized in the spring by the Eastern Tent Caterpillar (*Malacosoma americanum*). The caterpillars of this moth produce a silk tent in the fork of the tree, where they take shelter and molt, emerging from the tent to feed on the cherry leaves. In the late summer and fall it is the Fall Webworm (*Hyphantria cunea*) that builds a tent at the outer extremities of the branch, where the caterpillars feed on the leaves within the silken webs.

Thickets of blackberry (*Rubus spp.*) often dominate the bright understory of the Pioneer Forest. Catbrier (*Smilax spp.*) vines may also form impenetrable tangles. In the fall, Catbriers produce clusters of blue-black berries that persist through the winter, eaten by deer and grouse. The vines of Fox Grape (*Vitis labrusca*) are also common in open thickets. The combination of an open canopy and a thick understory is popular with birds including Eastern Towhees, Gray Catbirds, Chestnut-sided Warblers and Indigo Buntings. Eastern Cottontails and White-tailed Deer also frequent this habitat.

With time, forest herbs invade the young forest and some such as False Solomon's Seal (*Smilacina racemosa*) and White Snakeroot (*Eupatorium rugosum*) may become abundant. White Snakeroot with its display of large heads of bright white flowers may carpet the forest floor in September producing an impressive display.

Eventually shade tolerant seedlings of Red Maple (*Acer rubrum*), Northern Red Oak (*Quercus rubra*), Tuliptree (*Liriodendron tulipifera*), Serviceberry (*Amelanchier arborea*), Black Cherry (*Prunus serotina*), and other hardwoods begin to move in. After a number of decades have passed these long-lived species take over, producing the "climax" forest that will persist for centuries. The Black Locusts and Fire Cherries are shaded out by the taller trees and typically die. The standing skeletons of Black Locusts in many local forests tell of a past of farmland gone fallow.

SPRUCE-FIR FOREST

One of the most interesting and beautiful forest types in our area is the high-elevation Spruce-Fir Forest. These forests suggest the great northern evergreen forests and indeed it is likely that they are relicts of the glacial evergreen forest that probably covered much of this land 12,000 years ago. As the glaciers retreated north these evergreens moved to our highest peaks, beyond the deciduous tree line. Above approximately 5,400 feet the coniferous forest replaces the deciduous forest. These evergreen forests extend to the highest peaks of our area, including Roan High Bluff on Roan Mountain (elevation 6,267 feet) and Calloway Peak on Grandfather Mountain (elevation 5,964 feet). Our mountains do not extend above the *treeline* (the altitude limit for tree growth).

The shift from deciduous forest to evergreen forest is not abrupt but occurs over a transition zone of mixed evergreen and deciduous trees. This transition zone is easily seen as one drives up Highway 143 from the town of Roan Mountain to the crest of Roan Mountain. To the right of the road the lighter green deciduous forest gradually turns into the darker evergreen forest.

These high elevation forests receive high rainfall and are often covered in fog. They also experience extreme cold and high winds during the winter months. Locally, Spruce-Fir Forests are only found on the peaks of Grandfather Mountain and Roan Mountain. Other Spruce-Fir Forests in the region include Mount Mitchell to the southwest and Mount Rogers and Whitetop Mountain in Virginia. Further south are the Spruce-Fir Forests of the Smoky Mountains. Spruce-Fir Forests generally do not occupy a large area. The view from Grassy Bald across from the Roan High Knob allows one to see the relatively small size of this evergreen forest on Roan Mountain.

Unfortunately this unique community is one of the most endangered in the Southern Appalachians. All of these forests show a distressingly large number of dead trees. The reasons for this die-off are many, including the Balsam Wooly Adelgid (*Adelges piceae*), an introduced insect that attacks the Fraser Fir. Little cotton-like tufts on the trunks, branches, and twigs of the tree indicate the presence of this minute pest. Air pollution, including acid deposition and high ozone levels also appear to have a highly detrimental effect on both Red Spruce and Fraser Fir. Finally the specter of global warming may threaten this forest if deciduous trees are able to migrate into the community.

Trees

Two trees dominate this forest, Red Spruce (*Picea rubens*) and Fraser Fir (*Abies fraseri*). Red Spruce is found from the Southern Appalachians up through New England and into Canada, while Fraser Fir is limited to the Southern Appalachians. It is the Fraser Fir that has become the Christmas tree of choice for tree farmers in the local counties. The Fraser Fir is named after John Fraser, a Scottish botanist and contemporary of Andre Michaux during the 1790's. These two pioneer botanists were competitors, racing to "discover" new species of plants for their respective countries. Despite this competition Michaux and Fraser actually traveled together for a short period. However, Michaux found Fraser to be irritating due to his garrulous nature and his habit of collecting large quantities of common plants of little value, and the two botanists soon separated.

Fraser Fir and Red Spruce may be told apart by their needles. The Red Spruce has green, sharp pointed needles that are spirally arranged around the twig. The needles of the Fraser Fir have white stripes on their lower surfaces and are flattened with blunt "friendly fir" tips. Also the cones of Red Spruce hang down, while Fraser Fir cones are erect. Red Spruce naturally occurs at lower elevations than Fraser Fir and the fir is more common at the highest elevations. Interestingly, Red Spruce does not typically appear below 5,000 feet on the north side of Grandfather Mountain, but extends down to about 4,000 feet on the southern slopes. The mix of Red Spruce and Fraser Fir varies, in some areas Red Spruce is most common while in other areas Fraser Fir dominates.

Spruce-Fir Forests range from dense forests with a heavy canopy with a reduced shrub and herb layer to open forests with scattered trees and a heavy shrub layer. The latter is especially true in areas with many dead trees. Deciduous trees are rare in this community with stunted Yellow Birch (*Betula alleghaniensis*), Red Maple (*Acer rubrum*), and Fire Cherry (*Prunus pensylvatica*) occurring occasionally. Mountain Ash (*Sorbus americana*) may be common, appearing either as a shrub or a small tree. Some old trees attain heights approaching 30 feet. This northern tree has deciduous, pinnately compound leaves with up to 17 toothed leaflets. Mountain Ash produces a nice show of flowers in May with aromatic clusters of white flowers. It is in fall, however, that the Mountain Ash is most spectacular. As its leaves are shed, clusters of small, red, apple-like fruit produce a vivid display that robins and migrating thrushes take note of. Though bitter to our taste, these frugivorous birds find the fruits irresistible. It is thought that Roan Mountain may have been named for these "Rowan trees" that are common along its peaks.

Shrubs

The Catawba Rhododendron (*Rhododendron catawbiense*) is common in these forests, often forming dense colonies in open areas. Blueberries are also common shrubs. Bearberry (*Vaccinium erythrocarpum*) has dark red fruits that are unpalatable, while Highbush Blueberry (*Vaccinium constablaei*) has tasty bluish-black fruits. Blackberry is also common, especially in open areas. Smooth Blackberry (*Rubus canadensis*) is noteworthy in that its prickles are highly reduced and one is able to run a hand along its stems without injury. Other shrubs include Hobblebush (*Viburnum lantanoides [alnifolium]*), Red-berried Elder (*Sambucus pubens [racemosa]*), Mountain Holly (*Ilex montana*), and Mountain Maple (*Acer spicatum*).

Herbs

The floor of this forest is often covered with a living carpet of moss. Knight's Plume Moss (*Ptilium crista-castrensis*) is an attractive, showy moss with shiny, feathery fronds extending erect up to about 4 inches. Mountain Fern Moss (*Hylocomium splendens*) forms mats of branching, wiry stems, in places producing a thick turf of moss. Extensive beds of Spring Beauty (*Claytonia virginica or Claytonia caroliniana*) may cover the forest floor producing spectacular flower displays in early May. These beds may be seen on the Daniel Boone Scout Trail on Grandfather Mountain shortly past the Cragway Trail junction. Beds of Wood Sorrel (*Oxalis montana*) are also common. This herb is easily recognized by its shamrock-like leaves consisting of three heart-shaped leaflets. It produces an attractive 5-petaled white flower with pink veins in June and July. Smaller beds of Clinton's Lily (*Clintonia borealis*) and Canada Mayflower (*Maianthemum canadense*) are less common.

In open wet seepage areas, beds of Thyme-leaved Bluets *(Houstonia serpyllifolia)* may appear with their tiny opposite oval leaves and small blue 4-petaled flowers. Pink Turtlehead (*Chelone lyonii*), Michaux's Saxifrage (*Saxifraga michauxii*), Small Enchanter's Nightshade (*Circaea alpina*), Mountain St. John's wort *(Hypericum graveolens)*, Blue Ridge St John's-wort *(Hypericum mitchellianum)*, Bitter Cress (*Cardamine clematitis*), and Mountain Meadow Rue (*Thalictrum clavatum*) are also found in these wet seeps. Fall wildflowers include Whorled Wood Aster (*Aster acuminatus*), White Wood Aster (*Aster divaricatus*), and Cluster Goldenrod *(Solidago glomerata)*. Ferns include Southern Lady Fern (*Athyrium filix-femina [asplenioides]*) and Mountain Woodfern (*Dryopteris campyloptera*).

Local Spruce-Fir Forest Trails

Several local trails offer an excellent opportunity to visit our Spruce-Fir Forests. On Roan Mountain the approximately 2 mile stretch of the Appalachian Trail between the Carvers Gap parking area and the Rhododendron Gardens traverses some of the densest Spruce-Fir Forest in the area. The highest peak of Roan Mountain, Roan High Bluff is also covered in this forest. Unfortunately, much of the Spruce-Fir Forest on the highest ridges of Roan has died, producing thick shrub thickets.

On Grandfather Mountain the Grandfather Trail runs along the spine of the mountain, passing through a nice mosaic of dense Spruce-Fir Forest, open forest-shrub mix and rocky outcrops. If you ascend the southern side of the mountain on the Daniel Boone Scout Trail you can witness the transition from deciduous forest to an evergreen-deciduous mix to the evergreen forest. The Profile Trail on the northern side offers the same opportunity.

HEATH

The Heath community is dominated by woody shrubs. The term "heath" refers to the members of the plant family Ericaceae, which includes the blueberries, rhododendrons and azaleas. Heath communities are typically found on open ridges or south-facing slopes often associated with open metasandstone outcrops. The dense thickets of woody shrubs in this habitat make it impenetrable except for trails. While trees are present, they are typically stunted. Many of the areas where Heath communities occur today such as on the southeast side of Grandfather Mountain have in the past been logged and burned. It is not clear whether their occurrence today is due to these man-induced changes and whether the Heath is a successional stage eventually on its way to becoming a forest.

When entering the Heath habitat from the forest one becomes immediately aware of the higher temperatures, drier conditions, and stronger winds. It is likely that these extreme conditions limit tree growth. The shrubs found in the Heath are typically found in other habitats but here the shrubs rule. Highbush Blueberry (*Vaccinium constablaei*) is the common blueberry bush producing sweet, delicious fruit. Black Huckleberry (*Gaylussacia baccata*) is also found in this community. Huckleberries can be separated from blueberries by their resin dotted leaves and black fruits with ten seeds. Minnie-Bush (*Menziesia pilosa*) resembles a blueberry bush, however, instead of producing a juicy berry, it produces a dry capsule as does Male-berry (*Lyonia ligustrina*).

The Catawba Rhododendron (*Rhododendron catawbiense*) is common in the Heath. During the second half of May, the flowers of this shrub gives the Heath dramatic color. Mountain Laurel (*Kalmia latifolia*) is also common, usually beginning to flower in late May just as the Catawba Rhododendron are ending their flowering period. Pepperbush *(Clethra acuminata)* with its distinctive peeling reddish-brown bark is common, as are thickets of Black Chokeberry *(Aronia [Sorbus] melanocarpa)*. Finally, Mountain Ash *(Sorbus americana)* is often present, although not to the extent that it is found at the higher elevations.

Trees

There are several species of trees that are found scattered through the Heath, although they are typically short and have a stunted appearance. These include Red Spruce *(Picea rubens)*, Fraser Fir *(Abies fraseri)*, Fraser Magnolia *(Magnolia fraseri)*, Serviceberry *(Amelanchier arborea)*, Red Maple *(Acer rubrum)*, Fire Cherry *(Prunus pennsylvaticum)*, Sassafras *(Sassafras albidum),* and Mountain Holly *(Ilex montana).* Of particular interest is the presence of the rare Bigtooth Aspen *(Populus grandidentata)* in this community. This northern aspen, bearing leaves with large curved teeth, is found only in several counties in North Carolina, but is common in Canada.

Herbs

Due to the dense shrub layer, there is little in the way of an herb layer. Some herbs that occur in the odd open nook include Galax *(Galax urceolata [aphylla])*, Turkey Beard *(Xerophyllum asphodeloides)*, Dwarf Iris *(Iris verna)*, Wintergreen *(Gaultheria procumbens)*, Cow Wheat *(Melampyrum lineare)*, and Clubmosses *(Lycopodium spp.)*

Local Heath Communities

A number of beautiful Heath habitats are found on the southeastern slopes of Grandfather Mountain accessible from the Blue Ridge Parkway. These include the Cragway, Rough Ridge, Ship Rock and Beacon Heights. These Heaths are closely associated with open metasandstone outcrops (see Rocky Outcrops). The trail and boardwalk of Rough Ridge passes through one of the largest of the heath habitats ending up on the scenic outcrops of Ship Rock. Keep an eye out for Bigtooth Aspen on the way to Ship Rock.

High Elevation Rhododendron Bald

A second type of Heath is the high-elevation Rhododendron Bald. The term "bald" typically refers to a treeless area, either a Heath Bald dominated by shrubs or a Grassy Bald. In this community Catawba Rhododendron is the dominant shrub surrounded by a mosaic of habitats ranging from Spruce-Fir Forest to Grassy Balds to Rocky Outcrops. The most spectacular example of the Rhododendron Bald is the "Rhododendron Garden" of Roan Mountain at about 6,000 ft. This natural garden is probably the most extensive and unique stand of Catawba Rhododendron in existence. Smaller Rhododendron Balds are scattered all along the Roan Massif.

In mid-June the deep pink flowers of this shrub transforms this Heath Bald into an unforgettable vision. Perhaps it is this flowering display that prompted botanist Asa Gray to label Roan Mountain as the most beautiful mountain east of the Rockies. This rhododendron forms almost a pure stand with its dense cover allowing few other shrubs, trees, or herbs to get established. Occasional Red Spruce and Mountain Ash break through the shrub layer. Other shrubs include Roundleaf Gooseberry (*Ribes rotundifolia*) and Red-berried Elder (*Sambucus pubens [racemosa]*). The herb layer is restricted to the edges of the shrub thickets and appears to be limited to invaders from the surrounding Grassy Balds and Spruce-Fir Forests.

We don't really understand how these Heath Balds came into being, whether it was a natural process or whether grazing or logging played a factor. It appears, however, that these balds may now be in the process of changing. As trees invade the balds they shade out the shade-intolerant Catawba Rhododendrons, killing them as evidenced by the twisted dead rhododendron trunks under the invading evergreens. The National Forest Service has decided to try to maintain these "gardens" as Rhododendron Balds by cutting down the invading trees.

ROCKY OUTCROPS

Forest Outcrops

Rocky outcrops abound in this area from the highest peaks to the sheltered river valleys. Outcrops occurring in the forest typically are cooler, shadier, and wetter than the dry, open, exposed outcrops. Not surprisingly their plant communities are also very different. Forest outcrops are often covered by the large leathery lichen called Smooth Rock Tripe (*Umbilicaria mammulata*). This is one of the largest lichens in the world, some specimens measuring over 2 feet across. When dry they appear brittle, but when wet have a slimy, rubbery appearance. Rock tripes are edible, although from my experience their taste or lack of precludes their inclusion in any picnic.

Several ferns prefer these shady, rocky substrates. Rock Polypody (*Polypodium virginianum [vulgare]*), a small evergreen fern, is commonly seen on the surface of rocks. It has dark green, simple leaflets (the leaflets are not divided). Maidenhair Spleenwort (*Asplenium trichomanes*) and Mountain Spleenwort (*Asplenium montanum*) are found nestled in the rock crevices. These delicate ferns are uncommon and their presence often requires a close scrutiny of these shady, wet crevices.

Alumroot (*Heuchera villosa*) with its large maple-shaped basal leaves is a common herb found growing on shaded outcrops. From mid-summer to fall it produces flowering stalks with small white flowers. Wild Columbine (*Aquilegia canadensis*) also prefers these shaded rocky habitats, producing its distinctive red and yellow 5 spurred flower in the spring. Shaded rocky outcrops of different sizes are common in forests throughout the area. Many forest outcrops occur along the length of the Tanawha Trail of the Blue Ridge Parkway and along the trails of Grandfather Mountain.

Open Outcrops

Open outcrops are found on exposed summits and bluffs. At middle and low elevations, these outcrops are often dry environments shaped by wind, rain, heat and cold. Although trees may be present, they typically have a stunted appearance. Table Mountain Pine (*Pinus pungens*), the only pine restricted to the Appalachian region, is mostly limited to these open outcrops. It has two needles in each fascicle and persistent cones that may remain attached for years. This is a small pine often growing in a twisted growth form. Other trees that may occur include Pitch Pine (*Pinus rigida*), Chestnut Oak (*Quercus montana [prinus]*), Sourwood (*Oxydendron arboreum*), and Serviceberry (*Amelanchier arborea*). On the rocky outcrops of Linville Gorge, Carolina Hemlock (*Tsuga caroliniana*) often occurs.

Shrubs

Two kinds of rhododendron prefer these open outcrops, the Catawba Rhododendron *(Rhododendron catawbiense)* and Punctatum (*Rhododendron minus*). Punctatum is distinguished by its combination of small oval leaves and light pink flowers. Mountain Laurel (*Kalmia latifolia*), Male-Berry (*Lyonia ligustrina*), and thickets of Black Huckleberry (*Gaylussacia baccata*) are also common on outcrops.

A common prostrate shrub found on metasandstone is Sand Myrtle (*Leiophyllum buxifolium*). This evergreen shrub often spreads in a carpet-like fashion over an outcrop. It has small, thick, oval leaves and produces large numbers of small, white-pink flowers in May and June. The rocky peaks of Ship Rock on the Blue Ridge Parkway are covered by Sand Myrtle as are most of the exposed peaks in the Linville Gorge. Interestingly this plant also grows in the coastal sandy soils from New Jersey to South Carolina.

Another plant that grows in prostrate mats on exposed rock surfaces is Twisted-Hair Spikemoss (*Selaginella tortipila*). Spikemosses are non-flowering, spore producing vascular plants. Twisted Hair Spikemoss is moss-like with small scale-like leaves and many branches. During dry conditions it appears dead, however after a rain it revives and transforms in appearance. Unfortunately because of their preference for open, exposed rocks, both Sand Myrtle and Twisted-Hair Spikemoss have suffered from the trampling of oblivious hikers. Be aware of these species when walking on these outcrops.

Another low growing shrub is Dense-flowered St. Johns-wort (*Hypericum densiflorum*). Unlike most of our St. Johns-worts that are herbaceous, this one is a woody shrub with opposite, linear leaves. A rare Southern Appalachian endemic found in Linville Gorge is Hudsonia (*Hudsonia montana*). This small shrub has short linear leaves and yellow, solitary flowers that appear in June and July. Hudsonia appears to be maintained by periodic fire, undergoing sprouting and seeding after fire. It has been suggested that it requires a 10 to 15 year fire frequency to be maintained and controlled burns have been used to encourage its regeneration.

Herbs

Because of the hot, dry conditions on many outcrops, the number of herb species is often limited. Turkey Beard *(Xerophyllum asphodeloides)* with its clumps of long grass-like leaves only becomes obvious when it sends up its tall flower stalk. These stalks that appear in May and June may reach 4 feet with terminal clusters of white flowers. Patches of Turkey Beard can be found on Table Rock in the Linville Gorge.

Michaux's Saxifrage *(Saxifraga michauxii)* is noted for its reddish toothed basal leaves and branched stalk of tiny white flowers that appear in May and June. This plant is named for the famous French Botanist, Andre Michaux, who explored and collected plants on Grandfather Mountain in the late 1700's.

The delicate Pale Corydalis *(Corydalis sempervirens)* is often overlooked except in May when it produces exquisite pink and yellow flowers. It also has attractive finely divided, pale green leaves. Along rocky cliffs at the lower elevations, another member of the Fumitory or Poppy family, Wild Bleeding Heart *(Dicentra eximia)* flowers in May and early June.

High Elevation Rocky Outcrops

The high elevation rocky summits are exposed to cool temperatures, frequent fog, and high rainfall. These rocky peaks are subject to extreme weather conditions, including high winds and freezing temperatures. Trees, including Fraser Fir *(Abies fraseri)*, Red Spruce *(Picea rubens)*, Yellow Birch *(Betula alleghaniensis)*, Serviceberry *(Amelanchier arborea)*, and Mountain Ash *(Sorbus americana)* may be present, although they are usually stunted and do not occur in large numbers.

Shrubs tend to dominate these outcrops and include Catawba Rhododendron, Sand Myrtle, Blueberry, and Minnie Bush *(Menziesia pilosa)*. These shrubs are members of the heath family, Ericaceae, and thus this community could be considered a type of Heath community (see Heath). Common herbs include Michaux's Saxifrage, Alumroot, Twisted-Hair Spikemoss, Pale Corydalis, Three-toothed Cinquefoil *(Potentilla tridentata)*, Allegheny Stonecrop *(Sedum telephioides)*, Mountain Oat-Grass *(Danthonia compressa)*, and several species of sedge *(Carex spp.)*. Allegheny Stonecrop is especially obvious due to its thick, succulent, greenish-purple leaves and dense clusters of small, pink flowers that appear in July.

These high elevation rocky summits are of great interest due to the presence of a number of rare Southern Appalachian herbs that are found here. Heller's Blazing Star *(Liatris helleri)* has lance-shaped leaves and clusters of striking violet-blue flowers arranged on spikes that appear in July. Another rare species is Spreading Avens *(Geum radiatum)*. This member of the rose family is only found in several locales in Northwest North Carolina and Eastern Tennessee. It has large, toothed, basal leaves and large, yellow flowers. Mountain Bluets *(Houstonia montana)* look similar to the other bluets, but have deep purple flowers and shorter, ovate leaves.

Lichens are obvious on many of the rock faces and crevices, including several species of Cladonia *(Cladonia spp.)*. Cladonias are fruticose lichen, meaning that they have a stalked or shrubby appearance. Crustose lichens are those lichens that appear to be "painted" on the rocks. Many Cladonia have striking red fruiting bodies.

Common Toadskin *(Lasallia papulosa)* looks similar to rock tripe. It has blister-like pustules on its surface and sometimes appears in a red form. Folded Rock Tripe *(Umbilicaria caroliniana)* may also be seen on exposed outcrops at high elevations. This lichen has an interesting distribution, being found only in the Southern Appalachians and the Yukon Territory and Brooks Range of Alaska. This rock tripe is similar to the common Smooth Rock Tripe, except that it has crowded, folded lobes.

Local Rocky Outcrops

Open Rocky Outcrops are often associated with Dry Ridge Forest and Heath habitats. Outcrops are abundant in the Linville Gorge Wilderness. Table Rock, Hawksbill, and Babel Tower are just a few of the accessible Rocky Outcrops in the gorge that are excellent examples of this community. The southeastern slopes of Grandfather Mountain have a number of outcrops associated with Heath habitats, including the Cragway and Ship Rock. Flat Rock and Beacon Heights on the Blue Ridge Parkway offer easy access to outcrops.

Little Lost Cove Cliffs in the Pisgah National Forest has large outcrop formations with picturesque Table Mountain Pines as well as spectacular views of Grandfather Mountain and the Pisgah National Forest. High elevation Rocky Outcrops can be best experienced on the Grandfather Trail on Grandfather Mountain. This scenic trail passes through a mix of Spruce-Fir Forest and open outcrops along its ridge.

MOUNTAIN BOGS

Mountain Bogs are a highly variable community scattered around our area. About the only thing in common in all of these wetland communities is their wet, soggy nature, and the degree of wetness is even quite variable. Bogs are usually fed by some combination of groundwater seepage, rain, and snow. Wetlands fed by surface water are not technically considered bogs, however their appearance and plant composition often are quite "boggy". The soil is typically very acidic, thus influencing what plants can occur there. Mountain Bogs typically cover a small area, although some bogs, such as the Pineola Bog, reach sizes of over 50 acres.

Mountain Bogs are typically located on bottomlands or at the base of slopes and may be found far from running water. Bogs may also occur along ridges as evidenced by several small sphagnum bogs found along the ridges of Linville Gorge. Mountain Bogs can be open with few shrubs, closed with a dense canopy of shrubs or trees, or a mixture of the two. Many open bogs occur in cleared farmland that was probably once forested. Other bogs appear to be undergoing succession from open to closed. The Invershiel Bog over the past several decades has been invaded by a number of trees and shrubs and its appearance has changed dramatically. It is possible that the heavy development in this area is responsible for changing whatever conditions were responsible for maintaining an open environment.

Beavers may also play an important role in creating bogs. As abandoned beaver ponds fill in with silt, bog vegetation invades producing a "beaver bog". Areas below active beaver dams may also develop into bog-like wetlands. The beaver wetland at the Elk Valley Preserve is in the process of transforming from a freshwater marsh to a beaver bog. It is likely that before their extirpation in the early 1900's, beavers played a vital role in producing bog communities throughout the region. The recent recovery of the beaver in the Southern Appalachians has resulted in the increase of these wetland communities. Other local beaver bogs include the Boone Fork Bog and the Beech Creek Bog.

The plant most closely associated with bogs is Sphagnum Moss (*Sphagnum spp.*), with many species occurring in our area. Mats of these spongy mosses thrive in areas with poor drainage forming hummocks rising above the ground water. Sphagnum Moss is light green and has a branching pattern, although in the fall several species turn a striking red. Other plants such as Cinnamon Fern (*Osmunda cinnamomea*) and Royal Fern *(Osmunda regalis)* often grow on these hummocks, taking advantage of the somewhat drier conditions. These are large and impressive ferns with twice-cut leaves. Cinnamon Fern has lance-shaped, pointed leaflets, while Royal Fern's leaflets are oblong with blunt tips.

A characteristic plant of open bogs is the Cranberry (*Vaccinium macrocarpon*). This ground-hugging cousin of the blueberry is an unusual shrub in that it trails along the ground forming mats. It is easy to overlook as its leaves are quite small. It is most obvious in the fall when it produces its tart red berries. This is the cranberry grown commercially elsewhere. The best local example of a cranberry bog is the Invershiel Bog located at the junction of Highways 105 and 184 in Avery County.

The trees that may occur in Mountain Bogs are not limited to wet areas and are an interesting mix. They include Eastern Hemlock *(Tsuga canadensis)*, Red Spruce (*Picea rubens*), White Pine (*Pinus strobus*), Pitch Pine (*Pinus rigida*), Serviceberry (*Amelanchier arborea),* and Red Maple (*Acer rubrum).* Many of the shrubs, meanwhile, are wetland species. These include Possumhaw (*Viburnum nudum [cassinoides]*), Male-berry (*Lyonia ligustrina),* Winterberry (*Ilex verticillata*), Silky Willow (*Salix sericea*), Swamp Azalea (*Rhododendron viscosum),* Swamp Rose (*Rosa palustris*), Narrow-leaved Meadowsweet (*Spiraea alba*), and Hardhack (*Spiraea tomentosa*).

Possumhaw has deciduous, opposite leaves and terminal, broad clusters of white flowers. Its black fruits are also borne in clusters and appear raisin-like, thus its other name of Northern Wild Raisin. Male-berry resembles a blueberry, but produces terminal clusters of round capsules instead of fleshy fruit. Male-berry may form dense thickets in some bogs, such as Invershiel Bog. Winterberry looks quite similar to its cousin, Mountain Holly (*Ilex montana).* It is also deciduous, with finely toothed leaves, although it lacks the spur twigs found on Mountain Holly. Both species have red fruits, although the nutlets of Mountain Holly are grooved, while Winterberry's nutlets are smooth.

Silky Willow is a common wetland shrub, occurring in open bogs, fields, and along watercourses. It has long (up to 14 cm), toothed, lance-like leaves that have a silky growth on the undersides of the leaves. Willows often grow in clusters, with many stems emerging from the base. Swamp Azalea has deciduous leaves that resemble Flame Azalea (*Rhododendron calendulaceum*), although its leaves are shiny above. Swamp Azalea has fragrant, whitish-pink flowers that are quite sticky, thus it other name of Clammy Honeysuckle. It is also found along open rivers and streams. Like any self-respecting rose, Swamp Rose is well armed with a pair of hooked prickles at each node of the stem. It usually has seven, toothed leaflets and in midsummer produces showy, pink roses.

The Spiraeas are erect shrubs with alternate, deciduous, toothed leaves. Narrow-leaved Meadowsweet has a long cluster of small, white flowers, while Hardhack has a steeple-like cluster of pink flowers. Shrubs that may be found in bogs, but are not limited to wetlands, include Rosebay Rhododendron (*Rhododendron maximum*) and Mountain Laurel (*Kalmia latifolia*).

Herbaceous plants include Rough-leaved Goldenrod (*Solidago patula*), Golden Ragwort (*Senecio aureus*), Haircap Moss (*Polytrichum commune*), Bog Clubmoss (*Lycopodium inundatum*), and various sedges (*Carex spp.*), bulrushes (*Scirpus spp.*), and rushes (*Juncus spp.*). Haircap Moss is an erect moss, resembling a small pine tree. Bog Clubmoss is a creeping clubmoss with erect, bushy-topped fertile stems.

Mountain Bogs are a rare and threatened local community. The presence of rare plant and animal species (see Bog Turtle) in these bogs also relate to their importance. Most of our local bogs, including the Invershiel Bog and Pineola Bog, are located on private property and are surrounded by roads and development. Bogs that are accessible to the public include the Boone Fork Bog in Julian Price Park and the beaver wetland located in the Lees-McRae College's Elk Valley Preserve. The beaver bog in Elk Valley is in part a fresh water marsh, with many marsh plants, including Common Cattail (*Typha latifolia*), Bur Reed (*Sparganium americanum*), Arrowhead (*Sagittaria latifolia*), and Field Horsetail (*Equisetum arvense*). In time this marsh will fill in, becoming more bog-like. It is best to observe these bogs from afar as their sensitive nature does not tolerate trampling.

Another excellent bog is found in the Bluff Mountain Preserve in Ashe County. This wetland has actually been classified a Southern Appalachian Fen as opposed to a bog, due to its high pH (less acidic) nature and the dominance of sedges in place of sphagnum moss. This preserve, managed by the North Carolina Nature Conservancy, is open only during special guided tours due to its fragile nature.

Plate 1. Cove Forest, Grandfather Mountain

Plate 2. Dwarf American Beech Forest, Yellow Mtn.

Plate 3. Yellow Birch Forest, Snake Mountain

Plate 4. High Elevation Deciduous Forest, Yellow Mtn.

Plate 5. Mixed Oak Forest, Linville Gorge

Plate 6. Burned Dry Ridge Forest,
Linville Gorge

Plate 7. Spruce-Fir Forest,
Grandfather Mountain

Plate 8. Heath, Grandfather Mountain

Plate 10. Outcrop with Table Mountain Pine,
Pisgah National Forest

Plate 9. Rocky Outcrop, Linville Gorge

Plate 11. Mountain Bog, Invershiel Bog

Plate 12. Grassy Bald, Roan Mountain

Plate 13. Old Field, Elk Valley Preserve

Plate 14. Farmland, Watauga County

Plate 15. Grandfather Mountain, McRae Peak

Plate 16. Pisgah National Forest, Wilson Creek

Plate 17. Linville Gorge Wilderness

Plate 18. Linville River, Linville Gorge Wilderness

Plate 19. Roan Mountain, Spruce-Fir Forest

Plate 20. Roan Mountain, Rhododendron Heath

Plate 21. Hump Mountain, Avery County

Plate 22. Big Yellow Mountain, Avery County

Plate 23. New River, Ashe County

Plate 24. Elk River Falls, Avery County

Plate 25. Fraser's Sedge, *Cymophyllus fraseri*

Plate 27. Spiderwort,
Tradescantia subaspera

Plate 26. Jack-in-the-Pulpit,
Arisaema triphyllum

Plate 28. Turkeybeard, *Xerophyllum asphodeloides*

Plate 29. Fly Poison, *Amianthium muscaetoxicum*

Plate 30. Large-Flowered Bellwort, *Uvularia grandiflora*

Plate 31. Mountain Bellwort, *Uvularia puberula*

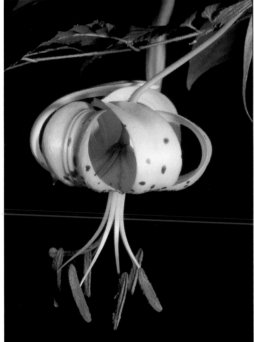

Plate 32. Turk's Cap Lily, *Lilium superbum*

Plate 33. Gray's Lily, *Lilium grayi*

Plate 34. Trout Lily, *Erythronium americanum*

Plate 35. Bluebead Lily, *Clintonia borealis*

Plate 36. Speckled Wood Lily, *Clintonia umbellulata*

Plate 37. False Solomon's Seal, *Smilacina racemosa*

Plate 38. Yellow Mandarin, *Disporum lanuginosum*

Plate 39. Canada Mayflower, *Maianthemum canadense*

Plate 40. Rosy Twisted Stalk, *Streptopus roseus*

Plate 41. Solomon's Seal, *Polygonatum biflorum*

Plate 42. Lily of the Valley, *Convallaria montana*

Plate 43. Indian Cucumber Root, *Medeola virginana*

Plate 44. Wild Leek (Ramp), *Allium tricoccum*

Plate 45. Wake Robin, *Trillium erectum*

Plate 46. Large Flowered Trillium, *Trillium grandiflorum*

Plate 47. Painted Trillium, *Trillium undulatum*

Plate 48. Crested Dwarf Iris, *Iris cristata*

Plate 49. Dwarf Iris, *Iris verna*

Plate 50. Pink Lady's Slipper, *Cypripedium acaule*

Plate 51. Showy Orchis, *Galearis spectabilis*

Plate 52. Large Purple Fringed Orchid,
Plantanthera grandiflora

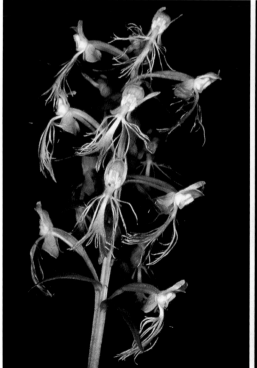

Plate 53. Green Fringed Orchid, *Plantanthera lacera*

Plate 54. Cranefly Orchis, *Tipularia discolor*

Plate 56. Puttyroot, *Aplectum hyemale*

Plate 55. Nodding Ladies' Tresses, *Spiranthes cernua*

Plate 58. Heartleaf Ginger, *Hexastylis shuttleworthii*

Plate 57. Wood Nettle, *Laportea canadensis*

Plate 59. Dutchman's Pipe, *Aristolochia macrophylla*

Plate 60. Pokeweed, *Phytolacca americana*

Plate 61. Spring Beauty, *Claytonia virginica*

Plate 62. Carolina Spring Beauty, *Claytonia caroliniana*

Plate 63. Giant Chickweed, *Stellaria pubera*

Plate 64. Fire Pink, *Silene virginica*

Plate 65. Mountain Meadow Rue, *Thalictrum clavatum*

Plate 66. Wood Anemone, *Anemone quinquefolia*

Plate 67. Virgin's Bower, *Clematis virginiana*

Plate 68. Wild Columbine, *Aquilegia canadensis*

Plate 69. Black Snakeroot, *Cimicifuga racemosa*

Plate 70. White Baneberry, *Actaea pachypoda*

Plate 71. Yellowroot, *Xanthorhiza simplicissima*

79

Plate 72. Mayapple, *Podophyllum peltatum*

Plate 73. Umbrella Leaf, *Diphylleia cymosa*

Plate 74. Blue Cohosh, *Caulophyllum thalictroides*

Plate 75. Fraser Magnolia, *Magnolia fraseri*

Plate 76. Tuliptree, *Liriodendron tulipifera*

Plate 77. Sweet Shrub, *Calycanthus floridus*

Plate 78. Sassafras, *Sassafras albidum*

Plate 79. Bloodroot, *Sanguinaria canadensis*

Plate 80. Dutchman's Breeches, *Dicentra cucullaria*

Plate 81. Squirrel Corn, *Dicentra canadensis*

Plate 82. Wild Bleeding Heart, *Dicentra eximia*

Plate 83. Pale Corydalis, *Corydalis sempervirens*

Plate 84. Cutleaf Toothwort, *Dentaria laciniata*

Plate 85. Stonecrop, *Sedum ternatum*

Plate 86. Allegheny Stonecrop, *Sedum telephioides*

Plate 87. Michaux's Saxifrage, *Saxifraga michauxii*

Plate 88. Alumroot, *Heuchera villosa*

Plate 89. Foamflower, *Tiarella cordifolia*

Plate 90. Miterwort, *Mitella diphylla*

Plate 91. Wild Hydrangea, *Hydrangea arborescens*

Plate 92. Witch Hazel, *Hamamelis virginiana*

Plate 93. Ninebark, *Physocarpus opulifolius*

Plate 94. Goat's Beard, *Aruncus dioicus*

Plate 95. Indian Physic, *Gillenia trifoliata*

Plate 96. Serviceberry, *Amelanchier arborea*

Plate 97. Wild Strawberry, *Fragaria virginiana*

Plate 99. Flowering Raspberry, *Rubus odoratus*

Plate 98. Common Cinquefoil, *Potentilla canadensis*

Plate 100. Fire Cherry, *Prunus pensylvanica*

Plate 101. Spreading Avens, *Geum radiatum*

Plate 102. Black Locust, *Robinia pseudoacacia*

Plate 103. Wood Sorrel, *Oxalis montana*

Plate 104. Wild Geranium, *Geranium maculatum*

Plate 105. Red Maple, *Acer rubrum*

Plate 106. Striped Maple, *Acer pennsylvanicum*

Plate 107. Mountain Maple, *Acer spicatum*

Plate 108. Yellow Buckeye, *Aesculus flava*

Plate 109. Spotted Jewelweed, *Impatiens capensis*

Plate 110. Pale Jewelweed, *Impatiens pallida*

Plate 111. Round-leaved Violet, *Viola rotundifolia*

Plate 112. Halbard-leaf Violet, *Viola hastata*

Plate 113. Common Blue Violet, *Viola sororia*

Plate 114. Canada Violet, *Viola canadensis*

Plate 115. Common Evening Primrose, *Oenothera biennis*

Plate 116. Spikenard, *Aralia racemosa*

Plate 117. Golden Alexander, *Zizia aptera*

Plate 118. Filmy Angelica, *Angelica triquinata*

Plate 119. Queen Anne's Lace, *Daucus carota*

Plate 120. Cow Parsnip, *Heracleum lanatum*

Plate 121. Sweet Cicely, *Osmorhiza claytonii*

Plate 122. Alternate-leaved Dogwood, *Cornus alternifolia*

Plate 123. Spotted Wintergreen, *Chimaphila maculata*

Plate 124. Indian Pipe, *Monotropa uniflora*

Plate 125. Pinesap, *Monotropa hypopithys*

Plate 126. Rosebay Rhododendron,
Rhododendron maximum

Plate 127. Catawba Rhododendron,
Rhododendron catawbiense

Plate 128. Punctatum, *Rhododendron minus*

Plate 129. Flame Azalea, *Rhododendron calendulaceum*

Plate 130. Pink Shell, *Rhododendron vaseyi*

Plate 131. Sand Myrtle, *Leiophyllum buxifolium*

Plate 132. Mountain Laurel, *Kalmia latifolia*

Plate 133. Dog Hobble, *Leucothoe fontanesiana*

Plate 134. Mountain Fetterbush, *Leucothoe recurva*

Plate 135. Trailing Arbutus, *Epigaea repens*

Plate 136. Wintergreen, *Gaultheria procumbens*

Plate 137. Deerberry, *Vaccinium stamineum*

Plate 139. Whorled Loosestrife, *Lysimachia quadrifolia*

Plate 138. Galax, *Galax urceolata*

Plate 140. Sweetleaf, *Symplocos tinctoria*

Plate 142. Common Milkweed, *Asclepias syriaca*

Plate 141. Bottle Gentian, *Gentiana clausa*

Plate 143. Poke Milkweed, *Asclepias exaltata*

Plate 144. Carolina Phlox, *Phlox carolina*

Plate 145. Waterleaf, *Hydrophyllum virginianum*

Plate 146. Fringed Phacelia, *Phacelia fimbriata*

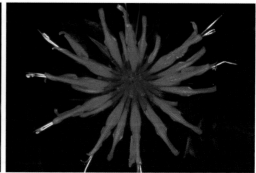

Plate 147. Forget-me-not, *Myosotis scorpioides*

Plate 148. Bee Balm, *Monarda didyma*

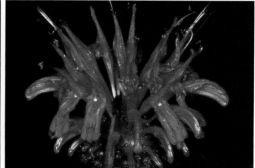

Plate 149. Wild Bergamot, *Monarda fistulosa*

Plate 150. Purple Bergamot, *Monarda media*

Plate 151. Heal-all, *Prunella vulgaris*

Plate 152. Horse Nettle, *Solanum carolinense*

Plate 153. Pink Turtlehead, *Chelone lyonii*

Plate 154. Small's Penstemon, *Penstemon smallii*

Plate 156. Appalachian False Foxglove, *Aureolaria laevigata*

Plate 155. Woolly Mullein, *Verbascum thapsus*

Plate 157. Common Lousewort, *Pedicularis canadensis*

Plate 158. Squawroot, *Conopholis americana*

Plate 159. One-flowered Cancer Root, *Orobanche uniflora*

Plate 160. Cow Wheat, *Melampyrum lineare*

Plate 161. Partridge Berry, *Mitchella repens*

Plate 162. Thyme-leaved Bluet, *Houstonia serpyllifolia*

Plate 163. Large Bluet, *Houstonia purpurea*

Plate 164. Hobblebush, *Viburnum lantanoides*

Plate 165. Maple-leaf Viburnum, *Viburnum acerifolium*

Plate 166. Possumhaw, *Viburnum nudum*

Plate 167. Common Elder, *Sambucus canadensis*

Plate 168. Red-berried Elder, *Sambucus pubens*

Plate 170. Southern Harebell, *Campanula divaricata*

Plate 169. Tall Bellflower, *Campanula americana*

Plate 171. Great Blue Lobelia, *Lobelia siphilitica*

Plate 172. Cardinal Flower, *Lobelia cardinalis*

Plate 173. Chicory, *Cichorium intybus*

Plate 174. White Snakeroot, *Eupatorium rugosum*

Plate 175. Boneset, *Eupatorium perfoliatum*

Plate 176. Joe-Pye-Weed, *Eupatorium fistulosum*

Plate 177. Pilewort, *Erechtites hieracifolia*

Plate 178. Bull Thistle, *Circium vulgare*

Plate 179. New York Ironweed, *Vernonia noveboracensis*

Plate 180. Green-headed Coneflower, *Rudbeckia laciniata*

Plate 182. Sneezeweed, *Helenium autumnale*

Plate 181. Heller's Blazing Star, *Liatris helleri*

Plate 183. Tall Sunflower, *Helianthus giganteus*

Plate 184. Small's Ragwort, *Senecio anonymus*

Plate 186. Ox Eye Daisy, *Chrysanthemum leucanthemum*

Plate 185. Curtis' Goldenrod, *Solidago curtisii*

Plate 187. White Wood Aster, *Aster divaricatus*

Plate 188. Heart-leaved Aster, *Aster cordifolius*

Plate 189. White Heath Aster, *Aster pilosus*

Plate 190. Purple-stemmed Aster, *Aster puniceus*

Plate 191. Curtis' Aster, *Aster curtisii*

Plate 192. Robin's Plantain, *Erigeron pulchellus*

Plate 193. Common Fleabane, *Erigeron philadelphicus*

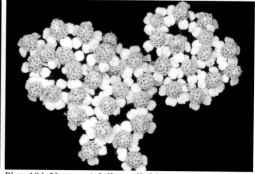
Plate 194. Yarrow, *Achillea millefolium*

Plate 195. Common Ragweed, *Ambrosia artemesiifolia*

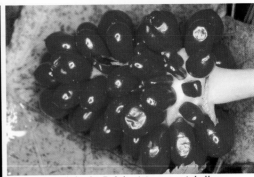

Plate 196. Jack-in-the-Pulpit, *Arisaema triphyllum*

Plate 197. False Solomon's Seal, *Smilacina racemosa*

Plate 198. Solomon's Seal, *Polygonatum biflorum*

Plate 199. Yellow Mandarin, *Disporum lanuginosum*

Plate 200. Tag Alder, *Alnus serrulata*

Plate 201. American Beech, *Fagus grandifolia*

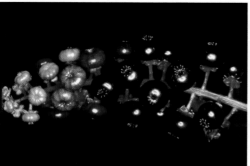

Plate 202. Pokeweed, *Phytolacca americana*

Plate 203. Virgin's Bower, *Clematis virginiana*

Plate 205. Umbrella Leaf, *Diphylleia cymosa*

Plate 204. White Baneberry, *Actaea pachypoda*

Plate 206. Serviceberry, *Amelanchier arborea*

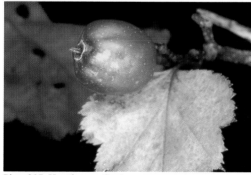

Plate 207. Hawthorne, *Crataegus sp.*

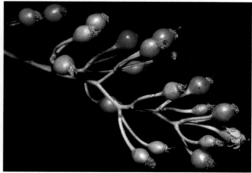

Plate 208. Multiflora Rose, *Rosa multiflora*

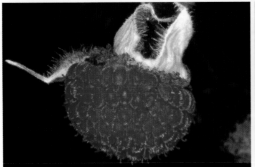

Plate 209. Flowering Raspberry, *Rubus odoratus*

Plate 210. Mountain Ash, *Sorbus americana*

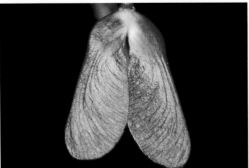

Plate 211. Red Maple, *Acer rubrum*

Plate 212. Devil's Walking Stick, *Aralia spinosa*

Plate 213. Flowering Dogwood, *Cornus florida*

Plate 214. Alternate-leaved Dogwood, *Cornus alternifolia*

Plate 215. Cranberry, *Vaccinium macrocarpon*

Plate 216. Poke Milkweed, *Asclepias exaltata*

Plate 217. Horse Nettle, *Solanum carolinense*

Plate 218. Partridge Berry, *Mitchella repens*

Plate 219. Hobblebush, *Viburnum lantanoides*

Plate 220. Maple-leaf Viburnum, *Viburnum acerifolium*

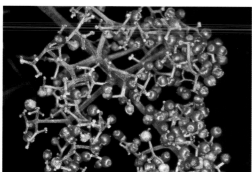

Plate 222. Carolina Hemlock, *Tsuga caroliniana*

Plate 221. Red-berried Elder, *Sambucus pubens*

Plate 223. Eastern Hemlock, *Tsuga canadensis*

Plate 224. Wild Leek (Ramp), *Allium trioccum*

Plate 225. Downy Rattlesnake Plantain,
Goodyera pubescens

Plate 226. Spotted Wintergreen, *Chimaphila maculata*

Plate 227. Rattlesnake Weed, *Hieracium venosum*

Plate 228. Maidenhair Spleenwort, *Asplenium trichomanes*

Plate 229. Mountain Spleenwort, *Asplenium montanum*

Plate 231. Ground Cedar, *Lycopodium tristachyum*

Plate 230. Cut-leaved Grape Fern, *Botrychium dissectum*

Plate 233. Sphagnum Moss, *Sphagnum sp.*

Plate 232. Shining Clubmoss, *Lycopodium lucidulum*

Plate 234. Haircap Moss, *Polytrichum commune*

Plate 235. Smooth Rock Tripe, *Umbilicaria mammulata*

Plate 236. Eastern Newt (aquatic phase),
Notophthalmus viridescens

Plate 237. Eastern Newt (red eft phase),
Notophthalmus viridescens

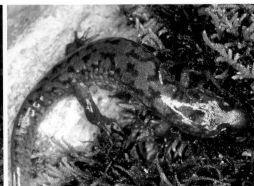

Plate 238. Spotted Salamander,
Ambystoma maculatum

Plate 239. Seal Salamander,
Desmognathus monticola

Plate 240. Blue Ridge Dusky Salamander, *Desmognathus orestes*

Plate 241. Pigmy Salamander,
Desmognathus wrighti

Plate 242. Northern Dusky Salamander,
Desmognathus fuscus

Plate 243. Blackbelly Salamander,
Desmognathus quadramaculatus

Plate 244. Blue-ridge Two-lined Salamander,
Eurycea wilderae

Plate 245. Spring Salamander, *Gyrinophilus porphyriticus*

Plate 246. Redback Salamander, *Plethodon cinereus*

Plate 247. Slimy Salamander, *Plethodon glutinosus*

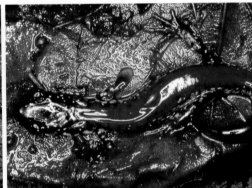

Plate 248. Jordan's Salamander, *Plethodon jordani*

Plate 249. Yonahlossee Salamander, *Plethodon yonahlossee*

Plate 250. Weller's Salamander, *Plethodon welleri*

Plate 251. Red Salamander, *Pseudotriton ruber*

Plate 252. American Toad, *Bufo americanus*

Plate 253. Spring Peeper, *Pseudacris crucifer*

Plate 254. Wood Frog, *Rana sylvatica*

Plate 255. Milkweed Tiger Moth, *Euchaetia egle*

Plate 256. Monarch Butterfly, *Danaus plexippus*

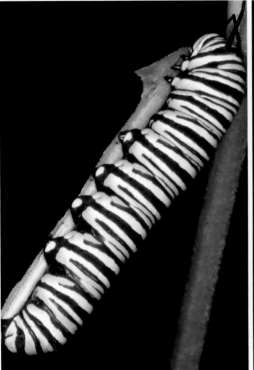

Plate 257. Monarch caterpillar,
Danaus plexippus

Plate 258. Pipevine Swallowtail caterpillar,
Battus philenor

Plate 259. Milkweed Beetle, *Tetraopes tetraophthalmus*

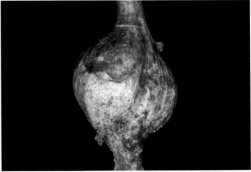

Plate 260. Goldenrod Fly Gall, *Eurosta solidaginis*

GRASSY BALDS

The high elevation Grassy Balds are dominated by herbaceous plants, especially grasses and sedges. These grasslands, occurring over 5,000 feet, are places of climatic extremes, intense sun during the summer months, high winds and low temperatures in the winter. They are typically moist due to high rainfall and frequent fog. Balds are also places of striking beauty with panoramic views and meadows of swaying grasses and wildflowers. Grassy Balds are well represented in our area including a series of balds across the Roan Mountain Massif and the balds on nearby Yellow Mountain.

Grasses, including Oat Grass (*Danthonia compressa*), Bent Grass (*Agrostis perennans*) and Hair Grass *(Deschampsia flexuosa)* dominate these open areas. These grasses typically grow in clumps creating a terrain of mounds or hummocks across the balds. A variety of sedges also inhabit the balds including *Carex debilis, Carex brunnescens,* and *Carex pensylvanica.* Sedges can usually be separated from grasses in several ways. The stems of sedges are mostly triangular and not jointed, while grass stems are round and jointed. Grass stems tend to be hollow, while sedge stems are solid. Finally the leaf sheaths of sedges are closed at the back, while in grasses they are open.

Interspersed among the grasses and sedges are a variety of other low-growing plants including Haircap Moss (*Polytrichum commune),* Three-toothed Cinquefoil (*Potentilla tridentata),* Cinquefoil (*Potentilla canadensis),* Thyme-leaved Bluets *(Houstonia serpyllifolia),* and Wild Strawberry (*Fragaria virginiana).* Other plants rise above the grasses, including Hay Scented Fern (*Dennstaedtia punctilobula),* Roan Mountain Rattlesnake Root (*Prenanthes roanensis),* Robbin's Ragwort (*Senecio schweinitzianus),* Golden Ragwort *(Senecio aureus),* Tassel Rue

(*Trautvetteria carolinensis*), and the abundant Filmy Angelica (*Angelica triquinata*). In late summer the balds are covered by Filmy Angelica with its large green-flowered umbels. When in flower, these umbels are often covered with an impressive number of insect pollinators. In the fall the skeletons of this angelica spread across the landscape.

The Grassy Balds of Roan Mountain include a number of rare plants. The beautiful Gray's Lily (*Lilium grayi*) is found scattered through the balds. This lily, named after the famous botanist Asa Gray, has a nodding deep orange-red flower with its petals in a more tubular shape than most lilies. This lily is not especially conspicuous until it flowers in late June. Appalachian Gentian (*Gentiana austromontana*) resembles Bottle Gentian (*Gentiana clausa*) except that its stems are densely hairy compared to the smooth stems of the Bottle Gentian. Finally Roan Mountain Bluet (*Houstonia montana*) may be found on rocky outcrops scattered through the balds.

The ridges and mountain domes where grassy balds occur are actually a mosaic of different habitats with one habitat merging into others. Among the Grassy Balds often are patches of Heath or shrub thickets, including Catawba Rhododendron (*Rhododendron catawbiense*), Highbush Blueberry (*Vaccinium constablaei*), Flame Azalea (*Rhododendron calendulaceum*), stunted American Beech (*Fagus grandifolia*), and Minnie Bush (*Menziesia pilosa*).

Of particular interest are the dense thickets of Green Alder (*Alnus crispa [viridis]*) on Roan Mountain. This bushy shrub has broad, ovate toothed leaves with ruffled margins. Its fruit is a brown woody, cone-like structure that appears in clusters. This plant, an inhabitant of the mountains of the northeast, appears to be a relict of the past glacial era. During colder times, this shrub was probably widespread, however as the temperatures warmed, populations of Green Alder migrated north, while a population retreated to the high, cool ridges of the Roan Massif. Interestingly it is not uncommon to find a pair of locally rare Alder Flycatchers (*Empidonax alnorum*) inhabiting these relatively small patches of alder thickets. Alder thickets can be easily found next to the parking area at Carver's Gap and along the Appalachian Trail between Round Bald and Jane Bald.

Patches of Spruce-Fir Forest and Northern Hardwood Forest also can be found scattered through the Grassy Balds and along its borders. The Appalachian Trail heading south from Carver's Gap goes through a nice series of Grassy Balds, forest and shrub communities.

A plant that appears to be invading the Grassy Balds is Allegheny Blackberry (*Rubus alleghenis*). This has created a dilemma for the National Forest Service which manages the balds of the Pisgah and Cherokee National Forests. Seeing blackberry as a threat to change the Grassy Balds into shrub habitat, the forest service have tried a number of management techniques including grazing sheep and weed eaters to keep the blackberry and other shrubs at bay. On Yellow Mountain the Nature Conservancy use cattle for the same reason. Thus it appears that the Grassy Balds are not naturally maintaining themselves, as most of these balds seem to be undergoing a succession to a shrub habitat. This leads to the current debate as to whether the Grassy Balds are indeed a natural community and how they were formed in the first place. The presence of several plant species unique to the balds suggests, however, that the Grassy Balds are a natural community.

It appears that at least some of the Grassy Balds were here when the first white settlers arrived on the scene. Origin theories include pre-settlement clearing and burning by Indians, clearing and grazing by early settlers, natural disturbances such as fire and wind, and changing climatic conditions. Also it has been suggested that grazing by herds of native large mammals such as Elk may have maintained the grassy nature of these balds, preventing invasion of shrubs and trees. Whatever their origins may be, Grassy Balds are a rare and highly threatened community deserving recognition and special care.

OLD FIELD

As a pasture or cropland is left fallow it will undergo changes or succession. As many herbaceous plants become established it is referred to as "Old Field". These plants include a variety of annuals, plants that live only one year, and perennials, plants that typically die back each fall and then sprout from the rootstock in the spring. Many of these colonizing plants are exotics or aliens, plants from Europe or Asia that have been introduced either intentionally or by accident. These include some of our best known plants such as Oxeye Daisy (*Chrysanthemum leucanthemum*) with its white flower head. This distinctive flower appears throughout the summer and into the fall. Old Field communities are also common along forest edges, roadsides or in any disturbed area. Because many of the plants in these communities spend most of the summer growing, many species do not flower until late August and September producing the colorful fall wildflower season.

A number of species do flower in the spring along roadsides and in fields. Most of these have yellow flowers and many are in the daisy family. In the early spring Golden Ragwort (*Senecio aureus*) may be abundant, producing a beautiful yellow field. Later in the spring, Small's Ragwort (*Senecio anonymus [smallii]*) begins to flower. The flowers of these two ragworts are very similar, but have different basal leaves. Golden Ragwort has round, heart-shaped leaves, while Small's Ragwort has linear-oblong leaves. Robin's Plantain (*Erigeron pulchellus*) flowers early in the spring, producing many-rayed, violet flowers. This small plant (usually less than 20 inches) typically has oval basal leaves. Common Fleabane (*Erigeron philadelphicus*) is taller (up to 30 inches), with clasping leaves going up the stem. Daisy Fleabane (*Erigeron annuus*) looks similar to Common Fleabane but does not have clasping leaves. It also flowers later, appearing in summer and fall.

Several species of hawkweed flower during the summer including Field Hawkweed (*Hieracium pratense [caespitosum]*) and Mouse Ear (*Hieracium pilosella*). Common Sow Thistle (*Sonchus oleraceus*) has a similar dandelion-like flower as the hawkweeds, but has deeply lobed leaves clasping the stem. It begins to flower in June.

The Buttercup family, Ranunculaceae, is also well represented in open areas. The yellow flowers of Creeping Buttercup (*Ranunculus repens*) may dominate a field in early spring, persisting throughout the summer. In the spring, Kidney-leaved or Small-flowered Crowfoot (*Ranunculus abortivus*) flowers, occurring in fields and forests.

Several members of the Rose family, Rosaceae, are widepread. Wild Strawberry (*Fragaria virginiana*) produces its white flowers with five petals early in the spring and its small but sweet strawberries appear early in June. Similar in appearance to Wild Strawberry is Common Cinquefoil (*Potentilla canadensis*). Common Cinquefoil or "Five-Finger" has a yellow flower and five leaflets, while Wild Strawberry has a white flower and three leaflets.

Colonies of Mayapple (*Podophyllum peltatum*) with their umbrella-like leaves and solitary white flower often stand out in early spring. As this plant is highly toxic it is left by cows and is often found in the middle of cow pastures. By mid-summer it produces its edible fruit. Another plant that often grows in highly visible colonies is Cow Parsnip (*Heracleum maximum [lanatum]*). This impressive member of the parsley family has large maple-like leaves and broad clusters of white flowers that appear in June. Cow Parsnip is often found on roadsides along fields and moist woods.

A common mint of open fields and forest edges is Heal-all (*Prunella vulgaris*). Heal-all produces small heads of purple flowers from early summer to fall and gets its name from its medicinal uses. Most mints have square stems, opposite leaves, and aromatic leaves. Other mints include Hyssop Skullcap (*Scutellaria integrifolia*), Purple Giant Hyssop (*Agastache scrophulariifolia*), American Pennyroyal (*Hedeoma pulegioides*), Henbit (*Lamium amplexaule*), and Ground Ivy or Gill-over the-ground (*Glechoma hederacea*).

Horse Nettle (*Solanum carolinense*) is not actually a member of the nettle family, but instead is in the same family as tomatoes, peppers, and tobacco. This is the nightshade family, Solanaceae, which includes the highly toxic Deadly Nightshade and Jimsonweed. Horse Nettle grows low to the ground and is covered by prickles. It produces white or violet, star-shaped flowers for most of the summer and in the fall a small yellow tomato-like fruit. Beware, while this plant has been used for medicinal purposes, it can be toxic.

A common roadside herb is Chicory (*Cichorium intybus*). The flower of this introduced composite is easily recognized by its distinctive shade of blue. Another common roadside immigrant is Black Mustard (*Brassica nigra*). Black Mustard with its racemes of small yellow flowers is in bloom all summer long. Its fruit is a four-sided pod containing spicy seeds that table mustard is derived from. Indeed the young leaves, flowerbuds, young seedpods, and seeds are all edible.

Wild Geranium (*Geranium maculatum*) has an attractive rose-purple flower with five petals and aromatic leaves with 3-5 deeply cleft lobes. Notice the darker purple lines running down the petal towards the center. These "nectar guides" direct insect pollinators to its nectar sources. Another attractive plant is the delicate Deptford Pink (*Dianthus ameria*) with its small, five-petal, deep pink flower rising from slender stalks.

A common group of plants in open fields and along roadsides are the Knotweeds or Smartweeds (*Polygonum spp.*). These members of the buckwheat family have dense spikes of small pink flowers and jointed stems. They flower throughout the summer and into the fall. Another widespread group is the Bedstraws (*Galium spp.*). Bedstraws usually grow in a spreading form, have their leaves in whorls of 4-8, and are often sticky to the touch. Their small flowers appear in branching clusters.

Phloxes can produce striking roadside flowering displays during the summer. Phloxes have vivid pink or purple five-petal flowers with long narrow tubes. Six species of Phlox occur in our area and while several such as Creeping Phlox (*Phlox stolonifera*) and Mountain Phlox (*Phlox ovata*) are found in moist woods, the others are found in moist open meadows and along roadsides. Garden Phlox (*Phlox paniculata*) is one of the most common, forming dense patches that flower from mid-summer into the fall.

Several common exotics include Bull Thistle (*Cirsium vulgare*), Yarrow (*Achillea millefolium*), Queen Anne's Lace (*Daucus carota*), Common Burdock (*Arctium minus*), and Woolly Mullein (*Verbascum thapsus*). Bull Thistle despite its prickly nature has an attractive pink-purple flower head. It is especially popular with insects and when in flower it is covered with bees, butterflies, and skippers. The flower heads of Yarrow and Queen Anne's Lace look similar as both have clusters of small white flowers. Queen Anne's Lace, however, has a flatter head and usually there is a purple floret in its center. Common Burdock is a broad herb, producing many purple, bristly, flower heads. Its fruit, a clinging bur, is well known for sticking to people's clothes and dogs' fur. Woolly Mullein is a tall, often over 5 feet, woolly-leaf plant with a showy spike of yellow flowers.

Several species of Milkweed, identified by their succulent, opposite, entire leaves and milky latex sap, are found in our area. The latex contains powerful heart poisons called cardenolides that discourage herbivores. Interestingly these same cardenolides have been used to treat congestive heart failure and atrial fibrillation in humans. Milkweeds produce large numbers of attractive flowers that are quite distinctive. Each flower has five downward facing petals and five erect hoods. Common Milkweed (*Asclepias syriaca*) often grows in dense colonies in open fields, while Poke Milkweed (*Asclepias exaltata*) is usually found along forest edges. When in flower during the summer, Milkweeds are very popular with pollinators, especially butterflies and skippers.

Milkweeds are also of special interest to several other insects. Adult Monarch Butterflies (*Danaus plexippus*) and Milkweed Tiger Moths (*Euchaetias egle*) lay their eggs on the leaves of Milkweed and the caterpillars feed on the leaves. These brightly colored caterpillars are not only immune to the toxins in the leaves, but they are able to store these poisons for their own defense. The adults of the Small Eastern Milkweed Bug (*Lygaeus kalmii*) lay their eggs on milkweed flower buds. The orange and black nymphs suck juices from the developing seeds and also are distasteful to predators. Later the adults may feed on the seeds. Often one finds dense colonies of small, globular, orange aphids on the milkweed stem. Aphids have tube-like mouthparts that suck the phloem sap of the milkweed. Red Milkweed Beetles (*Tetraopes tetraophthalmus*) feed and mate on milkweed leaves and flowers, while their larvae bore into and eat the roots.

A common non-woody vine found in fields and along roadsides is Virgin's Bower (*Clematis virginiana*). This vine with three leaflets is often confused with Poison Ivy (*Toxicodendron radicans*), however it has opposite leaves and its leaflets are coarsely toothed. Patches of Virgin's Bower can be profuse as its stems and leaf stalks wind and wrap around other plants. While Virgin's Bower produces an attractive cluster of white flowers in August, its clusters of wind-dispersed seeds with hair-like extensions are most noticeable. This distinctive fruit is often called Old Man's Beard.

Other vines include Common Morning Glory (*Ipomoea purpurea*) and Hedge Bindweed (*Calystegia sepium*). Both of these twining vines have distinctive large, showy, white, pink, or blue, funnel-shaped flowers. The leaves of Common Morning Glory are heart-shaped, while Hedge Bindweed has arrow-shaped triangular leaves.

As fields mature, briars often invade and form thickets. Several species of blackberry are common, including Tall Blackberry *(Rubus argutus),* Dewberry *(Rubus flagellaris),* and Swamp Dewberry *(Rubus hispidus).* In June, the blackberries produce attractive and aromatic displays of white flowers and in late July large, black, sweet fruit. Black Raspberry *(Rubus occidentalis)* is also occasionally found. Unlike the blackberries, its fruits come off easily, leaving a cone-shaped receptacle. Flowering Raspberry *(Rubus odoratus)* does not have prickles and produces very attractive large pink flowers. It produces small but sweet red raspberries in August and September. One plant that is often confused with blackberries is Multiflora Rose *(Rosa multiflora).* The leaf of this exotic from Asia usually has seven leaflets and its prickles are recurved. Unlike the blackberries it produces small apple-like "hips" that birds eat and disperse. Multiflora Rose is very aggressive and will take over a field, excluding native species.

Two species of elderberry, Red-berried Elder (*Sambucus pubens* [*racemosa*]) and Common Elder (*Sambucus canadensis*) are found in old fields and along forest edges. Red-berried Elder is most common above 4,000 feet. Both species have a similar compound leaf with 5-7 leaflets and produce showy terminal clusters of white flowers. Red-berried Elder, however, produces a cone-shaped cluster and a striking display of red fruits, while Common Elder produces a flat cluster of flowers and purple-black fruits. The fruits of the Red-berried Elder are inedible to people (but not birds) while the Common Elder fruits are edible when cooked. Another large, striking herb is Pokeweed (*Phytolacca americana*). This perennial with its succulent, alternate, entire leaves may grow over six feet tall and in the fall produces attractive racemes of dark purple fruits.

Fall Wildflowers

By late summer, old fields are in full bloom and the spectacular fall wildflower season is underway. Goldenrods often dominate these fields. There are some eleven species of goldenrod in our area and while many of these occur in open habitats, some do appear in forests. Tall Goldenrod (*Solidago canadensis [altissima]*), Late Goldenrod (*Solidago gigantea*), Gray Goldenrod (*Solidago nemoralis*), Rough-leaved Goldenrod (*Solidago patula*), Rough-stemmed Goldenrod (*Solidago rugosa*), and Elm-leaved Goldenrod (*Solidago ulmifolia*) have long terminal clusters of bright yellow flowers. Erect Goldenrod (*Solidago erecta*), Mountain Goldenrod (*Solidago roanensis*), and Silverrod (*Solidago bicolor*) have wand-like flower displays. Silverrod is unusual in that it is the only goldenrod with white flowers. Broad-leaved Goldenrod (*Solidago flexicaulis*) and Curtis' Goldenrod (*Solidago curtisii*) have flower clusters occurring along the stem. Tall Goldenrod, Late Goldenrod, Gray Goldenrod, Rough-leaved Goldenrod, and Rough-stemmed Goldenrod are the most common goldenrods of open fields.

Goldenrods are often blamed incorrectly for causing allergies. Goldenrods produce a heavy pollen grain that is carried off by pollinating insects. The real culprit is Common Ragweed (*Ambrosia artemisiifolia*). This inconspicuous herb with its aromatic, dissected leaves has small green flowers that produce small, wind dispersed pollen grains that cause hay fever.

Many goldenrods show a ball-like swelling on their stem. The Goldenrod Fly (*Eurosta solidaginis*) is responsible for this. The female fly lays an egg in the stem of the goldenrod that soon hatches into a larva. The saliva of the larva causes the stem of the goldenrod to produce an abnormal plant growth called a "gall". The larva develops inside the stem, feeding on plant tissue and the gall becomes golf ball sized. In the fall the larva chews an exit hole, but remains in the gall until the following spring when it pupates into an adult and departs. In the late fall as the goldenrod leaves fall off these galls become obvious. Opening the hard ball with a knife will reveal the worm-like larva within.

Asters may also form large beds in fields and along forest edges. At least 10 species may be found in our area. Asters produce daisy-like flowers in colors ranging from white to purple. A common aster in moist areas is the Purple-stemmed Aster (*Aster puniceus*). This showy aster has purple flowers, purplish stems, and large toothed leaves that clasp the stem. The bushy White Heath Aster (*Aster pilosus*) with its small white flowers and small lance shaped leaves is common in open fields. Heart-leaved Aster (*Aster cordifolius*) has numerous small pinkish-blue flowers and toothed, heart-shaped leaves and is usually found along rich forest edges. New England Aster (*Aster novae-angliae*) has larger 1-2 inch wide many rayed, blue flowers and is found in moist, open areas. Calico Aster (*Aster lateriflorus*) has small flowers with purplish disks and is found in fields and forest edges. Do not confuse Daisy Fleabane with the asters, as fleabanes have more than 40 flower rays, while most asters have 7-40 rays.

In addition to the goldenrods and asters, many other members of the daisy family are in bloom at this time, often growing in dense patches. Sneezeweed (*Helenium autumnale*) is one of the most common wildflowers at this time. Its yellow flowers have a knob-like disc and its 3-toothed petals droop around the disc. Sneezeweed gets its name by the historical use of its powdered leaves to induce sneezing. New York Ironweed (*Vernonia noveboracensis*) is quite at home in our mountains, often forming striking patches of purple in damp open fields. Ironweed may grow to heights of 9 feet and each plant produces an abundance of tubular, purple flower clusters. Boneset (*Eupatorium perfoliatum*) produces large clusters of dull-white flowers. It has distinctive wrinkled, opposite leaves that unite at the stem. Perhaps this feature is responsible for its name. Nonetheless, this herb has been used widely for medicinal purposes especially for colds and the flu. Similar in appearance to Boneset is White Snakeroot (*Eupatorium rugosum*). The flowers of White Snakeroot are whiter and its toothed leaves are egg-shaped and stalked. It prefers a more shaded environment, typically growing along forest edges.

Hollow Joe-Pye Weed (*Eupatorium fistulosum*) is another conspicuous wildflower at this time due to its large size and large number of purplish flower clusters. The toothed leaves of this plant occur in whorls of 3-6 along the stem. Joe Pye was an American Indian herb doctor who practiced in the 18th century. Equally showy is Tall Sunflower (*Helianthus giganteus*). Tall Sunflowers may reach heights of 10 feet with beautiful displays of yellow daisies with long rays. They tend to be found in moister locations. The smaller Thin-leaved Sunflower (*Helianthus decapetalous*) can be abundant on roadsides along woodland edges. Wild Lettuce (*Latuca canadensis*) is another giant, some plants towering over 10 feet. It has deeply lobed, toothed leaves and despite its size, its flower display of small pale-yellow flowers is less than impressive. As its name implies, the young leaves of this plant may be used in a salad. Several less attractive herbs include Horseweed (*Erigeron canadensis*) and Pilewort (*Erechtites hieracifolia*). These both have non-showy white flowers with brush-like tips.

Not all fall wildflowers are composites (members of the daisy family). In mid-summer Common Evening Primrose (*Oenothera biennis*) begins to flower. Spikes of long yellow flowers with four petals are produced into the fall. Individual flowers open in the evening and last only one day. A common orchid that appears in moist fields and edges is Nodding Ladies' Tresses (*Spiranthes cernua*). This orchid produces a spike of fragrant white flowers. In wet meadows and along open streams, spikes of brilliant blue flowers of Great Lobelia (*Lobelia siphilitica*) appear in early fall. Another lobelia, Indian Tobacco (*Lobelia inflata*) produces smaller, less showy light blue flowers in fields and open woods. Both of these lobelias have interesting medicinal properties. American Indians made a root tea from Great Lobelia to treat syphilis and used other plant parts to treat colds, headaches, worms, and sores. The dried leaves of Indian Tobacco were smoked to relieve respiratory problems. It was also used to induce vomiting, thus earning the name of "pukeweed". Today, lobeline, an alkaloid found in Indian Tobacco, is used in commercial anti-smoking lozenges and chewing gums as it is thought to be a non-addictive substitute for nicotine.

The displays of open-country wildflowers are widespread throughout our area, especially along our roadsides. In the fall it is often difficult to keep one's eyes on the road as they stray to the showy displays of wildflowers along the edges. A nice place to watch the progression of wildflowers in an Old Field community through the summer and fall is the Lees-McRae College's Elk Valley Preserve. The rich diversity of wildflowers during the summer attracts large numbers of butterflies while large numbers of goldenrods and asters produce a spectacular fall flower show.

BIRDS

The Southern Appalachians are well known for their great diversity of songbirds. Songbirds belong to the avian order Passeriformes and are also called perching birds. These are typically small birds and include the warblers, wrens, vireos, sparrows, tanagers, and finches. The great forests of the Southern Appalachians provide an important breeding ground for many species of neotropical migrants, those songbirds that spend the winter in the New World tropics.

Each spring this area is inundated with these tropical visitors and the forests become alive with their songs and bright colors. This is especially true of one of the most beautiful families of birds, the warblers (family Parulidae). Approximately 18 species of warblers breed in our area and they can be found in most of our habitats. Their arrival brings much joy to the bird watching community. This area is also a major migration route in the spring and fall as northern-breeding warblers move through in great numbers. Of course, many other groups of birds are also of great interest and beauty.

The dense forest can make bird watching difficult and frustrating for aspiring bird watchers. Even a bird as brilliant as a Scarlet Tanager can be hard to spot in the canopy of a forest. Patience is clearly a prerequisite for bird watching in this area. Hearing birds, however, is not a problem. The cacophony of bird song in our forests produces a rich variety of sounds from the melodic song of the Wood Thrush to the wispy song of the Black and White Warbler. Determining what bird is producing what song, however, can be a challenge, but one that with a bit of time is not insurmountable.

Residency

It is important to understand the residence status of a bird. There are four general categories. *Residents* breed and stay in an area for the entire year. *Summer Residents* breed in the area, but migrate to lower elevations or lower latitudes for the winter. This is our largest group of birds and includes all the warbler species. *Transients* are migrants that pass through the area in the spring and fall on their way to and from their breeding grounds in the north. *Winter Residents* are the smallest group, and includes several species that irregularly move down during the winter from the north.

Habitats

Most birds have specific habitat requirements and it is unlikely that you will see the same birds in a forest as you would in farmland. Listed below are the major habitat types and those birds common to each type.

Open Country

Throughout our area open country abounds, with farmland creating habitat for many species of birds. These open habitats vary from grassy pastures to old fields covered with goldenrods, asters, and small shrubs. Commonly seen soaring over these fields are Red-tailed Hawks (*Buteo jamaicensis*). Red-tailed Hawks belong to the group of hawks called buteos, due to their habit of soaring and circling on warm thermals and then dropping down on their prey. Small mammals make up the majority of their prey, although snakes and even insects are sometimes taken.

Turkey Vultures (*Cathartes aura*) can also be seen soaring over fields throughout the year, although they may be rare during cold spells in the winter. Turkey Vultures are easily recognized by the shallow V shape that their wings produce during soaring. Turkey Vultures have benefited greatly from the frequent road kills our highways provide. American Kestrels (*Falco sparverius*) are a rare breeder in the mountains and are most often seen perched on power lines in the fall.

Several aerial insectivores may be seen locally, including Barn Swallows (*Hirundo rustica*), Northern Rough-winged Swallows (*Stelgidopteryx serripennis*), and Tree Swallows (*Tachycineta bicolor*). Barn Swallows are especially common around farms and make use of local barns as shelters to make their mud nests.

Tree Swallows prefer open areas around water and forest edge. They can be seen at Valle Crucis Park, where they nest in the Bluebird boxes. Chimney Swifts (*Chaetura pelagica*) may also be seen in open areas, especially around rocky outcrops. This aerial acrobat has adapted well to man often breeding in the chimneys of buildings and homes. One of the largest breeding colonies in the area is on the Lees-McRae College campus in the old stone chimneys on campus. The evening and morning congregation of swifts on the campus is impressive.

In late August and early September flocks of migrating Common Nighthawks (*Chordeiles minor*) become a welcome sight over fields, parks, and lighted parking lots. The nighthawk, despite its name is not a true hawk, but a member of the "goatsucker" family Caprimulgidae that includes Whip-poor-wills and Chuck-will's-widows. They have also been called "bullbats" and even "flying toads". Nighthawks are typically "crepuscular", being active in the morning and evenings. They are most often observed at dusk, when they swoop through the air snaring flying insects, including mosquitoes, flying ants, beetles, and moths.

The fields themselves are home to Eastern Meadowlarks (*Sturnella magna*), American Robins *(Turdus migratorius)*, Song Sparrows (*Melospiza melodia)*, Chipping Sparrows (*Spizella passerina),* and Field Sparrows *(Spizella pusilla)*. The House Finch (*Carpodacus mexicanus)*, a native of the southwest, was introduced to the east and has become abundant in our area. Large flocks, with the red males and brown females, may be seen in open fields. In the winter, White-throated Sparrows (*Zonotrichia albicollis)* are common in weedy fields. Eastern Bluebirds (*Sialia sialis)* can be commonly seen on fences around farmland, while Eastern Kingbirds (*Tyrannus tyrannus)* perch on trees in open areas as they sally out for flying insects. In open areas around barns and houses House Wrens (*Troglodytes aedon)* often move in, making their presence known by their bubbling song. Northern Mockingbirds (*Mimus polyglottis)* may be found in open areas with scattered trees, although they are not nearly as common in the mountains as at lower elevations.

The number of Wild Turkeys (*Meleagris gallopavo)* in our area increased dramatically in the 1990's. Groups of turkeys are often seen cruising through fields and woodlands. These groups typically consist of females escorted by a "Tom". The male has a beard of hair-like feathers hanging from its breast. Turkeys like a mix of open field and forest with females nesting on the ground in the forest. Northern Bobwhites (*Colinus virginianus),* our only quail, are more common at lower elevations, especially in Christmas tree plantations.

Other open country birds include American Crows (*Corvus brachyrhynchos),* European Starlings (*Sturnus vulgaris),* Brown-headed Cowbirds (*Molothrus ater),* Red-winged Blackbirds (*Agelaius phoeniceus),* American Goldfinches (*Carduelis tristis),* Common Grackles (*Quiscalus quiscula),* and Mourning Doves (*Zenaida macroura).*

The Grassy Balds of Roan Mountain and Big Yellow Mountain are home to a mix of open country birds, including American Robins, Dark-eyed Juncos, Vesper Sparrows (*Pooecetes gramineus),* Barn Swallows, and Horned Larks (*Eremophila alpestris).* During the winter months, Snow Buntings (*Plectrophenax nivalis)* are sometimes found on these balds. The winter plumage of these arctic breeders is a mostly brown back and head, and a white breast and belly.

Forest Edge

This common habitat that borders homes, farms, and power lines produces a mix of shrubs, trees and open areas that many birds find attractive. In the lower shrubs Eastern Towhees (*Pipilo erythrophthalmus),* Gray Catbirds (*Dumetella carolinensis),* Brown Thrashers (*Toxostoma rufum),* Carolina Wrens (*Thryothorus ludovicianus),* Yellow Warblers (*Dendroica petechia),* Common Yellowthroats (*Geothlypis trichas),* and Northern Cardinals *(Cardinalis cardinalis)* are found. Gray Catbirds are especially obvious due to their vociferous nature, giving their plaintive *mew* calls while the males produce a patchwork song of varying phrases. Like their cousins the mockingbirds, catbirds are accomplished mimics of other species.

Carolina Wrens are also quite vocal with a resounding *teakettle-teakettle-teakettle* song. These charming birds are well known for their habit of nesting around and even in houses. They are regular residents of our back porch, nesting in any nook available.

The rare Golden-winged Warbler (*Vermivora chrysoptera)* is known to breed in our area in early successional habitats, preferring the brushy growth found along power lines and in clear cuts.

Mourning Doves, Chestnut-sided Warblers (*Dendroica pensylvanica),* Least Flycatchers (*Empidonax minimus),* Indigo Buntings (*Passerina cyanea),* Blue-Gray Gnatcatchers (*Polioptila caerulea)* and Northern Flickers (*Colaptes auratus)* frequent the trees along these edges. Chestnut-sided Warblers are common along forest edges and in brushy areas, where males sing their *please-please-please-to-meet-you* song. The rich chestnut sides and cocked tail are distinctive for this warbler.

Indigo Buntings also like these edges, enabling one to get nice views of the brilliant blue males. Males perch at the top of trees and sing a high pitched song of paired phrases. The brown female buntings are often confused with finches or sparrows. The Blue-gray Gnatcatcher (*Polioptila caerulea*) is recognized by its white eye-ring and long black and white tail that is often cocked. This active, small bird is more common at lower elevations. Northern Flickers are unusual woodpeckers in that they often forage on the ground on ants and other insects. Their white rump is obvious when in flight as is their dipping flight. These woodpeckers are quite vocal, giving a series of *wicker* notes as well as *klee-yer* calls.

One of most beloved edge species is the Ruby-throated Hummingbird (*Archilochus colubris*). The ruby-throat arrives in mid-April, when males begin to set up their fiercely defended territories. This hummingbird takes advantage of the many species of flowering plants that inhabit the edge. In particular, beds of Bee Balm and jewelweed flower as the young hummingbirds fledge, providing a vital food source as these birds prepare for their southward migration to Mexico and Central America. While the bulk of the ruby-throat's diet may be nectar, these hummers do feed on insects and will sally out to catch small flies. Ruby-throats typically leave our area in late September with the males leaving first and the females and young following later.

Edges are good places to see flocks of Cedar Waxwings (*Bombycilla cedrorum*). Waxwings are often heard first as they are quite vocal producing a high-pitched *zeee* call. Waxwings frequent all habitats in their quest for ripe fruit. While primarily a fruit-eater, it is not uncommon to find waxwings feeding over rivers and ponds on emerging aquatic insects such as mayflies. This behavior can be seen during the summer months on the Elk River just behind the Mill Pond dam.

Forest

The forest communities show the greatest diversity of birds. By understanding where birds are located in the forest layers, species identification is easier. The two common inhabitants of the forest floor are the Eastern Towhee (formerly known as the Rufous-sided Towhee) and the Ovenbird (*Seiurus aurocapillus*). The towhee can often be seen or heard scratching in the leaf litter in its quest for invertebrates. Also listen for its *sweep* call and *drink-your-tea* song. The Ovenbird with its large eyes, streaked breast, and terrestrial habits, make this warbler appear quite thrush-like. It makes its presence known by its explosive *teacher-teacher-teacher* song.

Ruffed Grouse (*Bonasa umbellus*) are also found on the forest floor. Grouse are usually seen as they explode out of the undergrowth when they are disturbed. The territorial males produce a drumming sound by beating their wings to attract females. In the summer it is not uncommon to run across a grouse hen with her young in tow. Ruffed Grouse are year-round residents and survive the winter by eating buds and shoots.

American Woodcocks (*Scolopax minor)* are difficult to see due to their nocturnal habits and cryptic coloration. Like grouse they are most often seen when flushed from the undergrowth, producing a whistling noise from their wings. Watch closely where they land, and it may be possible to observe this unusual sandpiper.

Where forests have a well-developed shrub layer, especially of rhododendron, many birds are found there. The Dark-eyed Junco (*Junco hyemalis)* is a common bird of the understory and is the bird "most likely to be seen" in the mountains. When disturbed it often flits about giving *chip* calls. It has a chunky body, sparrow-like light colored bill, and white outer tail feathers. Also listen for its one pitch, trill song.

The shrub layer is home to a number of warbler species. These include the Black-throated Blue Warbler (*Dendroica caerulescens*), Canada Warbler (*Wilsonia canadenis*), Hooded Warbler (*Wilsonia citrina*), and Worm-eating Warbler (*Helmitheros vermivorus)*. The beautiful Black-throated Blue Warbler is common and its buzzing *beer-beer-bee* song is easy to pick out. This species shows striking sexual dimorphism (different appearance of males and females) where the males display a rich blue back, black throat, and white belly, while the females are generally an olive drab with a pale eyebrow.

The Canada Warbler is common at mid and high elevations. The males have an attractive black necklace set off against a bright yellow throat and breast. Also a conspicuous eye-ring accents its large eyes. Its song is a rapid jumble sounding something like *chup-chuppity-swee-ditchee*. This active warbler will often expose itself when you enter its territory, giving a series of calls and displays.

The Hooded Warbler is easier to hear than see with its loud *wee-tee, wee-tee, wee-tee-you* song. Males have a bright yellow face with a dark black hood and throat. This warbler also has large eyes that are an adaptation for living in the shady understory. While cruising about, the Hooded Warbler rapidly flicks its tail open, exposing white outer tail feathers.

The Worm-eating Warbler is more common at lower elevations. The males and females of this stocky warbler look alike, with an olive-brown body and two pairs of black stripes on its buffy orange head. Males give an insect-like trill song.

A rare warbler of the dense rhododendron thickets, especially along creeks, is the Swainson's Warbler (*Limnothylpis swainsonii*). This shy warbler is difficult to see due to its habit of feeding on the ground in its dense habitat. Instead, listen for its loud *whee-whee-whip-poor-will* song.

The rich canopy of our forests contains the majority of bird species. This includes two species of vireo, the Blue-headed Vireo (*Vireo solitarius*) (formerly known as the Solitary Vireo) and the Red-eyed Vireo (*Vireo olivaceus*). The Blue-headed Vireo typically frequents the lower canopy, while the Red-eyed Vireo favors the higher canopy. The Blue-headed Vireo also moves in a slower, more deliberate manner than the more active Red-eyed Vireo. Both vireos are active songsters, producing long series of melodic phrases. The Blue-headed Vireo is one of the first migrants to appear in the spring and its song is a harbinger of the spring season.

The canopy warblers include the Black-throated Green Warbler (*Dendroica virens*), Blackburnian Warbler (*Dendroica fusca*), American Redstart (*Setophaga ruticilla*) and Northern Parula (*Parula americana*). Black-throated Green Warblers are the most common of this group. They are relatively tame and it is easy to watch them foraging for insects among the tree branches. Their wispy song is some variation of *zoo-zee-zoo-zoo-zee*.

Male Blackburnian Warblers sport a brilliant orange head and throat with a triangular black patch behind the eye. In our area this warbler seems to like woodlands with a mix of deciduous trees and evergreens, such as hemlocks or spruce. Their habit of foraging high in the canopy can make viewing tough on the neck.

The American Redstart is a striking warbler, the male showing a black, orange, and white plumage, while the female sports a gray, yellow, and white plumage. It has the unusual behavior of partly spreading its wings and fanning its tail as it actively forages through the canopy. Redstarts are also common along forest edges and are often found along streams. Redstarts are prolific songsters. Their songs are a series of high, buzzy notes and a single male may have a repertoire of several different songs.

The Northern Parula is heard more often than seen due to its habit of foraging in the upper canopy and its small size. It is a very vocal warbler, producing a rapid, buzzing trill that rises in pitch. They are most common in Cove Forests that have Eastern Hemlocks and along riparian corridors.

Two of our most spectacular birds that make their home in the forest canopy are the Scarlet Tanager (*Piranga olivacea*) and the Rose-breasted Grosbeak (*Pheucticus ludovicianus*). While these neotropical migrants occur throughout our forests, the Scarlet Tanager is more common in Mixed Oak Forests, while the Rose-breasted Grosbeak is more common in Northern Hardwood and Cove Forests. The brilliant plumage of the males makes them unmistakable. The females of the two species, however, are often overlooked or misidentified as the female Scarlet Tanager is yellow-olive, while the female grosbeak has a brown streaked body, resembling a burly sparrow. Interestingly, the male Scarlet Tanager molts in the fall, spending the winter with a female-like plumage. During this fall molt you may see unusual tanagers with a splotchy red-yellow plumage. Look for male Scarlet Tanagers perched at the top of trees giving their raspy, robin-like song. The Rose-breasted Grosbeak also produces a robin-like song, but it is more melodious and has been likened to "a robin that has taken voice lessons" by Peterson.

Three species of flycatcher are found in our woodlands. The small Acadian Flycatcher (*Empidonax virescens*), while difficult to see, is given away by its explosive *pizza* song. When seen, it is usually perched on a branch, where it sallies out to snare flying insects. It typically is found low in the canopy or in the understory. The Eastern Wood-Pewee (*Contopus virens*) is best recognized by its song, a slow *pee-a-wee*. The larger Great Crested Flycatcher (*Myiarchus crinitus*) is found in the high canopy in open woodlands.

The guild of bark gleaning birds is well represented in our forests. Woodpeckers include the Downy Woodpecker (*Picoides pubescens*), Hairy Woodpecker *(Picoides villosus)*, Pileated Woodpecker (*Dryocopus pileatus*), and the occasional Yellow-bellied Sapsucker (*Sphyrapicus nuchalis*). Red-Bellied Woodpeckers (*Melanerpes carolinus*) are more common at lower elevations.

The Downy Woodpecker is our smallest and most common woodpecker. During the fall and winter it often hangs out with chickadees and titmice in mixed species flocks. It advertises its presence with its distinctive, high pitched *pik* call. The Hairy Woodpecker with its white back and black and white wings looks similar to the Downy, however, it is larger and has a noticeably heavier bill.

Pileated Woodpeckers with their large size, red crest, and black body are easy to recognize and their loud calls consisting of a series of high-pitched notes are unmistakable. Yellow-bellied Sapsuckers are uncommon during the summer, being limited to Northern Hardwood areas, but become more frequent in the fall, when migrants swell their numbers. Their presence in an area is indicated by the rows of holes or "wells" that sapsuckers drill in a variety of trees to feed on the tree sap.

White-breasted Nuthatches (*Sitta carolinensis*) frequent deciduous forests while Red-breasted Nuthatches (*Sitta canadensis*) favor mixed evergreen-deciduous forests. Nuthatches travel in family groups and are often heard before being seen as they use their nasal *yank-yank-yank* call to communicate. The strong legs and long claws of nuthatches allow them to scamper up, down, and around tree trunks and branches in their quest for insects. Nuthatches are often found in mixed species flocks with chickadees and titmice during the fall and winter.

The enchanting Brown Creeper (*Certhia americana*) is another tree-hugger that works its way spirally up a tree. With its small, chunky, brown-streaked body, curved bill and long tail, the creeper is easy to recognize, but may be difficult to see as it is well camouflaged. Listen for its distinctive high pitched *see-see-see-sisi-see* song. Brown Creepers are most common at middle and high elevations.

The Black and White Warbler (*Mniotilta varia*) is a most unusual warbler, sporting a woodpecker-like black and white plumage and a nuthatch-like habit of creeping along branches and trunks probing for insects. This warbler busily works the bark of a tree, occasionally letting loose with its high-pitched *wee-see-wee-see-wee-see-wee-see-wee-see* song.

Two neotropical migrants, the Veery (*Catharus fuscescens*) and the Wood Thrush (*Hylocichla mustelina*), may have a drab plumage, but their songs may be the most beautiful of the forest birds. These two thrushes can be told apart by the heavily spotted breast of the Wood Thrush, compared to the lightly spotted breast of the Veery. The ethereal songs of these thrushes echo through the forests. The Veery produces a *ve-ur-ve-ur-veer-veer* song, while the Wood Thrush produces a flutelike song of melodic phrases with pauses between each phrase. During fall migration they are joined by their northern-breeding relatives, the Hermit Thrush (*Catharus guttatus*), Gray-cheeked Thrush (*Catharus minimus*), and Swainson's Thrush (*Catharus ustulatus*). At this time these thrushes show a strong liking for fruit and can often be found gorging themselves at fruiting trees and shrubs.

A common year-round forest resident is the Blue Jay (*Cyanocitta cristata*). Like most corvids, Blue Jays travel in noisy, family groups and their impressive vocal repertoire advertise their presence. Several other year-round residents play important roles in the forest bird community. The Carolina Chickadee (*Poecile carolinensis)* and the Tufted Titmouse (*Baeolophus bicolor)* form the nucleus of mixed-species flocks in the fall and winter. As groups of chickadees and titmice move through the forest foraging, other species including woodpeckers, nuthatches, and warblers join the chickadees. Observing a large mixed-species flock in action is an exciting event. In the summer, chickadees and titmice set up territories and both are cavity nesters. Both species feed on a variety of insects and seeds.

Several birds of prey are found in the forests. The Broad-winged Hawk (*Buteo platypterus)* is a chunky, crow-sized hawk with a tail with broad black and white bands. This buteo hunts from a perch on unsuspecting mammals, birds, and reptiles. In the fall, large numbers of broad-wings migrate down the Southern Appalachians on their way to the tropics. Viewing large "kettles" (circular formations of soaring hawks) of migrating Broad-winged Hawks in October on the Blue Ridge Parkway (Ship Rock MP 303) or in the Linville Gorge (Wiseman's View, Hawksbill, Table Rock, or Pinnacle Rocks) can be spectacular.

Cooper's Hawks (*Accipiter cooperii)* and Sharp-shinned Hawks (*Accipiter striatus)* may also be found in the forest, where the Cooper's is more common than the Sharp-shinned. These sleek accipiters feed primarily on birds, sweeping through the forest snaring birds with their feet. They are also well known for staking out bird feeders. During fall migration both species may be seen soaring, although they often soar at high altitudes where they are difficult to see.

Common nighttime birds of prey include the Great Horned Owl (*Bubo virginianus*), Eastern Screech Owl (*Otus asio),* and the Barred Owl (*Strix varia).* Great Horned Owls and Barred Owls are both large owls, but the Great Horned Owl has ear tufts and yellow eyes, while the Barred Owl lacks ear tufts and has striking dark eyes. While the Barred Owl keeps to the forest, the Great Horned Owl hunts in forest and field. The Eastern Screech Owl is a small owl, measuring some eight inches, and has yellow eyes and ear tufts. While it is difficult to see owls, hearing them is not. Great Horned Owls have their distinctive *Hoo-hoo-oo-hoo-hoo,* while the Barred Owl produces a haunting *who-cooks-for-you, who-cooks-for-you-all.* Eastern Screech Owls, meanwhile, make a descending wailing call with a trill at the end. Owls use these calls to mark their territories and for communication between breeding pairs.

Spruce-Fir Forest

This high elevation forest with its mix of trees and shrubs produces a smaller but distinct bird community. The Dark-eyed Junco is the most common bird of this community. Almost as abundant is the diminutive Golden-crowned Kinglet (*Regulus satrapa*). As you hike through these evergreen forests, listen for the high pitched *see-see-see* songs of this beautiful bird. Kinglets typically travel in family groups and are very active in their never-ending search for insects. Despite their abundance, Golden-crowned Kinglets can be frustrating to observe due to their constant movement through the dark spruce and firs.

The most vocal bird in this forest without question is the Winter Wren (*Troglodytes troglodytes*). Its loud, melodious song of a series of trills is impressive for such a little fellow. It is another tough one to spot as it lurks in the undergrowth.

Other birds that may be found in this evergreen forest include the Veery, Gray Catbird, Eastern Towhee, Red-breasted Nuthatch, Canada Warbler, Blue-headed Vireo, and Brown Creeper. Several locally rare species that may be found here include the Magnolia Warbler (*Dendroica magnolia*), Hermit Thrush (*Catharus guttatus*), Black-capped Chickadee *(Poecile atricapillus),* and the unusual Red Crossbill (*Loxia curvirostra*). Flocks of crossbills descend on spruce and fir, using their crossed bill to excise seeds from their cones. Their appearance is erratic and depends upon available cone crops. White-winged Crossbills (*Loxia leucoptera*) have also been seen on Roan Mountain and Grandfather Mountain but are less common than their red cousins, and are not known to breed in the area.

The diminutive Northern Saw-Whet Owl (*Aegolius acadicus*) occurs on Grandfather Mountain and Roan Mountain at the higher elevations in Spruce-Fir and Northern Hardwood Forests. Listen for its *too-too-too-too* repeated whistle-like call. This rare owl can be quite tame and will pay little heed to its admirer.

The rocky outcrops of these high elevation forests also provide important breeding sites for Common Ravens *(Corvus corax)* and the rare Peregrine Falcon *(Falco peregrinus)*. Ravens and crows can be difficult to separate. Ravens are larger with a long, wedge shaped tail. Probably the easiest way to separate the two is by their vocalizations, especially the distinctive croak call of the raven. During the summer, ravens can be seen soaring around the higher rocky peaks of Grandfather Mountain, while during the winter they often disperse to lower elevations to find food. The raven is clearly the king of the mountain, often mobbing Peregrine Falcons and Golden Eagles that invade their domain.

Peregrine Falcons, while not common in our area, can be observed from rocky overlooks at different elevations. They breed regularly on Grandfather Mountain, Big Lost Cove Cliffs in the Pisgah National Forest, and in Linville Gorge. Nesting areas are typically closed when these birds are breeding. Golden Eagles (*Aquila chrysaetos*) appear erratically in our area, usually in fall and winter, with no current breeding records. Eagles that are sighted are usually juveniles.

Heath

The shrub dominated heath communities such as the Cragway and Ship Rock on Grandfather Mountain attract birds that prefer dense undergrowth. These include the Dark-eyed Junco, Gray Catbird, Chestnut-sided Warbler, Canada Warbler, Veery, Indigo Bunting, Song Sparrow, and Eastern Towhee. The abundance of fleshy fruit in this community also attracts Cedar Waxwings, American Robins, and thrushes in the late summer and fall.

The Green Alder thickets on Roan Mountains are home to the Alder Flycatcher (*Empidonax alnorum*). Listen for its song, a descending *fee-bee'-o*.

Wetlands

A number of birds are associated with wetland habitats. The Louisiana Waterthrush (*Seiurus motacilla*) may be found walking along the shady streams of the forest coves. This warbler is unmistakable due to its habit of bobbing its tail and body as if bossa nova music is playing in its head. Acadian Flycatchers also frequent the understory along streams.

Along the rivers Eastern Phoebes (*Sayornis phoebe*) are common on open shorelines as they sally out over the water to capture insects. Their song is an emphatic *fee-bee*. Baltimore Orioles (*Icterus galbula*) may be found in open woodlands bordering rivers. Belted Kingfishers (*Ceryle alcyon*) with their distinctive rattle call are common along our rivers. These fish hunters stay here year round and their winter presence perched over icy rivers is sure to elicit some form of sympathy. Spotted Sandpipers (*Actitis macularia*) and Solitary Sandpipers (*Tringa solitaria*) also frequent open shorelines during their spring and fall migrations through our area.

Great Blue Herons (*Ardea herodias*), Green Herons (*Butorides virescens*), and Great Egrets (*Ardea alba*) may be found along open rivers during the summer months. A canoe ride down the New River offers a good opportunity to view these birds.

Our common breeding duck is the beautiful Wood Duck (*Aix sponsa*). The male Wood Duck with its colorful, crested head is unmistakable. This duck is unusual in that it nests in tree cavities and is thus associated with beaver ponds, man-made ponds, and rivers that are surrounded by forest. An excellent place to view these magnificent ducks is on Bass Lake on the Moses Cone Estate. Mallards (*Anas platyrhynchos*) and Canada Geese (*Branta canadensis*) have become common year-round residents around many man-made ponds and lakes, taking advantage of human handouts.

During migration a mix of waterfowl move through the area, although never in large numbers. These include the Common Loon (*Gavia immer*), Pied-billed Grebe (*Podilymbus podiceps*), Blue-winged Teal (*Anas discors*), Ring-necked Duck (*Aythya collaris*), Lesser Scaup (*Aythya affinis*), Bufflehead (*Bucephala albeola*), Hooded Merganser (*Lophodytes cucullatus*), and Red-breasted Merganser (*Mergus serrator*). Price Lake and Bass Lake on the Blue Ridge Parkway and the Mill Pond and Wildcat Lake in Banner Elk are good places to look for these waterfowl.

In brushy areas around beaver ponds and marshy wetlands, the Common Yellowthroat (*Geothlypis trichas*) is at home. Its *withchity-witchity-witchity-witch* song is difficult to miss. The male of this warbler sports a black mask, while the female is a duller yellow. This wren-like warbler may be glimpsed as it nervously flits through the brush. Also in open marshy areas, Willow Flycatchers (*Empidonax trailii*), Red-winged Blackbirds (*Agelaius phoeniceus*), and Song Sparrows (*Melospiza melodia*) may be found.

Transients

During the spring and fall months, local birdwatchers get the opportunity to observe migrants moving between their breeding grounds in the north and their southern wintering grounds. The fall months, between August and October, are especially rewarding as migrant bird numbers have swelled due to the influx of juveniles into the populations. This is a good time to pick up some new warbler species, although identification of these fall warblers can be tricky. Many species have lost their striking breeding plumage or are in their drab juvenile plumage.

Migrant warblers include the Tennessee Warbler (*Vermivora peregrina*), Golden-winged Warbler *(Vermivora chrysoptera),* Yellow-rumped Warbler (*Dendroica coronata*), Bay-breasted Warbler (*Dendroica castanea*), Magnolia Warbler (*Dendroica magnolia*), Prairie Warbler (*Dendroica discolor*), Palm Warbler (*Dendroica palmarum*), Blackpoll Warbler (*Dendroica striata*), Cape May Warbler (*Dendroica tigrina*) and Northern Waterthrush (*Seiurus noveboracensis*). A number of these warblers, especially the Tennessee Warbler, Palm Warbler, Yellow-rumped Warbler, and Magnolia Warbler are quite common in the fall. Other migrants include the Hermit Thrush, Swainson's Thrush, Gray-cheeked Thrush, Ruby-crowned Kinglet *(Regulus calendula)*, Philadelphia Vireo *(Vireo philadelphicus)*, Savannah Sparrow *(Passerculus sandwichensis)*, and Swamp Sparrow *(Melospiza georgiana)*.

Bird Feeders

Bird feeders are an excellent way to get close up views of many of our birds. A variety of seed-eating birds appear at feeders including forest and open country birds. While feeders are most active during winter, many birds will also use them in the summer. Rose-breasted Grosbeaks, a summer resident, will use feeders in the spring, summer, and fall, before it departs for southern climes. Some common feeder birds include House Finches, American Goldfinches, Tufted Titmice, Carolina Chickadees, White-breasted Nuthatches, Red-Breasted Nuthatches, Eastern Towhees, Indigo Buntings, Dark-eyed Juncos, Song Sparrows, Northern Cardinals, and Mourning Doves.

Feeders also attract several species that are often difficult to see, including the Pine Siskin (*Carduelis pinus*), Purple Finch (*Carpodacus purpureus*), and Evening Grosbeak (*Coccothraustes vespertinus*). Pine Siskins are erratic residents, moving in flocks throughout our area. Purple Finches and Evening Grosbeaks are winter visitors from the north. The appearance of a flock of Evening Grosbeaks at a feeder is a special event as these large seed eaters do not appear every year, but only during invasion years.

For those who do not have a bird feeder, Grandfather Mountain has bird feeders set up on the patio behind the museum. These feeders attract a large number of birds, including non-seed eating birds that are attracted to the bird activity. And of course, there will be several Red Squirrels lurking around the feeders to keep it entertaining.

MAMMALS

The different mammal groups are well represented in our area. Many of our mammals are widespread in the east, however a number of species are northern species with an Appalachian distribution. The Red Squirrel (*Tamiasciurus hudsonicus*) is found up the Appalachians, across Canada to Alaska and down the Rocky Mountains to New Mexico and Arizona. This feisty squirrel also known as a "boomer" is a common, visible inhabitant of our forests. It is also quite vocal, producing an impressive repertoire of sounds, including rattle, screech, growl, buzz and chirp calls that are used as alarm calls and territorial defense. Its chirp call sounds very similar to a bird. The Red Squirrel is smaller than the Grey Squirrel (*Sciurus carolinensis*) and has a white belly and a white eye ring. Its tail is also proportionately smaller and is often held erect. In winter a jaunty tuft of hairs grows from the tip of the boomer's ears. Boomers are found in the high elevation Spruce-fir Forests and also in deciduous forests. They seem to prefer deciduous forests with evergreen trees, especially Eastern Hemlocks. They are active during the day and throughout the year (they do not hibernate). Anyone who has spent much time around boomers quickly becomes enamored of them. Their highly territorial nature (both males and females defend territories from other squirrels and trespassing hikers) is highly amusing. Occasionally Red and Grey squirrels occupy the same area, however, the Red Squirrel dominates in the mountain forests while the Grey Squirrel is more common at the lower elevations and around human habitation.

Another common rodent of our forests is the Eastern Chipmunk (*Tamias striatus*). This five striped chipmunk is more at home on the forest floor, especially around rock piles where it digs its long burrow system.

Chipmunk burrow holes do not have dirt piled in front like groundhog holes and are quite small. Chipmunks are very noisy, producing a variety of chips and trills. A hiker is sure to elicit repeated chip calls from a chipmunk. If you get too close, the chip may expand to a trill alarm call accompanied by body and tail twitching. If chipmunks are caught away from their burrows they will take to the trees, however, they seem to prefer disappearing underground. Chipmunks do hibernate, although they may appear during the winter. They cache stores of seeds, including nuts that they eat during the winter.

One of our most interesting squirrels is difficult to see due to its nocturnal nature. The Southern Flying Squirrel (*Glaucomys volans*) is found in our deciduous forests, inhabiting tree cavities during the daytime hours. This is our smallest squirrel, possessing striking large black eyes ringed by black hairs. Probably the best way to watch flying squirrels is at a bird feeder after dark. Their presence is often given away by their high-pitched chip calls. They are capable of incredible acrobatic and gliding feats. By use of the membranes that stretch from their wrists to their ankles they are able to make sharp turns and swoops. They are also very agile, scampering up and down trees.

Another flying squirrel, the Northern Flying Squirrel (*Glaucomys sabrinus*) is more commonly found in the high elevation Spruce-Fir Forests of Roan Mountain and Grandfather Mountain. This rare squirrel, larger than its southern cousin, is believed to be a relict of cooler times when it was probably more widespread. Now its populations are fragmented throughout the Southern Appalachians and its numbers appear to be declining.

The largest member of the squirrel family, the Woodchuck (*Marmota monax*) inhabits open country. This proverbial harbinger of spring is also known as the Groundhog and Whistle Pig. This large, grayish-black ground squirrel is common along the Blue Ridge Parkway, appreciating the mowed roadsides that produce excellent herbage. They are also common on farmland, much to the ire of local farmers because of their burrowing habits. Large burrow systems are used for breeding, shelter from predators, sleeping, and hibernation. Their burrows are obvious due to their habit of leaving excavated dirt around the burrow entrance. Burrows may be found in open fields or in bordering forests. Woodchucks are ravenous, as they need to lay down a thick layer of fat for their winter hibernation. They typically emerge in March from their long winter sleep. Although Woodchucks prefer staying on the ground do not be surprised to see one up a tree. This is usually the last resort for escaping a ground predator such as a dog.

Several inconspicuous rodents frequent our forests. The Deer Mouse (*Peromyscus maniculatus*) is the most common forest mouse, although it is often found with the White-footed Mouse (*Peromyscus leucopus*). At lower elevations, the White-footed Mouse becomes more common. The Deer Mouse has large eyes, dark gray body, whitish belly, and a bicolored tail that is dark above and white below. The White-Footed Mouse looks similar to the Deer Mouse, but has white feet and its tail is indistinctly bicolored. These two species of mice have similar habits and appear to occupy the same ecological niche. Both are nocturnal, often nest in trees, and are omnivorous, feeding on seeds, fruits, buds, fungi, and a wide variety of arthropods. Short-lived in the wild, these mice are capable of impressive reproduction. One pair of wild caught mice produced 13 litters in slightly over a year. That forests are not overrun by these mice is attributed to their popularity with many predators, including snakes, hawks, owls, weasels, foxes, and bobcats.

The Allegheny Woodrat (*Neotoma magister*) looks like a large mouse (not very ratty looking) with a densely haired tail. This forest dweller is an attractive creature with large eyes, and soft, brown-gray fur with black-tipped hairs. Woodrats are well known for building impressive houses of twigs, sticks, and debris that may be over six feet in diameter and three feet high. These houses may have many entrances leading to the inner nest of grass and bark. Woodrats are also obsessive collectors of objects, including human artifacts, and it is this habit that has earned them the nickname of packrats.

At the higher, cooler elevations, Southern Red-backed Voles (*Clethrionomys gapperi*) are common in the Spruce-Fir Forests and Northern Hardwood Forests. Despite the severe weather at these elevations, they are active day and night even during the coldest times of the year. These short-tailed mice have a reddish back and gray sides. This northern species extends up the Appalachians, throughout Canada, and down the Rocky Mountains. Red-backed Voles feed on seeds, fungi, bark, and leaves.

In open country, including old fields and pastures, the Meadow Vole (*Microtus pennsylvanicus*) is the most common rodent. This vole, known as a "gopher" by the local farmers, has a short tail, small rounded ears, and a chunky body. The Meadow Vole is also a northern species occurring throughout most of the northern United States and Canada, extending all the way to Alaska. This vole is active day and night, producing surface runways through the grass. They also have underground runways. Meadow Voles are highly prolific breeders, and have been known to produce 17 litters in one year. They are an important prey for many predators, including snakes, owls, hawks, raccoons, foxes, bobcats, and weasels. Voles, due to their taste for tree seedlings, also play an important role in keeping certain species of trees from colonizing fields.

A number of species of mammals are associated with wetlands including rivers, streams, and ponds. Of particular interest is the American Beaver *(Castor canadensis)*. This large rodent (some males may exceed weights of over 50 pounds) was extirpated (wiped out) from our area, but reintroduction programs have been successful and over the last several decades beavers have once again become an important part of our landscape. Beavers prefer a woodland area with small streams that they can dam. The dams are composed of logs, branches, bushes, mud, and leaves. These dams are repaired regularly and may stand for many years. The resulting beaver ponds produce an open wetland habitat that may include bog-like areas in addition to ponds. These wetlands attract many animals and provide excellent breeding grounds for many insects, fish, amphibians, and birds.

Beaver living quarters may be a lodge located in the pond or they may dig dens in stream banks. The entrances are below the surface of the water. Beavers feed primarily on the bark and outer wood layers of a variety of deciduous trees, leaving their telltale sign of gnawed tree trunks. Beavers are unusual among rodents in that they are monogamous and the male and female are mated for life. The young may stay with their parents for up to two years and are taught the way of the beaver by their parents. Once mature the young leave the family and wander, looking for a stream to begin their dam and family. While beavers are predominately nocturnal, they can be seen swimming in the evening and early morning. Several places that beavers are commonly seen are Bass Lake on the Moses Cone Estate, the Elk Valley Preserve, and the Mill Pond in Banner Elk.

Another wetland species often confused with the beaver is the Muskrat *(Ondatra zibethicus)*, especially when swimming in a pond. Muskrats are much smaller than beavers, look a bit rat-like, and have a laterally flattened, nearly naked tail that is not obvious until they leave the water. Muskrats get their name from the secretions that they use in marking territories and attracting mates. Muskrats are accomplished swimmers being able to swim backwards or forward and can swim long distances underwater. They can also remain underwater for up to 20 minutes. Like beavers, muskrats build tunnel dens in stream and pond banks.

A common carnivore along our rivers and streams is the Mink (*Mustela vison*). The best opportunity to see a mink would be along one of the larger rivers such as the Elk, Watauga, New, or Linville Rivers. While mink are generally nocturnal, they can be seen venturing out at dawn and dusk. These members of the weasel family are about two feet in length with a thick, glossy, dark brown coat. Mink are active predators feeding on a variety of terrestrial and aquatic prey, including fish, amphibians, snakes, crayfish, birds and mammals. They also store food and one den was found to contain 13 dead muskrats, 2 ducks, and a coot.

Another member of the weasel family, Mustelidae, is the River Otter (*Lutra canadensis*). River Otters were extirpated in our area, but appear to be making a comeback. River Otters are brown, long-bodied, muscular mammals with webbed feet. They are always associated with aquatic environments and are excellent swimmers. Due to their secretive nature, River Otters are difficult to see, although their distinctive tracks and scats may indicate their presence. The scats often contain crayfish and fish remains. Otters live in family groups and are active, amusing creatures. They are well known for their playful nature, including tobogganing. They slide down snow covered stream banks into the water over and over again, forming a slippery track. River Otters have been observed in the New River in Ashe County, where an otter reintroduction program has been successful. Hopefully this fascinating mammal will soon become a common denizen in all of our watersheds.

The Raccoon (*Procyon lotor*) is often associated with wetland areas. Raccoons feed on a variety of plant and animal foods, but are best known for "feeling" for food with their sensitive forepaws in streams. This would include crayfish, salamanders and aquatic insect nymphs. Raccoons are by no means limited to watercourses. They are found throughout our forests and feed on a wide variety of plant and animal foods. They take advantage of the fruit of many plants and their seed-filled droppings are often seen along trails. Raccoons have adapted well to man-inhabited areas and have become common on local farms and near houses. Ironically, the large number killed on our local roads is evidence of their success.

Possibly the most confusing mammal group in our area is the shrews. These small, active, black or brown mammals are often misidentified as rodents. They are "insectivores", members of the primitive mammal order Insectivora. Unlike the herbivorous rodents, shrews are meat-eaters, feeding on invertebrates, salamanders, and the occasional mammal. Unlike rodents who have large gnawing incisors and elaborate molars, shrews have a mouth full of simple, sharp pointed teeth, well suited for killing small animals. Their snouts are more elongated than rodents, their eyes and ears are very small, and they have a velvety coat. Shrews are active day and night, feeding constantly to fuel their high metabolism. Watching a shrew in action is amusing as it frenetically searches every nook and cranny for food. Unlike moles who spend most of their time underground, shrews live along surface runways, cruising around and under rocks, logs and leaf litter. Lifting up a rock will often reveal a tubular shrew tunnel.

About 6 species of shrew live in our area, including the Pygmy Shrew (*Sorex hoyi*), the smallest mammal in North America, weighing about as much as a dime. One of the most common shrews locally is the Northern Short-tailed Shrew (*Blarina brevicauda*), one of the larger shrew species. In our area this shrew is slate black and has a short, hairy tail. This shrew is especially interesting in that it is one of the few poisonous mammals in the world. Its salivary glands produce a toxin that paralyses the shrew's prey when bitten. The shrew may then cache the immobilized prey for later consumption. The Northern Short-tailed Shrew is a voracious feeder, capable of eating its body weight in food each day. Short-tailed Shrews, like all shrews, have a short life span, living only about 20 months. Males are capable of breeding at the early age of 7 weeks and females born in the spring are able to breed later in the summer.

The shrew's insectivore cousins, the moles, are well represented in our area. Three species, the Hairy-tailed Mole (*Parascalops breweri*), the Eastern Mole *(Scalopus aquaticus),* and the Star-nosed Mole (*Condylura cristata*) are found here, with the Hairy-tailed Mole being limited to western North Carolina. While moles resemble shrews, their enlarged forefeet with outward facing palms are distinctive. Moles are also voracious eaters, feeding on earthworms and other invertebrates. Moles occasionally feed above the ground but seeing a mole above ground is unlikely. Locating their ridged tunnels isn't, however. Moles build two types of tunnels, surface tunnels for feeding and deeper tunnels that they use for nesting and winter activity. Moles are active day and night, year-round. The Star-nosed Mole is particularly interesting due its sensitive nose with its crown of tentacles. This mole often feeds in streams using its nose tentacles to find prey. There is some evidence that this mole may use electroreceptors in these rays to locate prey.

One animal that is not difficult to see in our area is the Eastern Cottontail (*Sylvilagus floridanus*). Forest edges, old fields, and brier patches produce ideal habitat for this highly recognizable lagomorph. Cottontails are herbivorous and feed on a wide variety of grasses and forbs (broad-leaved herbs). During the winter they may feed on twigs and bark. Rabbit cuttings are identified by a 45-degree angle cut on a twig.

Recently a new species of cottontail, the Appalachian Cottontail (*Sylvilagus obscurus*) was named. Originally considered to be a race of the New England Cottontail (*Sylvilagus transitionalis*), this cottontail is more of a forest dweller than the Eastern Cottontail. Unfortunately the differences between the two are not obvious in the field. The Appalachian Cottontail is slightly smaller, has shorter ears, and more black on its back. This secretive rabbit appears to prefer Northern Hardwood Forests and Spruce-Fir Forests, although it has not been well studied.

Two species of skunk are found in our area, the Striped Skunk (*Mephitis mephitis*) and the smaller Eastern Spotted Skunk (*Spilogale putorius*). The Striped Skunk or "polecat" is the larger of the two skunks and usually has two white stripes running down its back to the base of the tail. Striped Skunks are nocturnal and their slow locomotion makes them susceptible to getting squashed on highways. These skunks are well known for their accuracy in spraying their pungent musk. Interestingly it is possible to lift up a Striped Skunk by its tail and not get sprayed IF you pull it up BEFORE it everts its musk gland nipple. Good luck! Striped Skunks have few predators although the Great Horned Owl (*Bubo virginianus*) has few qualms about tackling a skunk.

The Eastern Spotted Skunk or "civet cat" is an attractive small skunk with a series of white spots on its head and body. Spotted Skunks are often found living in rock piles in forests and farms. Unlike the stockier Striped Skunk, Eastern Spotted Skunks are good climbers and are able to feed in trees. This skunk is well known for its unique behavior of balancing on its front feet when it is about to spray. Spotted Skunks and Striped Skunks have different secretions and the Eastern Spotted Skunk's musk is considered to be more pungent. Both species of skunk are omnivorous and feed on a wide variety of invertebrates, amphibians, snakes, birds, eggs, small mammals, carrion, and plant matter. While rooting and digging in the leaf litter they seem to be oblivious to their surroundings and it is possible to approach them closely (but not too closely).

The mix of forests and fields in our area is also very attractive to the Virginia Opossum (*Didelphis virginiana*). This marsupial is easily recognized by its frizzy, gray hair and long, scantily haired tail. Although they are usually seen on the ground, opossums are able to climb trees, using their prehensile tails to grab on to branches. Opossums are well known for their wandering and this may in part explain their wide range. The death-feigning act of possums is quite convincing. During this act, heart and respiration rates decrease dramatically, although they do appear to maintain some degree of sensory awareness. Opossums are omnivorous with the majority of their food coming in the form of animal matter, including insects, snails, crayfish, snakes, birds, and rodents. Despite their relatively large size, opossums have a short life span, living just over a year. They make up for this by their prolific reproduction, breeding twice a year with litters of 6 to 9 young.

One of the mammals most identified with our mountains is the Black Bear (*Ursus americanus*). Large forest tracts with rocky outcrops produce excellent bear habitat. Black Bears have large home ranges, with males larger than females. Radiotelemetry studies in the Pisgah National Forest found average home ranges of 61.0 km^2 for males and 16.9 km^2 for females. Black Bears are omnivorous and opportunistic in their diet. Their diet varies with the seasons, taking advantage of ripening fruits during the summer and fall. Blueberries and acorns are especially important, as they are widespread and abundant. In late November, Black Bears retreat to dens in tree hollows, hollows in the ground, or in thickets. Although not considered to show true hibernation (dropping body temperature to within $1°$C of the ambient temperature), Black Bears drop their metabolism, heart rate, and respiration significantly. Their body temperature drops about $7°$C. Interestingly, it is during the winter that the female gives birth. Between one and fours cubs are born, although two cubs are most common. Females are the sole caretakers of the cubs and they remain with their mother throughout the summer, fall, and often the winter. Bears are typically shy creatures and avoid contact with humans.

Red Fox (*Vulpes vulpes*) and Gray Fox (*Urocyon cinereoargenteus*) are both found in our area, the Red Fox being found in more open country and the Gray Fox in forests. These two foxes may be similar in appearance as some Red Foxes have a gray pelage. The Gray Fox has a black-tipped tail, however, while the Red Fox's tail is white-tipped. Both foxes feed primarily on cottontails and mice, but will also feed on fruit in the summer. The Gray Fox is also known as the "tree fox" due to its ability to climb trees. They are able to leap from branch to branch as well as shinning up a tree like a bear. The Red Fox did not appear in the southeast until colonial times and it is likely that our Red Foxes are descendents of introduced foxes from Europe. Their success is due in large part to the clearing of forest for farmland.

Another canid, the Coyote (*Canis latrans*), is a newcomer to our area. Coyotes are currently expanding their range eastward from their native west. This range expansion has been helped by intentional and unintentional releases of western Coyotes in the east. The absence of its main competitor the Gray Wolf (*Canis lupus*) and excellent habitat have allowed this resourceful canid to proliferate. Coyotes seem to prefer the broken open country of farmland with forest edge, habitats rich with their preferred prey, rabbits and rodents. It is possible that Coyotes will partially fill the niche left vacant when wolves were extirpated from our area at the end of the 19th century. They may also become important in controlling Raccoon and opossum numbers, though competition from Coyotes may have a negative effect on our fox and Bobcat populations.

Two weasels, the Long-tailed Weasel (*Mustela frenata*) and the Least Weasel (*Mustela nivalis*) are found in our area. The Least Weasel is less than 10 inches long and is North Carolina's smallest carnivore, while the Long-tailed Weasel is usually over a foot long with a long black-tipped tail. The Least Weasel is a northern species that extends down the Appalachians, while the Long-tailed Weasel is found throughout North America. Both species are secretive and seeing one is a fortunate occasion. They are voracious predators and often kill their prey with a bite to the back of the skull. I had one fascinating observation of a Long-tailed Weasel pursuing a chipmunk. The weasel chased the chipmunk up a tree, the chipmunk then jumped down to the ground and climbed another tree. This occurred three times until the weasel finally caught the chipmunk on the ground and quickly killed it. The weasel then calmly picked up the chipmunk in its mouth and disappeared into the forest.

The Bobcat (*Lynx rufus*), although rarely seen, is the common native cat in our area. Bobcats are usually brownish in color with small dark spots. The backs of the ears are black with a white spot and its tail is short. The wide expanses of forest, thick undergrowth, and rocky ledges in our mountains provide good habitat and shelter for this secretive cat. Bobcats feed primarily on rabbits and rodents, although the occasional deer may be taken. Interestingly bobcats seem to have little aversion to living near humans. Their presence can often be determined by the presence of their scat, which contains the hair of its prey. The scat may or may not be covered. Bobcats also make "scrapes" that are typically used for scent marking territories. Bobcats are also well known for their eerie mating screams in late winter and spring.

Of particular interest is the increase of Mountain Lion (*Puma concolor*) sightings in the area. A local survey of Mountain Lion sightings resulted in over 70 reported sightings in Avery, Watauga, Mitchell, and Ashe counties between 1998 and 2002. Most of these sightings have been in forested areas, with many around farms. Interestingly, many of the cats described were dark in color, with a charcoal pelage. Reports of Mountain Lions in other parts of the eastern North America, including the mountains of Virginia have also surfaced, although hard evidence such as photographs, footprint casts, or a body has been lacking.

The Mountain Lion is native to our area, but was considered extirpated by the beginning of the 19th century. Locals, however, have argued that the "painters" never disappeared from the mountains. It is not clear whether the lions that are now roaming our area are remnants of these survivors, introduced cats, western cats that have expanded their range, or some combination of the above. This impressive cat, distinguished from the Bobcat by its larger size and long tail, may also owe its resurgence to the local increase of its primary prey, the White-tailed Deer. It will be interesting to see the predator-prey dynamics between these two species in the future.

The White-tailed Deer (*Odocoilius virginianus*) is our only native deer and is easily recognized by the white underside of its tail. Since the early 1980's this widespread deer has dramatically increased its numbers in our area, due to restocking efforts and game management. It prefers a mix of woodlands, forest edge, and open fields and is common around farms. Deer are most often seen in the morning and evening, although they may stay active all night. They typically bed down in dense cover during the day. Deer are browsers, although they feed on a wide variety of plant matter, including fruit, acorns, and herbs. White-tailed Deer breed in the fall, and it is at this time that the bucks mark and defend territories. It is common to see the bark of small trees scraped off by the buck's antlers at this time. Females give birth to one to three young in the spring and the fawns are spotted for four or five months. The young remain with the doe for at least a year, with females often remaining for two or more years.

The changing face of mammal diversity and abundance in our area may also include the Elk (*Cervus elaphus*) in the future. This large deer with its impressive antlers in the male was extirpated from our area in the mid-1800s.

In 2001 an experimental herd of Elk were released in the Smokies and it is conceivable that if this project is successful, additional Elk may someday be released in the Pisgah National Forest. The high elevation Grassy Balds and surrounding forests of the Roan Massif could provide suitable habitat for this majestic ungulate. The success of these introduced herds however, may be affected by a nematode worm that White-tailed Deer carry. This parasite, known as brain worm, attacks the brain, spinal cord, and lungs and while not fatal to deer, is usually lethal to Elk.

Approximately 11 species of bats are found in our area, however, it is often difficult to identify individual species as they swoop around snaring insects out of the air. Common bats that may occur around homes, include the Big Brown Bat *(Eptesicus fuscus)*, Eastern Pipistrelle *(Pipistrellus subflavus)*, and Little Brown Myotis *(Myotis lucifugus)*. Big Brown Bats have wingspans over 12 inches, while Little Brown Myotis and Eastern Pipistrelles are small bats with wingspans less than 10 inches. The Eastern Pipistrelle is one of our most common bats. Its yellowish brown color separates it from the Little Brown Myotis. These bats are entirely insectivorous, catching flying insects on the wing. During the day bats may take shelter behind window shutters, in attics, or in shelters in trees or rock crevices.

During the winter some bats hibernate in local caves and mines. The Black Rock Cave on Grandfather Mountain has a substantial population of the endangered Virginia's Big Eared Bat *(Corynorhinus townsendii virginianus)* that winter there. Other local hibernating bats include the Eastern Pipistrelle, Little Brown Myotis, Big Brown Bat, and Northern Myotis *(Myotis septentrionalis)*. During hibernation a bat drops its body temperature to just above the ambient temperature and its metabolism drops dramatically. During the winter bats may awaken and move around the cave or mine. Eastern Pipistrelles, however, may remain immobile for long periods of time as evidenced by the droplets of water that condense on their bodies. Abandoned mines provide suitable hibernaculums for a number of species of bats, but because they are extremely vulnerable at this time, hibernating bats should not be disturbed.

REPTILES

Snakes

The cool, cloudy climate of the Southern Appalachians reduces the diversity of reptiles compared to the piedmont and coastal plain of North Carolina. Many piedmont reptiles start becoming rare at about 2,000 feet. Reptiles are best represented in our area by the snakes, with about 12 species occurring in the high country. Some of these species are very common, including the Eastern Garter Snake *(Thamnophis sirtalis)*. This slender snake varies in color and is usually some shade of yellow, green or brown. It can be best identified by the light stripes running down the body. If picked up, this snake is likely to excrete a foul-smelling musk from glands located at the base of its tail and will vigorously do its best to wipe you with it. Garter Snakes are most common in moist habitats and near water. They appear in the spring and remain active into the fall.

The Northern Water Snake *(Nerodia sipedon)* is also a common local snake. Although this snake is often found along and in rivers, ponds, and creeks, it is not uncommon to find it basking away from water. In our area it is typically brown with dark blotches running down the back and dark bars along its sides. It is a stocky snake and may reach lengths of over 3 feet. Unfortunately for this snake, its blotched pattern gives it a superficial resemblance to several venomous species such as Copperheads and Cottonmouths. Thus they are often killed when encountered. Probably the best characteristic to separate the Northern Water Snake from the venomous species is its head. Venomous snakes have large triangular heads while this water snake has a slender head not much wider than its neck. The Northern Water Snake is not partial to being picked up and will bite.

Another snake associated with water is the Queen Snake (*Regina septemvittata*). This slender snake has a dark brown dorsum with three faint black stripes running down the body. It also has a yellowish belly and lip. Queen Snakes often bask on rocks or limbs along shallow streams, but can also be found under rocks along the stream edge. They discharge a pungent musk when handled. Queen Snakes have a strong preference for crayfish as evidenced by a study that found only crayfish as food for 63 Queen Snakes. These snakes are viviparous (do not lay eggs), giving birth to up to 15 young. The Eastern Ribbon Snake (*Thamnophis sauritus*) is also found along streams, although this snake is uncommon in the mountains.

A snake that is often found around houses and farms is the Black Rat Snake (*Elaphe obsoleta*). This is an impressive, attractive snake with a glossy black body and long length often exceeding 6 feet. Rat Snakes have a distinctive bread loaf body shape thus separating this species from the similar round-bodied Black Racer (*Coluber constrictor*). Rat Snakes, as their name implies, are fond of mice and rats and thus are often found around and in houses and barns. Rat Snakes are welcome guests in my basement, where they feast on my unwelcome mice guests. The presence of shed skins often betrays their presence. Black Rat Snakes also have a taste for bird eggs and nestlings and are excellent climbers. Black Rat Snakes are harmless and typically will remain still when approached. If harassed they will rattle their tail and bite if picked up. Young Black Rat Snakes are commonly seen in the late summer and fall. These hatchlings are not black like the adults but have an attractive dark blotch pattern on a lighter body. With time the blotches begin to fade and the body coloration becomes black.

One of the easiest local snakes to identify is the Ringneck Snake (*Diadophis punctatus*). This small gray-black species has a distinctive yellow collar and a yellow undersurface. Ringneck Snakes are commonly found under logs and stones in moist habitats. They can also be found in houses, garages, and basements as they use these areas for winter shelters. These snakes are docile and can be handled without fear of being bitten.

Another small snake is the diminutive Worm Snake (*Carphophis amoenus*). One of the smallest North American snakes at less than one foot, this snake has a brown body, small pointed head, a light pinkish undersurface, and a tail with a spine-like point. It has a strong resemblance to an earthworm, which happens to be its primary food. This docile species is also found under rocks and logs, coming out at night to stalk its prey.

Perhaps the most attractive snake in our area is the Eastern Milk Snake (*Lampropeltis triangulum*). It has large gray or brown blotches and a pale Y or U shape at the back of its head. Its underside has a black and white checkered pattern. This blotched color pattern resembles that of the venomous Copperhead, leading to its unnecessary persecution. Milk Snakes are found in both forests and pastures and will also inhabit rural buildings in its quest for rodents. Although most common at middle and lower elevations, these snakes have been found at over 5,400 feet on Roan Mountain and Grandfather Mountain.

The Redbelly Snake (*Storeria occipitomaculata*) is a small snake with a tan, brown, or gray upper body and its distinctive reddish-orange belly. It also has a characteristic white spot below its eye and three spots on its nape. Redbelly Snakes are found in moist forests and bogs, but are quite secretive and are most often found under rocks and logs. These snakes are nocturnal, feeding on slugs and worms. They also eat snails after extracting them from their shells.

Venomous snakes are not common in our area. Copperheads (*Agkistrodon contortrix*) are rarely found at the higher elevations, typically occurring below 3,000 feet. Even at these lower elevations, Copperheads are not common, often being confused with the Northern Water Snake. Copperheads have stout bodies with hourglass shaped blotches and large, triangular heads. They possess a heat-sensing pit on each side of the head, between the eye and nostril, although I wouldn't suggest looking too closely for them. Young Copperheads have a distinctive yellow tail tip. Copperheads are most common in forests.

The only other local venomous snake is the Timber Rattlesnake (*Crotalus horridus*). Like the Copperhead, it has a large triangular head with pits. This large, blotched rattlesnake once occurred up to the highest elevations, but has become rare in our area. They are usually found in forests, where they prey on a wide variety of rodents. They have most often been observed on the rocky slopes of Linville Gorge. Although these rattlesnakes are highly venomous, they are not dangerous unless provoked. Timber Rattlesnakes spend the winter in rock crevices and are known to return to the same winter hibernation dens, where a number of individuals congregate.

Turtles

Three very different species of turtle, the Snapping Turtle, the Eastern Box Turtle, and the Bog Turtle, are found in our area. The Snapping Turtle (*Chelydra serpentina*) is easily recognizable by its large size, long saw-toothed tail, and a carapace with three rows of keels running down the back. It is also known for its bad temperament and willingness to bite when harassed. Snapping Turtles rarely bask out of water, instead bask while floating on the surface. While Snapping Turtles inhabit ponds and lakes in the area, they often are found crossing roads as they wander from pond to pond. These turtles are omnivorous, feeding on a wide variety of animals, plants, and carrion. They even appear to be partial to grapes. Snapping Turtles lay their eggs on land in a shallow nest. Nests are often dug up by raccoons, and the opened, leathery, white shells are left scattered about.

The widespread Eastern Box Turtle (*Terrapene carolina*) is found throughout our area and has the distinction of being the official state reptile of North Carolina. This handsome turtle has a dome-shaped carapace that has a yellow and black mottled color pattern. Males have a concave plastron and red eyes, while females have a flat plastron and brown or yellow eyes. Although primarily terrestrial, these long-lived turtles can often be found alongside and even in small creeks. After rains they are often found crossing roads, much to their detriment. They feed on a variety of plant leaves and fruits and also small animals. When harassed the box turtle will promptly withdraw its head, legs and tail within its shell, closing it tightly with hinges at the front and rear of its plastron.

The Bog Turtle (*Clemmys muhlenbergi*) is our smallest turtle reaching only 4 inches in length. It is also quite rare, being limited to scattered Mountain Bogs. It is dark in color with a large bright orange or yellow blotch on each side of the head. Bog Turtles have an interesting distribution being found in the northeast, are absent in West Virginia, north Virginia, and Maryland, but then reappear in the Southern Appalachians. Bog Turtles prefer open sphagnum bogs where they can burrow in the thick moss. This secretive behavior makes them difficult to locate. It is likely that Bog Turtles were once more common in our area. The draining of many bogs and the hunting of beavers, resulting in fewer beaver bogs, have undoubtedly reduced the numbers of this noble turtle. It currently has protected status in the state.

Lizards

Lizards are relatively scarce in our high country, being limited to the lower elevations. One point of confusion is that locals call salamanders "lizards". Five-lined Skinks (*Eumeces fasciatus*) can be found on rocky outcrops at the lower elevations, including Little Lost Cove Cliffs in the Pisgah National Forest. This quick lizard has smooth glossy scales and a long sleek body with five light stripes running down its body. Juveniles are especially striking as they have a brilliant blue tail. Adults have a brown tail. The tails of skinks break off very easily. These "automized" tails wriggle violently producing a distracting display to potential predators. Skinks are often seen basking on warm days, but also can be found under rocks and logs.

Eastern Fence Lizards (*Sceloporus undulatus*) may also be found at lower elevations in the drier open forests as along the ridges of Linville Gorge. Unlike the Five-lined Skink, that stays on the ground, fence lizards like to perch up on rocks, logs, and the lower trunks of trees. These lizards are brown with wavy dark bands on each side of the body. Unlike the smooth scaled skink, this lizard has keeled scales, giving it a spiky appearance. Adult males have brilliant blue coloring on their throat, chin, and sides. These males are highly territorial, defending their turf with head-bobbing displays and combat.

One place of particular interest is the Wilson Creek Gorge in the Pisgah National Forest in Caldwell County. Some 14 species of reptiles have been found in this area of steep, rugged, rocky slopes and dry woodland. Unusual species found include the Carolina Anole (*Anolis carolinensis*), Ground Skink (*Scincella lateralis*), Southeastern Five-lined Skink (*Eumeces inexpectatus*), and the Southeastern Crowned Snake (*Tantilla coronata*). The combination of favorable conditions, including fissure shelters, abundant rocky basking sites, and warmer evening and winter temperatures are responsible for the range extensions of these species and the overall diversity of reptiles in this unique area.

AMPHIBIANS

Salamanders

The diversity and abundance of salamanders in our area is impressive. A short search for these long tailed amphibians typically yields many species and individuals. The Southern Appalachians show the greatest diversity of salamanders in the world. Salamanders have probably inhabited the Appalachians for over 200 million years. This vast time span and factors such as climate change and topographical variation has resulted in the radiation of this group into many species. The distribution of salamanders is also quite interesting. Some species have very limited ranges, while others are widespread and occur in many states. Our climate is also kind to these moisture-loving vertebrates. Salamanders are susceptible to drying out and are able to take in water through their skin. Indeed, moisture seems to be a critical factor as salamander numbers decline as habitats become drier. Salamanders are typically most abundant in Northern Hardwood and Cove Forests, especially along creeks. Salamanders are locally called "spring lizards" due to their occurrence around springs and wet areas. High rainfall, cool temperatures, and an abundance of mountain streams are the perfect formula for making our region "Salamander Central".

Many of our local salamanders belong to the family Plethodontidae or the "lungless" salamanders. This salamander family includes members of the *Desmognathus, Eurycea, Gyrinophilus, Pseudotriton,* and *Plethodon* genera. All plethodontids lack lungs, respire through their skin, and have nasolabial grooves (tiny grooves running from the nostril to the lip). These grooves play a key role in smell during courtship. While most salamanders have aquatic larvae, members of the genus *Plethodon,* including the Slimy Salamander, Redback Salamander, Jordan's Salamander, Ravine Salamander, Weller's Salamander, and Yonahlosee Salamander, lay their eggs on land. Eggs are laid under rocks, logs, and rotting stumps and are often protected and brooded by the female. The young hatch as small salamanders.

The abundance of salamanders in aquatic and terrestrial habitats suggests that they play a pivotal role in the ecology of these communities. They are major predators of a variety of invertebrates and are prey for many vertebrate species. They are clearly an important component in the food webs of our rivers, streams, and forest floor.

The local salamanders fall into two general ecological categories, the full-time aquatic species and the more terrestrial species. Aquatic species tend to have triangular, keeled tails, while the terrestrial species have rounded tails. Many terrestrial species, however, inhabit the sides of creeks and are more than willing to take the plunge. Aquatic species include the Black-bellied Salamander (*Desmognathus quadramaculatus),* Shovel-nosed Salamander (*Desmognathus marmoratus),* and the Seal Salamander (*Desmognathus monticola).* These salamanders typically remain under rocks during the day and venture out at night to feed. Scanning a creek at night with a flashlight is an excellent way to see them out and about. These "*Desmognathans*" show a characteristic light diagonal line running from their eye to their jaw.

The Black-bellied Salamander is a robust salamander up to 8 inches in total length with a dark mottled back, black belly, and one or two rows of light dots along the lower side of the body. It has a compressed, keeled tail characteristic of the more aquatic species. Hatchlings are not hard to find and can be recognized by six to eight pairs of light spots running down the back. Black-bellied Salamanders are often found in swift moving streams and catching them can be a challenge. At night this salamander may leave the water and forage along the stream edges.

Shovel-nosed Salamanders have a strong resemblance to their close relative, the Black-bellied Salamander. They have a dark back with two rows of light blotches, while their bellies are dark gray with a light central area. Their tail is even more keeled than the Black-bellied Salamander and they have a flatter snout. Herpetologist Bernard Martof made an interesting field observation involving the Shovel-nosed Salamander. He found a Northern Water Snake swallowing a trout. In the trout was a large Shovel-nosed Salamander. In this salamander was a smaller Shovel-nosed Salamander. And in this salamander were several aquatic insects. So goes the food chain.

Seal Salamanders are smaller (up to 6 inches) aquatic salamanders with a greenish-gray color, a dark wavy pattern on their backs, light belly, and a keeled tail. Seal Salamanders attach their clusters of eggs to rocks or other substrates in running water and are often found with the eggs. Young seals have four pairs of reddish orange spots down their backs and small external gills.

Our most impressive aquatic salamander is the Hellbender (*Cyptobranchus alleganiensis*), the largest North American salamander. The origin of the name Hellbender is uncertain although it has been attributed to an early fisherman who concluded that "it was a creature from hell where it's bent on returning". This relict of an ancient lineage of salamanders grows up to about 30 inches and is characterized by its large flat head, short legs, and wrinkled folds of slimy skin running along their sides. Hellbenders emerge at night from under cover to forage for crayfish and small fish. Hellbenders can and will bite when handled, so beware. Hellbenders inhabit the larger local rivers such as the Watauga and the Elk Rivers.

The most abundant of the terrestrial salamanders is the Blue Ridge Dusky Salamander (*Desmognathus orestes [ochrophaeus]*). This salamander, previously known as the Mountain Dusky Salamander, can be confusing as it shows amazing variation in color and markings. Some individuals sport bright colors and dorsal patterns while other individuals are brown and nondescript. All have rounded tails and mottled bellies. In moist forests and along stream banks the number of these salamanders can be impressive. It is not uncommon to find two or three Blue Ridge Dusky Salamanders together under a rock. Like most terrestrial salamanders, Blue Ridge Dusky Salamanders remain under rocks, logs, or litter during the day and emerge at night to feed. This widespread salamander may be found at all elevations in our area, including the higher peaks above 5,000 feet.

The Northern Dusky Salamander (*Desmongnathus fuscus*) is also variable in appearance, but is typically dark brown with a dorsal spotting pattern and a mottled belly. It resembles the Blue Ridge Dusky Salamander, but has a keeled tail. Northern Dusky Salamanders may be found in streams, along stream banks, and in moist ravines.

Jordan's Salamander (*Plethodon jordani*) is another common species in our moist forests. This large salamander (up to 7 inches) varies in appearance over its range throughout the Southern Appalachians, but in our area they show an overall black color. They are widespread and occur from the lowest to the highest elevations. Large oval glands behind their jaws are a good way to identify this species. Like most of the terrestrial salamanders, Jordan's Salamander feeds on a wide variety of invertebrates, including mites, worms, millipedes, centipedes, spiders, insects, and spiders. They are active from spring to fall, retreating to underground winter quarters when the temperature drops below freezing.

Similar in appearance and size to the Jordan's Salamander is the Slimy Salamander (*Plethodon glutinosus*). This black salamander has small white spots scattered over its body. Glands on its body and tail produce a sticky slime similar to that of a slug. These secretions act to discourage predators and make handling these handsome salamanders a messy affair. Slimy Salamanders are most common below 4,000 feet.

The Yonahlossee Salamander (*Plethodon yonahlossee*) is another large *Plethodon* with a brick red back and gray splotched side. This attractive salamander was initially discovered along the Yonahlossee Road, now Highway 221, in Avery County. Its range is limited to northwest North Carolina, northeast Tennessee, and several counties in southern Virginia.

The Redback Salamander (*Plethodon cinereus*) is a small *Plethodon* with a slender body and a reddish dorsal stripe extending from the head to the tail. It also has a mottled black and white belly. This widespread salamander occurs throughout the northeast to the Great Lakes and into Canada. Redback Salamanders are well known for their territorial behavior. Both males and females mark territories with glandular secretions and feces.

The Ravine Salamander (*Plethodon richmondi*) is another small, slender *Plethodon* species. This long salamander has a dark body with brassy flecks and small legs that are widely separated. These salamanders are most active in the spring and fall, retiring to underground retreats during the hot summer months.

The high elevation Spruce-Fir Forest is the home of the Weller's Salamander (*Plethodon welleri*) and the Pigmy Salamander *(Desmognathus wrighti)*. The Weller's Salamander is named after its discoverer, the herpetologist, Worthington Weller, who died on Grandfather Mountain in 1914, while collecting salamanders. This attractive, small salamander is black with gold flecks on its back. Populations of this species are isolated on different mountaintops throughout its range. These relict populations suggest that this species was once more widespread. It is especially common in the Spruce-Fir

Forests of Grandfather Mountain, occurring under rocks, logs, litter, and the bark of stumps.

The most diminutive of our salamanders, the Pigmy Salamander, is around 2 inches long with a coppery bronze coloration with a herringbone pattern running down its back. Its rounded tail is shorter than its body. During the day this salamander remains under litter, bark, rocks, and logs, but at night it emerges and commonly climbs trees and other vegetation. Here they feed on small invertebrates and avoid the larger, predatory salamanders.

The Blue Ridge Two-lined Salamander (*Eurycea wilderae [bislineata]*) is one of our most attractive salamanders with a yellow-orange color with two black lines running down the back. In some individuals the black lines are broken up into spots. Breeding males have two pointed flaps of skin hanging over their lip (cirri) running from their nostrils, giving this little salamander a vampire-like appearance. These structures are involved with smelling and are used to locate females. Breeding males also have unicuspid teeth with which they bite females, injecting male gland secretions into the female's circulatory system. After the breeding season, the males replace their unicuspid teeth with the typical bicuspid teeth. This salamander can be found in streams, along stream banks, and in moist woodlands. Like most salamanders, Blue-Ridge Two-lined Salamanders are capable of tail autonomy or losing their tail. This is an effective defensive strategy, especially when attacked by snakes. In one study on this salamander, 32% of the salamanders collected had autonomized tails.

Spring Salamanders (*Gyrinophilus porphyriticus*) also prefer wet environments, typically being found in small springs and streams. This large (5-8 inches), stout salamander has a striking orange-red body with small dark flecks. It also has a distinctive light line running from its eye to its nostril and a black and white mottled pattern on its jaw margins. The bright coloration of this salamander is likely a warning signal as it is capable of producing a noxious skin secretion to deter predators. Spring Salamanders are well known for their habit of eating other salamanders both as adults and as larvae.

The Red Salamander (*Pseudotriton ruber*) sports a red body with black spots. This large (up to 7 inches), stout salamander has a short tail and short legs. Red Salamanders overwinter in springs or streams and disperse to moist terrestrial sites in the spring. Like Spring Salamanders, Red Salamanders also prey on smaller salamander species and produce toxic skin secretions that are concentrated along the back. It has been suggested that the Red Salamander,

Spring Salamander, and Eastern Newt are part of a Mullerian Mimicry complex. Members of this complex benefit from each other by their similar red warning (aposomatic) coloration that advertises their toxic nature. In other words, if you see any red salamander, do NOT eat it.

Spotted Salamanders (*Ambystoma maculatum*) belong to the family of Mole Salamanders, Ambystomatidae, a group of round headed, stout-bodied salamanders with conspicuous costal grooves (vertical furrows on the side of the body). This large (up to 10 inches), handsome salamander has two rows of yellow spots running down the body to the tip of the tail. This striking coloration functions as a warning to potential predators as this salamander also produces toxic skin secretions. Spotted Salamanders spend most of their time underground but emerge on rainy nights to feed on the forest floor. In late winter, after rains, Spotted Salamanders move to woodland vernal pools to breed. After this brief breeding frenzy, this salamander is rarely seen. Their egg masses may be clear, but usually have a cloudy, white appearance. The larvae develop quickly in these pools and by June they metamorphose and leave the pools for their terrestrial life. Spotted Salamanders often share their breeding pools with Wood Frogs (*Rana sylvatica*). This is not a friendly coexistence as the Wood Frog tadpoles feed upon the Spotted Salamander embryos. Interestingly, experiments have shown that white egg masses are less vulnerable to predation than clear egg masses. It is believed that Spotted Salamanders return to their natal pools to breed.

One of the most conspicuous of our salamanders is the Eastern Newt (*Notophthalmus viridescens*). After a rain it is not uncommon to find a bright orange newt trucking through the forest. This salamander is unusual in that it has a land and water stage in its life cycle. The young are born in ponds where the aquatic larvae develop. The larvae then transform into the terrestrial "Red Eft" with their granular rough orange skin with red spots. Red Efts produce toxic skin secretions that discourage many predators (see above). After several years on land the eft returns to its breeding pond and transforms into the aquatic form with an olive green color, red spots, and a long flattened tail. It is in this form that the newt breeds with eggs being laid singly on aquatic vegetation.

Frogs and Toads

Although there is not a great diversity of frogs and toads in our area, several species are quite common. The American Toad (*Bufo americana*) is the most common toad being found in a wide variety of habitats. Summer evenings often bring these toads out in gardens and backyards in their quest for insects and other invertebrates. These amphibians are conspicuous by their large warts and large parotoid glands behind their eyes. These warts and glands do secrete a poison that deters predators (including dogs). Unless eaten, these toads are harmless, although when picked up they often urinate on their handler. Nonetheless their voracious appetites make them a welcome inhabitant of any backyard. This widespread toad reaches its largest size in the mountains, with females being larger than males. They also show wide color variation from brown to a striking orange-red. They breed in temporary pools, with eggs appearing in long strings. The tadpoles develop quickly and metamorphose into small toadlets the same summer.

One of our most common frogs is the Wood Frog (*Rana sylvatica*), a northern species that extends down the Appalachian chain. A dark mask behind its eye identifies this handsome frog. Dorsolateral folds, two ridges running down the back, are well developed and there are a series of horizontal stripes on its legs. After heavy rains in late February and early March, these frogs congregate in shallow pools to breed. These pools can often be located by listening for the Wood Frog's quack-like call, as the males call in the females. Large numbers of globular egg masses are laid in these small pools. Each egg is transparent and the developing tadpole is easy to see. The tadpoles develop quickly and after about 45 days the small froglets move out of the pool to live a terrestrial existence. Because they lay their eggs in shallow pools it is often a race for the tadpoles to develop before the pool dries out. The Wood Frog is one of the most terrestrial of frogs, often occurring far from water in moist forests.

The most common frog around ponds is the Bullfrog (*Rana catesbeiana*), also our largest frog reaching 8 inches in size. These frogs typically have a greenish-brown color with large blotches on their backs and lack the dorsolateral folds found in the other "ranid" frogs. Bullfrogs live and breed around ponds. Their deep "*jug-o-rum*"calls can be heard in the spring and early summer. Unlike the Wood Frog, the Bullfrog tadpole takes at least a year to develop before it metamorphoses into an adult. These tadpoles can be quite large often reaching 4 inches in length. Bullfrogs are voracious predators and will eat anything they can cram into their wide mouths, including small snakes.

The Pickerel Frog (*Rana palustris*) is also found near water, although it prefers aquatic habitats in shaded wooded areas. This hard to catch frog is easily identified by the square, brown spots all over its body and its well-developed dorsolateral folds. It is about 3 inches in length and has striking patches of yellow under its thigh and groin. These "flash colors" may startle potential predators. Its call is a low-pitched snore that is repeated. Pickerel Frogs produce skin secretions that make them distasteful and their distinctive coloration may warn potential predators.

The Green Frog (*Rana clamitans*) is found along streams and ponds and has a greenish brown color. It resembles a small Bullfrog but has dorsolateral folds that extend down to the middle of the back. Its presence is usually betrayed by its explosive "*c'tung*" mating call that has been aptly described as sounding like a loose banjo string. They also give a high-pitched "*squeenk*" call when startled. Unlike the Pickerel Frogs that deposit their egg masses on stems of plants in the water, Green Frog egg masses are laid on the water surface. The tadpoles attain a large size and metamorphose in late summer.

The most common treefrog (family Hylidae) is the Spring Peeper (*Pseudacris [Hyla] crucifer*). Easy to hear but difficult to locate, this little frog (about 1 inch) inhabits woodlands and pond edges. Choral groups, with their distinctive, high-pitched "*peep*", call day and night beginning in early spring and continuing throughout the summer. This frog has a distinctive X-shaped mark on its back and its long toes have prominent sucker-like toepads. Spring Peepers breed in ponds, pools, and ditches laying single eggs that are attached to vegetation or other submerged objects. Metamorphosis takes from 3 to 4 months. The Gray Treefrog (*Hyla chrysoscelis*) is less common than the Spring Peeper. This treefrog, recognized by its mottled gray coloring and a bright yellow pattern on the concealed surfaces of its hind legs, is typically found at lower elevations.

FISHES

It is ironic that the two best known species of fish in this area, the Rainbow Trout (*Oncorhynchus mykiss*) and the Brown Trout (*Salmo trutta*), are both introduced game species. The Rainbow Trout is a native of northwestern North America, while the Brown Trout is a native of Europe, Asia, and northern Africa. Populations of these species of "*salmonid*" (family Salmonidae) have been maintained by stocking, although they may breed locally when the conditions are suitable. Rainbow Trout show a pinkish lateral stripe down its side and fin spots on all of its fins. The Brown Trout lacks the lateral stripe, has a body speckled with black and red and has fin spots only on its dorsal (top) fin. The Brown Trout is more tolerant of warmer waters and siltation (the presence of silt runoff on river and stream bottoms) and is more widespread in our area. Both species may attain large size and Brown Trout may weigh more than 15 pounds.

The Brook Trout (*Salvelinus fontinalis*) is our native trout. This beautiful fish is identified by a white margin on all but its dorsal fin. Its sides are covered with red spots surrounded by blue halos and it is usually less than 10 inches. The Brook Trout has the strictest habitat requirements of the three species of trout, needing cold, fast flowing streams with a high oxygen content and is intolerant of pollution and siltation. It is the "wildest" of the trout, often being found in remote streams surrounded by rhododendron thickets. It is also likely that competition from Rainbow and Brown Trout have pushed the "Brookie" out of many of its historical streams. The ecology of the Brook Trout is closely linked to its primary food, the aquatic insects that dwell in our mountain streams. These include mayfly, stonefly, and caddisfly nymphs that reside on the rocky stream bottoms and also the flying adults that lay their eggs in the stream. Brook Trout migrate upstream to breed, requiring a clean gravel bed to make their nest and lay their eggs. The females lay up to 5,000 sticky eggs in a male's territory. The eggs adhere to the gravel and are also covered by more gravel by the female. The embryos overwinter in the cold, oxygen-rich water and hatch the following spring.

Another group of fish well represented in our rivers and streams are the members of the minnow family Cyprinidae. This is the largest family of fish and while we typically think of minnows as small fish some members of this family can attain a large size. However in our area most of these minnows are rather small. All have one dorsal fin, abdominal pelvic fins, cycloid scales, and a lateral line running down their sides. In our area we have about a dozen minnow species and they are typically the most numerous fish in any stream or river. Species include the Central Stoneroller (*Campostoma anomalum*), Rosyside Dace (*Clinostomus funduloides*), Whitetail Shiner (*Cyprinella galactura*), Warpaint Shiner (*Luxilus coccogenis*), River Chub (*Nocomis micropogon*), Tennessee Shiner (*Notropus leuciodus*), Silver Shiner (*Notropus photogenis*), New River Shiner (*Notropus scabriceps*), Mountain Redbelly Dace (*Phoxinus oreas*), Bluntnose Minnow (*Pimephales notatus*), Blacknose Dace (*Rhinichthys atratulus*), Longnose Dace (*Rhinichthys cataractae*) and the Creek Chub (*Semotilus atromaculatus*).

The Central Stoneroller is one of our most abundant minnows, found in clear, cold rocky streams with numerous riffles. This stocky minnow reaches a size of 9 inches and has a subterminal mouth (mouth below the head) with a distinctive hard edge that it uses to scrape algae off of rocks.

A common, small (up to 4 inches) minnow is the Blacknose Dace. This minnow has an elongate slender body, a pointed snout with a subterminal mouth, and a black stripe on its side running from the snout to the tail separating a dark top from a lighter belly. The Longnose Dace has a fleshy snout that extends far beyond its subterminal mouth and an indistinct black stripe on its side. The Longnose Dace prefers fast moving streams, while the Blacknose Dace is found in streams, beaver ponds, and pools.

One of the most beautiful of our local minnows is the Warpaint Shiner. This fish has a striking red bar running vertically on its opercle (the flap behind the eye that covers the gills) and breeding males have a red snout and upper lip. This fish has the interesting habit of feeding at the surface on terrestrial insects that have fallen into the water.

The Creek Chub is found in streams and rivers and is best identified by a large black spot at the front of the dorsal fin. It is a stout fish with a large terminal mouth (mouth at end of head) that extends beyond the front of the eye. Creek Chubs feed on a wide variety of aquatic and terrestrial invertebrates and algae.

River Chubs are robust minnows with large subterminal mouths. The breeding males have a hump on their heads and bumpy tubercles on their snout. They are common in rivers and fast moving creeks. Male River Chubs are famous for their nest building. Carrying stones in their mouths they build oval or circular gravel mounds. Some mounds attain diameters of over 40 inches and may be 7 inches high. One measured mound weighed in at 235 pounds! The highly impressed females lay their eggs in the top of the mound.

The shiners of the genus *Notropus* are the second-largest genus of freshwater fishes in North America. They are recognized by having eight dorsal fin rays, scales on the nape about the same size as on the upper side, and the absence of barbels (fleshy projections around the mouth). Individual species are difficult to tell apart, as most of the species are small (less than 5 inches) and have slender, silver bodies. It is often important to use the range of individual shiner species to help in identification. The New River Shiner has a very restricted range, occurring only in the New River drainage, while the Tennessee Shiner and Silver Shiner are more widespread and are found in many drainages.

Three species of suckers (family Catostomidae) are found locally, the Northern Hogsucker (*Hypentelium nigricans*), the White Sucker (*Catostomus commersoni*) and the Black Redhorse (*Moxostoma duquesnei*). The Northern Hogsucker is the most common occurring in most of our rivers and streams. This is a burly sucker with a large rectangular head that is concave between the eyes. Its subterminal mouth has large fleshy lips that it uses to root around for food along the streambed like an aquatic pig. In clear streams, one can easily watch this sucker as it forages on the bottom. Hogsuckers are one of our largest fish, reaching a size of up to 2 feet.

Several species of catfish are found in our area. Catfish (family Ictaluridae) are identified by their lack of scales, four pairs of whisker-like barbels around their large mouths, and a sharp spine in their pectoral and dorsal fins. Most catfish are nocturnal, using their barbels to feel around the bottom in search of food. Catfish come in a variety of sizes from the small madtoms to the large species that are popular in recreational fishing.

Bullheads are medium sized catfish usually less than two feet in length. The Brown Bullhead (*Ameiurus nebulosus*) has a mottled pattern and has 5-8 large saw-like teeth on the rear of its pectoral spine. Brown Bullheads are found in ponds and rivers and are a popular game fish. They have a broad distribution and have been widely introduced outside their native range. Brown Bullheads show a high degree of parental behavior. Parents guard the eggs and once the eggs hatch into larvae, they keep close tabs on their youngsters, herding them in tight schools. Strays are picked up in the mouth of a parent and returned to school.

Large catfish in our area include the Channel Catfish (*Ictalurus punctatus*) and the Flathead Catfish (*Pylodictus olivaris*). The Channel Catfish has been introduced throughout the United States and is widely stocked in farm ponds. It is most likely the catfish on your plate in a restaurant. This highly adaptable catfish, while native to rivers, does well in ponds and lakes. In our area it is most common in farm ponds, where it is a popular game fish. The Flathead Catfish is native to the Mississippi River basin and in our area is only found in the New River. This large catfish can reach 60 inches in length and may weigh more than 95 pounds. Flathead Catfish are found in deep river holes that have shelter such as logs. Females can produce as many as 100,000 eggs, while the males guard the eggs until they hatch.

The Margined Madtom (*Noturus insignis*) is a small, gray catfish reaching a size of only up to 6 inches. Madtoms can be found in ponds, lakes, creeks, or rivers. When harassed the madtom erects its pectoral and dorsal spines. These spines are surrounded by sheaths that contain venom, and handling a madtom is likely to be a painful experience. Madtoms feed on a wide variety of invertebrates and carrion.

Two species of sculpin (family Cottidae) are found in our area, the Banded Sculpin (*Cottus carolinae*) and the Mottled Sculpin (*Cottus bairdi*). These sculpins are small fish with large heads and mouths and big eyes. They have two dorsal fins, fan-shaped pectoral fins, and pelvic fins occurring under their pectoral fins. Sculpin prefer clean, fast-moving streams with rocky substrates. They are difficult to see as they are well camouflaged and live among the rocks on the bottom.

Three species of darter (family Percidae) are found in our area, the Greenside Darter (*Etheostoma blennioides*), Kanawha Darter (*Etheostoma kanawhae*), and Greenfin Darter (*Etheostoma chlorobranchium*). The genus *Etheostoma* is the largest genus of North American fish and the greatest diversity of darters occurs in the Southern Appalachians. Darters resemble sculpins in that they have two dorsal fins, large pectoral fins, a broad snout, and are small, bottom dwellers. The males of many species are very colorful and are among the most beautiful of our freshwater fish. The Kanawha Darter is especially attractive, with broad green bars on its side, alternating with thin orange bars. This rare species is only found in the New River drainage in North Carolina and Virginia.

Sunfishes (family Centrarchidae) are the easily recognized, deep-bodied fishes that many young anglers have put their first hooks into. They are very popular as game fish and have been widely introduced throughout North America and the world. The Bluegill (*Lepomis macrochirus*) is one of the most widespread fish in North America and commonly occurs in ponds throughout our area, except for some high elevation ponds. The Bluegill has a small mouth, a dark spot at the posterior base of the dorsal fin, and a bluish-black opercular lobe from which it gets its name. Bluegill may become abundant in small ponds, due to the absence of predators. In these ponds the Bluegill remain small in size.

Occurring in the same ponds as the Bluegill is the Largemouth Bass (*Micropterus salmoides*). This is the largest sunfish, although in the mountains it does not attain the "lunker" size of lower latitudes. Largemouth Bass have an elongated body and a large mouth that extends beyond the rear margin of the eye. These fish feed on a variety of invertebrates and will also eat frogs and other fish, including Bluegill.

Smallmouth Bass (*Micropterus dolomieu*) can be distinguished from the Largemouth Bass by appearance and habitat. It has a smaller mouth that does not extend past the eye and it is found in rivers not ponds. Smallmouth Bass require clear, unsilted water and are a good indicator of stream health. They are a popular game fish in the local rivers at lower elevations, especially the New River.

Rock Bass (*Ambloplites rupestris*) are found in rivers and creeks. Rock Bass have a short, stocky body with brownish coloration and red eyes. They prefer a rocky substrate and are often found in deeper water around shelter. Finally, the Redbreast Sunfish (*Lepomis auritus*) is also found in a number of our streams and rivers. The belly of this sunfish is orange in males and yellow in females. It has a long opercular flap that is black.

LOCALES

Northwestern North Carolina has many beautiful, accessible natural areas. Even better, most are free. Some areas require hiking on steep, rocky trails while others are short, easy walks. Always be aware of what is involved for the different hikes and locales. I have listed below some of the most popular locales that are for the most part easy to get to, have maintained trails, and have excellent natural properties. This list is by no means complete but is a starting point. Use maps to locate destinations before setting out and take detailed, topographic maps on hikes. The *North Carolina Atlas & Gazetteer* by Delorme Mapping is a good way to become familiar with the region.

BLUE RIDGE PARKWAY

The Blue Ridge Parkway through Ashe, Avery, Burke, Caldwell, and Watauga counties is an impressive stretch of the parkway both in terms of views and variety of habitats. Between milepost 249 (junction with NC 18) and milepost 317 (junction with US 221) almost all of the mountain habitats are found or are accessible.

FLAT ROCK (mp 308.3) - This 0.7 mile loop trail first moves through a Mixed Oak Forest with impressive Northern Red Oaks. The open forest floor has a rich herb layer that is rewarding in the spring and early summer when many of the herbs flower. These include Galax, Lily-of-the-Valley, Bluebead Lily, Wild Sarsparilla, Indian Cucumber Root, Fly Poison, Blue Bead Lily, and Squawroot. The trail then opens up onto an open scenic area of metasandstone outcrops (elevation 4110 ft), with a heath community of Catawba Rhododendron, Mountain Laurel, Blueberry, Black Huckleberry, Mountain Ash, Serviceberry, and stunted Pitch Pines. Depressions in the rocks host mats of spike moss.

BEACON HEIGHTS (mp 305.3) - This 0.7 mile round trip trail first moves through a dry Mixed Oak Forest dominated by Chestnut Oak and Northern Red Oak. Fraser Magnolia, Red Maple, and Witch Hazel are also found along with a thick shrub layer of Rosebay Rhododendron and Mountain Laurel. The trail leads to several metasandstone outcrops with vegetation similar to Flat Rock, but also includes Red Spruce. This trail offers an opportunity for bird watching and the outcrops are good viewing spots for migrating raptors in the fall.

TANAWHA TRAIL (mp 305 – mp 297) - This trail runs 13.5 miles along the parkway from Beacon Heights to Julian Price Park, passing through a variety of habitats including Cove Forest, Mixed Oak Forest, open pasture and Heath. The trail traverses the southeastern flank of Grandfather Mountain, offering the opportunity to experience the mid-elevation forests of Grandfather along easy to moderate trails. The stretch between Wilson Creek (mp 302.8) and Rough Ridge (mp 303.6) is prime Cove Forest with a great diversity of trees including Eastern Hemlock, Black Cherry, Fraser Magnolia, Red Spruce, Yellow Birch, Sweet Birch, Tuliptree, Red Maple, Sugar Maple, Striped Maple, Yellow Buckeye, and American Basswood. In the spring and early summer this trail has a nice diversity of forest herbaceous wildflowers, especially in the seepage areas. This trail also passes over Ship Rock (see below).

The northern stretch of this trail between Boone Fork (mp 299.9) and Julian Price Park (mp 297) passes through a mix of forests and open fields. The National Park Service allows cattle grazing in these fields to maintain the pastures along the trail. The cattle are docile and are not a concern to the wary hiker. These fields offer a good opportunity to experience the fall wildflowers and open country birds.

ROUGH RIDGE / SHIP ROCK (mp 302.8) - This area is one of the best examples of the Heath habitat in our area. Rough Ridge and Ship Rock are rugged outcrops of tilted metasandstone. The trail from the Rough Ridge parking area first passes through Cove Forest before it opens onto Rough Ridge (elevation 4460 ft.) In open areas Sand Myrtle covers the large rocks, surrounded by thickets of Catawba Rhododendron, Mountain Laurel, Highbush Blueberry, Mountain Ash, Fetterbush, Black Chokeberry, and Bearberry.

After leaving Rough Ridge the trail winds through a dense habitat of small trees and shrubs. Stunted trees include Red Spruce, Red Maple, Fraser Magnolia, Serviceberry, American Chestnut, Sassafras, and the locally rare Bigtooth Aspen. Shrubs include Catawba Rhododendron, Mountain Laurel, Highbush Blueberry, and Blueberry. The herb layer includes Galax and Wintergreen.

The trail finally emerges onto the rocky ledges of Shiprock (elevation 4580 ft). Large mats of Sand Myrtle and blueberry thickets dominate. These outcrops are an excellent vantage point for witnessing the fall raptor migration, especially Broad-winged Hawks in October. Common Ravens are also a frequent sight as they soar above the peaks of Grandfather Mountain. Ship Rock also offers a panoramic view of the Wilson Creek area of the Pisgah National Forest. On clear days distant skyscrapers of Charlotte are visible to the east.

JULIAN PRICE PARK (mp 296-297) - This 4,200 acre park boasts some of the most impressive scenery and habitats of the Blue Ridge Parkway. Elevation ranges between 3,400 and 4,000 ft. The 4.9 mile Boone Fork Loop Trail is an excellent way to explore this park. Begin the trail by crossing the Boone Fork Creek bridge in the Price Park Picnic Area (milepost 296.4). A trail map is posted at this point. If you take the loop trail counter clockwise you will be heading up the Boone Fork Creek. You will first pass an interesting bog area. This open area is good for bird watching especially in the fall when flocks of migrant songbirds pass through. Beaver activity is also obvious.

The trail then moves up along Boone Fork Creek. Aside from its scenic qualities this is also an excellent area for spring and summer wildflowers. Keep a lookout for the rare Kidney-leaved Twayblade orchid growing under the heavy Rosebay Rhododendron thickets. Eventually the trail moves west leaving the Boone Fork Creek to run along the smaller Bee Tree Creek and through a beautiful Cove Forest dominated by Yellow Birch. Salamanders are abundant in the small feeder creeks and along the trail. Eventually the trail passes through several pastures and then back into forest where it comes out in the Price Park campground.

PRICE LAKE (mp 296.7) - This 47 acre impounded lake is one of the best areas for locating migrating and wintering waterfowl, including Common Loons, Pied-billed Grebes, Double-crested Cormorants and numerous species of ducks. A 2.3 mile loop trail runs around the lake passing through mature Mixed Oak Forest. This is an excellent trail for forest bird watching.

MOSES CONE MANOR (mp 291.9) - This 3,516 acre tract, once the pride of textile magnate, Moses Cone, is now the pride of the Blue Ridge Parkway. The estate includes Flat Top Mountain (elevation 4,558 ft.), Rich Mountain, two impounded lakes, Trout Lake and Bass Lake, and vast forests. The estate is accessible through roads, hiking trails and carriage trails. The 25 miles of scenic carriage trails below the Cone Manor House pass through a beautiful Mixed Oak Forest of Northern Red Oak, White Oak, Chestnut Oak, White Pine, Eastern Hemlock, Black Cherry, Sweet Birch, Tuliptree, Fraser Magnolia, Red Maple, Striped Maple and Pignut Hickory. The understory is dominated by Rosebay Rhododendron with the occasional Catawba Rhododendron and Mountain Laurel.

A number of these trees and shrubs were planted during Moses Cone's time. He was especially fond of White Pine, Eastern Hemlock, Sugar Maple, and Catawba Rhododendron. Herbaceous wildflowers, including Bluebead Lily, False Solomon's Seal, Solomon's Seal, and Wake Robin, are common in the spring. Bird watching along these carriage roads is especially rewarding in the spring and summer. Bass Lake is an excellent place to get stunning views of Wood Ducks and Beavers are often seen cruising about.

Contact: Blue Ridge Parkway, Bluffs District, 2284 Blue Ridge Parkway, Blowing Rock, 28605, (828) 295-7591. www.blueridgeparkway.org

Maps: NPS Blue Ridge Parkway- Price Park Trails, Tanawha, Cone Park Carriage Trails; USGS Boone

GRANDFATHER MOUNTAIN

In terms of scenery, wildlife, variety of habitats, and trail systems, few natural areas can compare to this grand mountain. It is also home to many rare species, including the Northern Flying Squirrel, Virginia Big-eared Bat, Northern Saw Whet Owl, Weller's Salamander, and Heller's Blazing Star. As the highest peak in the Blue Ridge Mountains (Calloway Peak, elevation 5,964 ft.), Grandfather Mountain serves as a fitting centerpiece to our high country. Although Grandfather Mountain encompasses some 100,000 acres and extends into the Pisgah National Forest and beyond, visitors typically recognize the mountain as the slopes sandwiched between the Blue Ridge Parkway and NC 105. This area is owned and managed by Grandfather Mountain Incorporated and the Nature Conservancy. Grandfather Mountain maintains some 12 miles of trails (permit required) that pass through some 3,000 acres of backcountry including the highest peaks.

Grandfather Mountain runs in a northeast to southwest direction. The western side of the mountain is north facing and is thus cooler and wetter than the south-facing eastern side. The Profile Trail is the only trail on the western side, passing through diverse Cove and Northern Hardwood Forests that include White Ash, Black Cherry, Yellow Birch, American Beech, Eastern Hemlock, and Yellow Buckeye. This trail is a wildflower bonanza in spring as the banks along the trail are home to numerous herb species, including Yellow Mandarin, Dutchman's Breeches, Squirrel Corn, Crested Dwarf Iris, Umbrella Leaf, Fringed Phacelia, Blue Cohosh, Black Snakeroot, Mountain Lettuce, Foamflower, Canada Mayflower, and Painted Trillium. The trail is also rich in breeding warblers, including Black-throated Blue, Canada, Blackburnian, Ovenbird, and Black-throated Green Warblers. The trail eventually winds into a high elevation Northern Hardwood Forest before it merges into the Spruce-Fir Forest at the Grandfather Trail.

The Daniel Boone Scout Trail and the Nuwati Trail access the eastern side of the mountain. The forests on this drier, south-facing side are mostly Mixed Oak, although patches of Cove Forest occur in the valleys and sheltered slopes. The Nuwati Trail parallels the pristine Boone Fork Creek that originates in the Boone Fork Bowl. The Cragway Trail splits off the Nuwati Trail and winds through a scenic Heath community of rocky outcrops and shrubby growth. This trail is especially worthwhile in spring when the Catawba Rhododendrons are in flower.

The Daniel Boone Scout Trail begins at the Tanawha Trail of the Blue Ridge Parkway and climbs some 2.6 miles and 1,844 feet to the summit of Calloway Peak. The lower elevations are Mixed Oak Forest that is replaced by a lush Northern Hardwood Forest above 4,600 feet. The last stretch of the trail passes through a dense high elevation Spruce-Fir Forest.

The Grandfather Trail runs along the ridge of the mountain for some 2.4 miles. This ridge consists of metasedimentary rock dominated by metasandstone and metaconglomerate. The Profile Trail and the Daniel Boone Scout Trail lead to the Grandfather Trail, although the easiest access is by driving up the mountain to its trailhead near the swinging bridge or use the Black Rock Trail.

The Grandfather Trail runs through a mix of high elevation habitats including Spruce-Fir Forest and Rocky Outcrops all above 5,200 feet. The Spruce-Fir Forest includes Red Spruce, Fraser Fir, Mountain Holly, Hobblebush, Bearberry, and Mountain Ash and is the home to the rare Weller's Salamander. This is also a good spot to look for Magnolia Warbers, Red Crossbills, and Hermit Thrush during the summer.

The exposed stacks of huge boulders are often covered by Heath species such as Sand Myrtle, Catawba Rhododendron, Minnie-Bush, and Blueberry. The rare Heller's Blazing Star is also found nestled in these outcrops. This trail passes by MacRae Peak (elevation 5,939 ft.) and ends at Calloway Peak (elevation 5,964 ft). This is a land of high winds, cold temperatures, and heavy precipitation, as evidenced by the stunted growth of vegetation in exposed areas. Be prepared for the elements and a steep, rocky trail, but also some incredible scenery.

Contact: *Grandfather Mountain, P.O. Box 129, Linville, NC, (828) 733-2013. www.grandfather.com*

Maps: Grandfather Mountain Trail Map (free with paid permit); USGS Grandfather Mountain, Valle Crucis, Boone

WILSON CREEK - PISGAH NATIONAL FOREST

The Pisgah National Forest is the largest national forest in North Carolina, with a total of 495,000 acres. It is divided into districts with the Grandfather Ranger District covering some 187,000 acres within McDowell, Burke, Avery, Watauga, and Caldwell Counties. The 76,000 acres of the Toecane Ranger District also contains holdings in Avery and Mitchell Counties along the Tennessee border. Within a district there is a historical patchwork of private and public properties so that portions of the national forest are often split from each other. Where the Pisgah National Forest comes into contact with the Tennessee border the national forest becomes the Cherokee National Forest.

One of the largest and wildest areas of the Grandfather Ranger District is the Wilson Creek Area, east of Grandfather Mountain in Avery, Burke and

Caldwell counties. A number of forest service roads from the Blue Ridge Parkway and US 221 make this area accessible, although it is easy to get lost in the maze of roads and trails. The Wilson Creek Area Trail Map available at local outdoor stores is essential for enjoying this splendid area. The Wilson Creek area runs along the eastern edge of the Blue Ridge Mountains with elevations ranging from around 4,000 ft. down to 1,100 ft. as the Appalachians merge into the piedmont along the Blue Ridge Escarpment.

Outstanding features of this area are its pristine creeks, scenic rocky outcrops, extensive forests, and abundant wildlife. Wilson Creek, Harper Creek, Gragg Prong Creek, and Lost Cove Creek are especially impressive for their scenic qualities and wildlife, including large numbers of Brook Trout and other fish. Trails follow the creeks, however, be prepared to get wet as the trails cross the creeks repeatedly. A number of waterfalls are found on these creeks with five major waterfalls on Harper Creek alone. It is interesting to follow Wilson Creek from its headwaters on Grandfather Mountain (Blue Ridge Parkway mp 302.8) through the national forest where Gragg Prong Creek, Lost Cove Creek, and Harper Creek all feed into Wilson Creek. Lower Wilson Creek and Wilson Creek Gorge can be visited by taking forest service road 1328 off of NC 2 between Lenoir and Morganton. In August 2000 Wilson Creek was awarded federal Wild and Scenic Designation and a Wilson Creek Visitor Center in the Edgemont Community opened later that year.

Equally impressive are the "cliffs", which include Big Lost Cove Cliffs and Little Lost Cove Cliffs. Both cliffs can be accessed by trails of about 1 to 1.5 miles. Big Lost Cove Cliffs is often closed during the summer due to nesting Peregrine Falcons on its cliffs. These cliffs offer spectacular views of the Pisgah National Forest looking towards Grandfather Mountain. On the cliffs are Table Mountain Pines with thickets of Punctatum and Blueberry. Spikemoss forms mats in depressions on the ledges.

Although much of this area was logged and burned in the early 1900's, the forest has grown back and is now rich and diverse. Most of the forest is Mixed Oak with Chestnut Oak, Northern Red Oak, Scarlet Oak, and Pitch Pine dominating. American Chestnut sprouts are common along with White Pine, Eastern Hemlock, Pignut Hickory, Sourwood, Black Gum, Witch Hazel, Sassafras, Fraser Magnolia and Red Maple. The presence of Sourwood and Black Gum with their striking, red fall leaves make this an especially attractive place to visit in the autumn. Mountain Laurel is abundant and its flowering in early June can be spectacular. Along the creeks, Tag Alder is common and wildflowers such as Pale Corydalis, Fire Pink, Yellowroot, and Broad-leaved Waterleaf produce nice flowering displays in the spring and Cardinal Flower in the fall.

This area is also very attractive to wildlife. Harper Creek and Lost Cove are Black Bear sanctuaries and Mountain Lions have been seen in this area. White-tailed Deer, Long tailed Weasels, Red and Gray Fox, Red and Grey Squirrels, and Eastern Chipmunks arc all common here. This area is also excellent for bird watching as the broad elevation range produces a nice mix of lower and middle elevation birds.

Contact: Grandfather Ranger District, P.O. Box 519, Marion, N.C. 28752, (828) 652-2144. www.cs.unca.edu/nfsnc/

Wilson Creek Visitor Center (828) 757-0005.

Maps: USFS Wilson Creek Area Trail Map; USGS Chestnut Mountain, Grandfather Mountain.

LINVILLE GORGE WILDERNESS AREA

The 10,975 acres of the Linville Gorge Wilderness Area are located in the Pisgah National Forest in Burke County. A designated wilderness area is managed to maintain its natural character and while hiking, hunting, fishing, and camping are allowed within its borders, roads, timber harvesting, and mechanical vehicles are prohibited. Linville Gorge is located on the edge of the Blue Ridge with elevations ranging from 1,300 feet on the lower end of the Linville River to 4,120 feet on Gingercake Mountain. Uplift of the surrounding mountains and millions of years of carving by the Linville River have produced one of the deepest gorges in the east. The eastern rim of Linville Gorge consists of a series of rocky peaks, running from north to south. These include Gingercake Mountain, Sitting Bear Mountain, Hawksbill Mountain (elevation 4020 ft.), Table Rock Mountain (elevation 3,920 ft.), The Chimneys, and Shortoff Mountain. The western rim consists of the long Linville Mountain. Two forest service roads access the eastern and western sides of the gorge, Kistler Memorial Highway on the west and Forest Service Road 210 on the east.

An excellent view of the scenic east rim can be seen from Wiseman's View off Kistler Memorial Highway. Linville Falls, located at the northern end of the gorge, is accessible either from Kistler Memorial Highway or the

Blue Ridge Parkway. All of the peaks and the river are accessible by an extensive trail system, and possession of the Linville Gorge Wilderness map is highly recommended before embarking on any trip within the gorge. Be warned however, many of these trails are poorly marked and steep.

The diverse topography, wide elevation range, rocky peaks, and river ecosystem produces a great diversity of plant communities, including Mixed Oak Forest, Cove Forest, Dry Ridge Forest, Rocky Outcrop, Mountain Bog, and Riparian communities. The steep terrain hindered logging and old growth forests are still common along many of the lower slopes. The forests along the rims are Dry Ridge Forests with Chestnut Oak, White Oak, Scarlet Oak, and Northern Red Oak. Pines are also common, including Pitch Pine, Virginia Pine, and White Pine. Carolina Hemlock, Sourwood, Black Gum, and Red Maple are also found in these dry forests. The herb layer includes Galax, Wintergreen, Indian Cucumber Root, and Trailing Arbutus.

Down the slopes of the gorge, Cove Forests take over. American Basswood, Sweet Birch, Eastern Hemlock, Cucumber Magnolia, Fraser Magnolia are mixed with Northern Red Oak and Chestnut Oak. The herb layer becomes more diverse and includes Fire Pink, Small's Penstemon, False Solomon's Seal, Bloodroot, Crested Dwarf Iris, Whorled Loosestrife, Heartleaf Ginger, Sweet Cicely, and Bluebead Lily.

Along the Linville River Sycamores appear and Eastern Hemlocks shade the banks of the river. Tag Alder lines the river and Ninebark, Common Elder, and Yellowroot also appear. Eastern Phoebes and Acadian Flycatchers are common along the river. The Conley Cove Trail off Kistler Memorial Highway passes from Dry Ridge Forest to Mixed Oak Forest to Cove Forest to Riparian Forest and is an excellent way to experience some of the common habitats of the gorge.

The open rocky outcrops and peaks of Linville Gorge are popular due to their outstanding scenic value, but are also fascinating communities in themselves. Scattered trees include Chestnut Oak, Sourwood, Pitch Pine, Eastern Hemlock, Carolina Hemlock, and Serviceberry. Table Mountain Pines are restricted to these rocky outcrops, often perched picturesquely on exposed outcrops. Shrubs include Catawba Rhododendron, Punctatum Rhododendron, Mountain Laurel, Male-Berry, and thickets of Black Huckleberry. Low-growing mats of Sand Myrtle and Dense-flowered St. John's-wort are also common. Accessible rocky outcrops include Babel Tower and Wiseman's View on the eastern rim and Table Rock and Hawksbill on the west rim.

In 2003 a wildlife platform was opened on Pinnacle Rocks on Kistler Memorial Highway just outside the wilderness area. This platform offers a spectacular view of the southern end of the gorge and is an excellent viewing point for the fall raptor migration.

In the fall of 2000 a fire swept through the eastern side of Linville Gorge, burning thousands of acres. The fire began on the Cabin Trail and traveled south to the lower end of the gorge. The fire moved from the rim down to the river in many places even jumping the river in several spots, although the western side was for the most part left unscathed. The fire was primarily restricted to the ground, with relatively few trees killed but many shrubs were charred. The regeneration of these burned areas has been rapid and impressive. Pine seedlings and rhododendron and Mountain Laurel root sprouts are abundant while herbaceous plants are taking advantage of the open ground layer. These dry oak communities are clearly fire-adapted and many species appear to benefit from the occasional fire. Linville Gorge is an excellent place to observe first-hand the ecological process of fire succession.

Contact: Grandfather Ranger District, P.O. Box 519, Marion, NC, (828) 652-2144. www.cs.unca.edu/nfsnc/

Maps: USFS Linville GorgeWilderness; USGS Linville Falls, Ashford.

ROAN MOUNTAIN

The Roan Mountain massif is one of the most impressive natural areas in the Southern Appalachians. Roan's natural appeal dates back to the 1790's when botanist Andre Michaux spent a week on Roan and was delighted to find an abundance of Flame Azaleas in bloom. Botanist Asa Gray and Professor Elisha Mitchell visited Roan Mountain in the mid 1800's, and were equally taken by its beauty and diversity. Today, the appeal of Roan Mountain continues due to its exceptional ecological diversity, including the largest expanse of high elevation Grassy Balds in the Southern Appalachians, its threatened Spruce-Fir Forest, and a significant number of rare plant and animal species. The preservation of this mountain has thus become a high priority. Groups such as the Southern Appalachian Highlands Conservancy, a regional private land trust, and the United States Forest Service, have been working together to ensure that this area will be protected and managed to maintain the natural integrity of the mountain.

Roan Mountain is typically referred to as a "massif" as it is actually a large mountainous mass consisting of a series of peaks, forming the backbone of the Unaka Mountain range. The rock formation of the massif consists of pre-Cambrian gneiss. The highest point of the massif is 6,286 feet, located near the Roan High Bluff overlook, and the entire ridgeline is above 5,000 feet. Located in Avery and Mitchell Counties in North Carolina and Carter County in Tennessee, Roan Mountain straddles the North Carolina/Tennessee border. The Toe River drains the North Carolina side of the mountain, while the Doe River drains the Tennessee side.

Roan Mountain is managed by the Toecane Ranger District of the Pisgah National Forest and the Unaka Ranger District of the Cherokee National Forest. Access to Roan Mountain may be from the Tennessee side (TN 143 from the junction with US 19E in Roan Mountain) or from the North Carolina side (NC 261 from Bakersville). The two highways meet at the state line at Carver's Gap (elevation 5,512 ft), where a parking lot is located. The Appalachian Trail also crosses Carver's Gap at this point, where it runs along the ridge of the massif, making it accessible for day hikers. The approximately 17 mile stretch of the Appalachian Trail that passes over the highlands of Roan is considered to be one of the most scenic parts of the entire trail. Be prepared for the possibility for severe weather and plan for steep, rocky trails.

The Roan Mountain massif boasts a rich diversity of high elevation communities. This includes some 850 acres of Spruce-Fir Forest, Grassy Balds, Heath Balds, Green Alder thickets, and high-elevation Northern Hardwood Forest. The Spruce-Fir Forest can best be explored by heading south on the Appalachian Trail from Carver's Gap, climbing up about 1.3 miles to Roan High Knob. The Spruce-Fir Forest along the trail is dense with a closed canopy and an open understory dominated by a carpet of mosses. Patches of dead trees in spots produce patches of heavy undergrowth of Smooth Blackberry, Red-berried Elder, Bearberry, Catawba Rhododendron, and Mountain Ash, as well as Red Spruce and Fraser Fir saplings. Stop at seepage areas to find Pink Turtleheads, Mountain Meadow Rue, Thyme-leaved Bluets, and Michaux's Saxifrage. Bird life includes Golden-crowned Kinglets, Brown Creepers, Winter Wrens, Red-breasted Nuthatches, Blue-headed Vireos, Veerys, and Dark-eyed Juncos.

Heath Balds are scattered over Roan Mountain, but the most popular is the 600 acre Rhododendron Gardens located on the crest near Roan High Bluff. At Carver's Gap, the Rhododendron Gardens Road leads to a parking area at the gardens. It is also possible to hike 2.0 miles on the Appalachian Trail south to the parking area. A series of loop trails pass through the heavy growth of Catawba Rhododendron that make up the heath bald. This area is spectacular when the rhododendrons are in bloom in mid-June. It is well worth the crowds to experience this natural event. If one is lucky enough to be there on a warm, sunny day, the air hums with the sound of nectar-loving insects as they gorge on the rhododendron flowers.

The Cloudland Trail also begins at the Rhododendron Gardens parking lot and runs along this high elevation crest, ending at the summit of Roan High Bluff (elevation 6,267 ft.) This trail passes through Spruce-Fir Forest and patches of Heath Balds and Grassy Balds. The trail is about 1.5 miles long (one way).

To experience the Grassy Balds, head north on the Appalachian Trail from Carver's Gap. Between Hump Mountain and Carver's Gap, the AT runs some 8 miles over a series of Grassy Balds and patches of Heath Balds. The scenery is spectacular with breathtaking panoramic views. Leaving Carver's Gap the AT passes through patches of Spruce-Fir Forest and Heath Balds until it reaches Round Bald (elevation 5,826 ft.) Here it is possible to get a view to the southwest of Mount Mitchell (elevation 6,685 ft.), the highest mountain in the eastern United States. Oat Grass, Bent Grass, and sedges dominate this bald in addition to Filmy Angelica and other low-growing plants including Cinquefoil and Wild Strawberry.

Beyond Round Bald the AT drops to Engine Gap, where thickets of Catawba Rhododendron, Highbush Blueberry, Allegheny Blackberry, and Flame Azalea take over. The AT then begins the climb to Jane Bald. This is a good area to find small patches of the rare Gray's Lily growing among the shrubs and blackberry. Beyond Jane Bald, the Grassy Ridge Bald spur trail leaves the AT. This dead end trail passes through heavy heath thickets before it emerges into the open bald of Grassy Ridge. The summit of Grassy Ridge (elevation 6,200 ft) provides incredible panoramic views. Between Engine Gap and Grassy Ridge, patches of Green Alder thicket occur and it is often possible to spot Alder Flycatchers here. There is also a Green Alder thicket at the parking area at Carver's Gap.

The AT then passes across the Yellow Mountain Gap heading north to the Grassy Balds of Little Hump Mountain (elevation 5,549 ft.) and Big Hump Mountain (elevation 5,587 ft.) This stretch of the trail passes through patches of Northern Hardwood Forest, fields, and thickets. The AT beyond Big Hump Mountain descends through a high elevation Northern Hardwood Forest that includes thick stands of American Beech. The AT then descends through mostly

Cove Forest until it emerges at US 19E in Tennessee (elevation 2,900 ft), a distance of 13.3 miles from Carver's Gap.

Contact:Toecane Ranger District, US Forest Service, P.O. Box 128, Burnsville, NC 28714, (828) 682-6146. www.cs.unca.edu/nfsnc/
  Appalachian Trail Conference, P.O. Box 807, Harper's Ferry,WV 25425, (304) 535-6331. www.appalachiantrail.org/
  Maps: Carver's Gap, Bakersville, Iron Mountain Gap,White Rocks Mountain.

BIG YELLOW MOUNTAIN

Located in Avery County, Big Yellow Mountain is part of the Roan Highlands, however as it not on the Appalachian Trail it is often overlooked by hikers. Big Yellow Mountain (5,540 ft.) is best known for its panoramic, dome-shaped summit of Grassy Balds. Vegetation includes several species of grass, including Mountain Oat Grass, sedges, and low growing herbs such as Wild Strawberry and Three-toothed Cinquefoil. The scenery from the summit is one of the best in our high country, including parts of the Roan Massif and the Blue Ridge Mountains. Big Yellow Mountain is owned and managed by The Nature Conservancy and Southern Appalachian Highlands Conservancy. Management practice includes the use of low-level cattle grazing to maintain the grass bald, preventing invasion by blackberry and other shrubs. It is likely that Elk once were important grazers on these balds and perhaps they will return in the near future.

There is more to Big Yellow Mountain than the Grassy Balds. Along the edges of the bald, shrub thickets dominate, including interesting patches of stunted American Beech. On the slope below the summit, an old growth forest of Yellow Birch, Northern Red Oak, and Sugar Maple is found in the preserve. The trees found in this forest are grand. Although not especially tall, due to the high elevation and exposure, the great age of these oaks and birch is obvious due to their great girth and their twisted growth forms make them more striking. The absence of rhododendron at this elevation allows for an open understory with abundant wildflowers. In the early spring, Spring Beauty forms carpets before the trees leaf out, while Gray's Lily is found in open patches along the edges of the woodland.

Access to Big Yellow Mountain is a bit tricky due to the presence of private property around the mountain. There is a spur trail running east from the Appalachian Trail south of Little Hump Mountain to Yellow Mountain. Access to the AT south of this spur trail may be made from the Overmountain Victory Trail located on Roaring Creek Road, south of Minneapolis, NC on US 19E. The Nature Conservancy and Southern Appalachian Highlands Conservancy also offer field trips to the preserve on a regular basis.

Contact:The North Carolina Nature Conservancy, One University Place, 4705 University Drive, Suite 290, Durham, NC. (919) 403-8558. www.nature.org/ wherewework/northamerica/states/northcarolina/

Southern Appalachian Highlands Conservancy, 34 Wall Street, Suite 802, Asheville, NC 28801,(828) 253-0095. www.appalachian.org/

Maps: USGS Carver's Gap

VALLE CRUCIS PARK

Located in the scenic town of Valle Crucis on Broadstone Road, this park ,though small in size, has a nice variety of habitats, including fields, forest edge, and riparian forest. Wetlands include creeks, a pond, and the Watauga River. The forest along the river includes some large trees, including Sycamores. Walking paths make for easy strolls along the river, creek, and fields.

Valle Crucis Park is best known for its impressive bird life. The river attracts many riparian species and the birds are well habituated to the presence of people, resulting in easy viewing. Some birds that breed in the park include Killdeers, Black-billed and Yellow-billed Cuckoos, Eastern Kingbirds, Least Flycatchers, Willow Flycatchers, Tree Swallows, Eastern Bluebirds, Carolina Wrens, Yellow Warblers, Common Yellowthroats, Baltimore Orioles, Orchard Orioles, Eastern Meadowlarks, and Song Sparrows. Unusual bird species seem to always be cropping up in the park and a trip to the park during spring and fall migration is worthwhile.

Contact:Valle Crucis Community Park, (828) 963-9239
Maps: USGS Valle Crucis

HEMLOCK HILL

This impressive stand of old growth Eastern Hemlock is located in Banner Elk on the Lees-McRae College campus on the south side of the Elk River. It can be accessed by the gravel road off of Hickory Nut Gap Road just past the intersection of Highway 184. Park behind the Mill Pond dam. The ¼ mile Hemlock Hill trail begins across the road from the bridge. This 20 acre forest is dominated by towering Eastern Hemlocks. Core samples have determined that many of these giants are over 500 years in age. In addition to the hemlocks, this cool, north-facing slope forest is home to a number of northern hardwoods, including Yellow Birch, Sugar Maple, American Beech, and Black Cherry. Red Maple, Fraser Magnolia and Mountain Holly are also common. The shrub layer consists of an impenetrable layer of Rosebay Rhododendron.

Hemlock Hill is an excellent location for bird watching and due to the heavy evergreen canopy, several high elevation birds more typical of Spruce-Fir Forests are found here. These include Golden-crowned Kinglets, Winter Wrens, Brown Creepers, and Red-breasted Nuthatches. A walk through this forest on a cool, foggy summer morning is enchanting.

Contact: Lees-McRae College, P.O. Box 128, Banner Elk, NC, (828) 898-5241. www.lmc.edu

Maps: USGS Elk Park

ELK VALLEY PRESERVE

Located on the Elk River in Avery County, the 70 acre Elk Valley Preserve is owned and managed by Lees-McRae College. The Elk Valley Biological Station, an ecological research and teaching center, is located on the preserve. The preserve is located on Puckett Road off of NC 194, between Banner Elk and Elk Park. The public is welcome to visit the preserve, but please respect designated research sites.

The preserve has a variety of communities, including Cove Forest, Riparian Forest, Pioneer Forest, and Old Field. Wetland habitats include the Elk River, feeder streams, a beaver pond, and a freshwater marsh. The marsh is an Eastern Newt and American Toad breeding site, while a series of ephemeral pools also provide breeding grounds for Wood Frogs and Spotted Salamanders. A trail system runs through the preserve and a boardwalk runs to the edge of the beaver pond and marsh. A trail runs along the Elk River through a Riparian Forest that includes Yellow Birch, Black Cherry, American Hornbeam, and Yellow Buckeye. The understory of this forest is rich in wildflowers from spring to the fall.

Wildlife viewing is excellent due to the variety of habitats and the presence of water. Wood Ducks and Great Blue Herons are found in the wetlands, warblers frequent the woodlands, while sparrows and goldfinches are at home in the fields. The fields are especially scenic in the late summer and fall when goldenrods and other fall wildflowers are in bloom. At this time the fields are alive with butterflies and other pollinators.

Contact: Division of Natural Sciences, Lees-McRae College, P.O. Box 128, Banner Elk, NC 28604, (828) 898-8787. www.lmc.edu
    Maps: USGS Elk Park

ELK RIVER FALLS

Located in Avery County in the Pisgah National Forest (Toecane Ranger District), the Elk River Falls, while popular with locals, remains unknown to most visitors to the high country. This may be due to its location, which is a bit off the beaten track. To reach the falls, head to Elk Park on US 19E and then turn on SR 1303. Turn again at Elk River Road (SR 1305). After 4 miles the road ends at a parking area with several picnic tables on the banks of the Elk River. The river here is wide, shallow, and gentle. The short trail to the falls begins just past the parking area following the river downstream. The trail descends to the base of the 50 foot falls where hikers may walk out on large rocks to get an excellent view. Be careful, the rocks are often quite slippery.

For a longer hike, leave the falls and follow the trail downstream along the river's edge. This trail passes through a riparian habitat of Cove Forest with heavy rhododendron thickets. Spring wildflowers are common; keep an eye out on the rock faces for rare ferns such as Ebony Spleenwort and Mountain Spleenwort. Beaver activity is obvious along the trail and bird life is abundant. The trail ends as it runs into a forest service road. You can then loop back on this road to the parking area. The entire loop is approximately a mile.

Contact: Toecane Ranger District, Pisgah National Forest, P.O Box 128 Burnsville, NC 28714, (828) 682-6146. www.cs.unca.edu/nfsnc/
    Maps: USGS Elk Park

MOUNT JEFFERSON

Located in Ashe County, Mount Jefferson looms over the towns of West Jefferson and Jefferson. Rising some 1,600 feet over the surrounding landscape, the summit of Mount Jefferson at 4,400 feet offers panoramic views of Ashe County and the Blue Ridge Mountains to the east. Mount Jefferson is a remnant of the ancient Ashe Plateau, lying along the drainage divide between the north and south forks of the New River. It is composed primarily of amphibolite and gneiss. The mountain is well known for its rocky outcrops and "caves". It is believed that these caves were used as shelters by escaped slaves on the Underground Railroad.

Access to Mount Jefferson is through NC 1152 off of US 221 between West Jefferson and Jefferson. The road winds almost to the top of the mountain, allowing one to see the changes in vegetation with increasing elevation. Mount Jefferson is heavily forested with Mixed Oak Forest of Chestnut Oak and Northern Red Oak, including some old growth forest. This forest was once thick with American Chestnut trees as evidenced by chestnut sprouts in the understory. The Summit and Rhododendron trails run along the crest of the mountain, through a Dry Ridge Forest. On the exposed crest the trees are stunted by high winds and cold temperatures. The shrub layer is heavy with abundant Rosebay Rhododendron, Catawba Rhododendron, and Mountain Laurel. These shrubs produce a succession of flower displays with Catawba Rhododendrons flowering in early June, Mountain Laurel later in June, and finally Rosebay Rhododendron in early July. Below the drier ridge forest, Cove Forests appear on the northern slope with Red Maple, Tuliptree, and American Basswood appearing. Below Luther Rock an isolated stand of Bigtooth Aspen appears.

Contact: Mount Jefferson State Natural Area, P.O. Box 48, Jefferson, NC 28640, (336) 246-9653. www.ils.unc.edu / parkproject / visit / moje / home.html
Maps: USGS Jefferson; NCPR Mount Jefferson State Natural Area

BLUFF MOUNTAIN PRESERVE

Located in Ashe County, Bluff Mountain is part of the chain of peaks that includes Tater Hill, Elk Knob, Three Top Mountain, Paddy Mountain, Phoenix Mountain, and Mount Jefferson. These mountains form the six-mile

Long Hope Valley and contain the headwaters of the North Fork of the New River. Bluff Mountain has a number of plant communities, but is best known for its Rocky Outcrop and Mountain Bog communities. The cliffs are home to a number of rare species, while the open bog contains unusual plants, including sundew. Overall some 25 endangered, rare or threatened flowering plant species are found on the preserve.

Bluff Mountain Preserve is owned and managed by The Nature Conservancy. Due to its ecologically sensitive nature visitation is limited to guided tours through the North Carolina Chapter field trip program or through the Ashe County Chamber of Commerce volunteer-led visits.

Contact: North Carolina Nature Conservancy, One University Place, 4705 University Place, Suite 290, Durham, NC 27707, 919-403-8558. www.nature.org/ wherewework/northamerica/states/northcarolina/

Ashe County Chamber of Commerce, 6 N Jefferson Ave., West Jefferson, NC, 28694, (336) 246-9550. www.ashechamber.com

Maps:Warrensville

THREE TOP MOUNTAIN GAME LAND

Three Top Mountain is part of the amphibolite mountain group found in Ashe and Watauga Counties (see Bluff Mountain). Owned and managed by the North Carolina Wildlife Resources Commission, the three rocky peaks of the mountain's ridge form a distinctive sight in Ashe County. With elevations from 3,000 to 4,800 feet there is a variety of habitats from Mixed Oak Forests to open, Rocky Outcrops. A number of rare plants, including Heller's Blazing Star, are found on the exposed cliffs. This large expanse of natural area (2,289 acres) is also attractive to many bird species for breeding and during migration.

The game lands may be reached by taking NC 88 west from Jefferson to Creston. Turn left on Three Top Road (SR 1100). After two miles, pass over Three Top Creek and there will be a parking area and an access road to the Wildlife Game Lands on the left.

Contact: North Carolina Wildlife Resource Commission, 1701 Mail Service Center, Raleigh, NC 27699, (919) 733-7291. www.216.27.49.98

Maps: USGS Warrensville.

THE NEW RIVER

Designated a National Scenic River, the New River is probably the best known of the rivers that drain northwest North Carolina. Running from its headwaters in the Blue Ridge Mountains, the New River winds north into Virginia and eventually into the Kanawha and Ohio rivers. Eventually its waters end up in the Mississippi River and the Gulf of Mexico. Ironically the New River, named by Peter Jefferson, father of Thomas Jefferson, is considered to be the oldest river in North America.

The best way to experience the New River is to canoe or kayak downstream. Fortunately several outfitters and the New River State Park facilitate this option. The most popular stretch of the river is the 26.5 mile designated scenic section in Ashe and Alleghany Counties. The South Fork of the New River makes up 22 miles of this stretch, until the North Fork joins in for the final 4.5 miles. The New River State Park consists of three river access areas within the scenic section that contain campsites. The three sites are located approximately 10-15 miles apart, thus are about one day's canoe ride between the camping areas. Several roads also cross the river and river outfitters will rent canoes, kayaks, and set up shuttles to pick up customers along the river at designated take out points. Be aware of water levels as in late summer water levels tend to be low and the trip can be a rocky affair.

Aside from where the New River passes through state parkland, the river travels mainly through private property. This includes residential areas, farmland, tree plantations, and forest. For the most part the scenery is good. There is some nice riparian habitat including large Sycamore trees and the wildflower displays along the river can be excellent. Be sure to bring binoculars as the bird life is abundant and the open nature of the river makes for easy viewing. Birds found along the river include Green Herons, Great Egrets, Belted Kingfishers, Wood Ducks, Spotted Sandpipers, Eastern Phoebes, Willow Flycatchers, Least Flycatchers, Tree Swallows, Warbling Vireos, Baltimore Orioles, Red-winged Blackbirds, American Goldfinches, Song Sparrows, and the odd Osprey. Also be on the lookout for Beavers, Muskrats, Mink, and River Otters.

Contact: New River State Park, P.O. Box 48, Jefferson, NC 28640, (336) 982-2587. www.ils.edu/parkproject/visit/neri/home.html

Maps: USGS Jefferson, Laurel Springs, Mouth of Wilson; NCPR New River State Park

TENNESSEE

Geographical borders are constructs of man and do not reflect borders of natural communities. Thus the communities we find in northwestern North Carolina extend beyond our borders to our neighbor to the west, Tennessee. The proximity of many excellent natural areas in northeast Tennessee, make visits across the state line rewarding. The Cherokee National Forest is as impressive as the Pisgah National Forest in North Carolina for its diverse communities and trail systems. For exploring this interesting area I highly recommend: *Wilderness Trails of Tennessee's Cherokee National Forest. 1992. edited by William H. Skelton. The University of Tennessee Press, Knoxville.* This is a comprehensive guidebook to the natural areas of the Cherokee National Forest with detailed descriptions, highlights, and directions. For the naturalist looking to "go west" into Tennessee, this guide is a must.

Some excellent natural areas that are less than an hour drive from Avery, Mitchell, or Watauga Counties, include Big Laurel Branch Wilderness, Pond Mountain Wilderness, Doe River Gorge Scenic Area, Unaka Mountain Wilderness, Rogers Ridge Scenic Area and Primitive Area, and Flint Mill Scenic Area and Primitive Area.

Contact: Supervisor's Office, USDA Forest Service, Cherokee National Forest, P.O. Box 2010, Cleveland, TN 37320, (615) 476-9700; Unaka Ranger District, USDA Forest Service, 1205 N. Main Street, Erwin, TN 37650, (615) 743-4452; Watauga Ranger District, USDA Forest Service, Route 9, Box 2235, Elizabethton, TN 37643, (615) 542-2942. www.southernregion.fs.fed.us/cherokee/

Maps: Elizabethton, Watauga Dam, Doe, Carter, Holsten Valley, Grayson, Laurel Bloomery.

EPILOGUE

Even the casual visitor to northwestern North Carolina, quickly becomes enamored with its nature. The rich diversity of its life, the scenery, and the vast expanses of natural areas make this area one of the most biologically exciting areas in North America. The beauty of our area attracts countless visitors, but also is a place that an increasing number of people want to call home. Ironically this desire to live in a beautiful region, often results in the inadvertent despoiling of it. Exploitation of our region is not new, as evidenced by the large logging operations that once gave Linville the nickname of "Stumptown".

Nature, however, is resilient and the recovery of our forests has been one of nature's miracles. Human development, however, produces new problems to our natural communities. Fragmentation of forests by development is changing the ecology of many a mountainside and valley. Mountain ridges that had never seen development are being cleared and covered with homes and riddled with roads. Farmland is being converted to housing developments and the buffer zones of rivers are being cleared for homes. Development is also producing serious erosion and sediment problems in our waterways, threatening the high water quality that our aquatic life requires. One of the greatest challenges to our local communities is how we deal with this growth to minimize its impact on the very nature that attracted so many of us to this area in the first place.

Fortunately this region possesses large tracts of protected natural areas, including National Forest and National Park Service lands. But even these areas face serious threats such as introduced species, air pollution, and global warming. Natural resource personnel working with limited funding face their own challenges in the management of these precious areas.

The importance of protecting the natural integrity of our region has not gone unrecognized. Numerous citizens and regional land trust organizations have worked diligently to identify and protect important natural areas. These actions have made a difference and hopefully all of us who enjoy the natural assets of our region will become involved and supportive of this ongoing preservation process.

What conservation education must build is a universal curiosity to understand the land mechanism. Conservation may then follow.

Aldo Leopold

SUGGESTED FIELD GUIDES
AND REFERENCE BOOKS

PLANTS

Newcomb'sWildflower Guide. 1977. L. Newcomb. Little, Brown and Co., Boston.
  Although this guide is specific for the northeast, it works extremely well for our
  area. Except for a number of endemics, this guide has the majority of our flower-
  ing herbs, shrubs, and vines. The key system is clear and easy to use. For anyone
  interested in identifying our local wildflowers, this book is a must.

Manual of theVascular Flora of the Carolinas. 1968. A.E. Radford, H.E. Ahles, &
  C.R. Bell. The University of North Carolina Press, Chapel Hill.
  The bible for plant identification in the Carolinas. This book is not for everyone
  as the keys and plant descriptions are highly technical. Nonetheless the scope of
  this book is impressive and the county distributions are extremely helpful, as are
  the flowering, fruiting, and habitat information.

Guide to theVascular Plants of the Blue Ridge. 1989. B. Eugene Wofford. The
  University of Georgia Press, Athens.
  Excellent keys of our regional flora and habitat info for each species make this
  comprehensive book very useful for our area. There are no pictures, but its light
  weight makes it very manageable in the field.

Wildflowers of the Southern Mountains. 1998. R.M. Smith. University of
  Tennessee Press, Knoxville.
  This non-technical guide focuses on herbaceous plants with descriptions of some
  1,200 mountain species found from Maryland to Georgia. A pictorial key based

on flower shape is used to identify plants to family or genus. The 600 color photos are outstanding.

Wildflowers of the Shenandoah Valley and Blue Ridge Mountains. 1979. O.W. Gupton & F.C. Swope. University Press of Virginia, Charlottesville.
The wildflowers are separated by color with nice photographs of the flowers. Also includes flowering times and interesting information about the different species.

Wild Flowers of North Carolina. 1968. W.S. Justice & C. R. Bell. The University of North Carolina Press, Chapel Hill.
Although this guide displays wildflowers from throughout the state, the mountain region is well represented including a number of rare mountain species. Flowering and state distribution information is included.

Wildflowers in Color. 1965. A. Stupka. Harper Colophon Books, New York.
This is an excellent guide to over 250 herbs, shrubs, vines, and trees of the Southern Appalachians. Includes identification, flowering, fruiting, and habitat information. Includes many of our common species.

Wildflowers of the Blue Ridge Parkway. 1997. J.A. Alderman. The University of North Carolina Press. Chapel Hill.
This compact guide includes 275 species of wildflowers using flower color and shape for identification. The guide includes specific sites along the Blue Ridge Parkway for wildflower viewing.

A Field Guide to Wildflowers. 1968. R.T. Peterson & M. McKenny. Houghton Mifflin Company, Boston.
This general wildflower guide uses a flower color and form key. I prefer the Newcomb's Guide, although this guide is useful as a backup.

Wildflowers of the Southern Appalachians: How to Photograph and Identify Them. 1996. K. Adams & M. Casstevens. John F. Blair Publisher, Winston Salem.
For those with the photography bug, this is the book for you. Includes photo tips for each species and of course beautiful photos.

Fern Finder. 1981. A.C. Hallowell & A.C. Hallowell. Nature Study Guild, Berkeley.

This nifty little guide has a nice key to many of our local ferns. Ferns can be confusing to key out and this small book is a good way to begin.

Ferns. 1984. B. Cobb. Houghton Mifflin Company, Boston.

Excellent overall guide to the ferns. Includes physical descriptions and habitat information. Also contains sections on clubmosses, spikemosses, horsetails, and quillworts.

A Field Manual of the Ferns & Fern-Allies of the United States & Canada. 1985. D. Lellinger. Smithsonian Institution Press, Washington, D.C.

Despite its title the size of this guide may limit its usefulness in the field. None-theless, it is probably the most thorough guide to the ferns of North America. Unlike the other fern guides, it uses photographs of the different species.

A Field Guide to the Trees and Shrubs of the Southern Appalachians. 1994. R.E. Swanson. The Johns Hopkins University Press, Baltimore.

My favorite guide to our local trees and shrubs. An easy to use key, nice illustrations, and thorough species descriptions, distributions, and habitat information. Pick this one up.

A Field Guide to Eastern Trees: Eastern United States and Canada, Including the Midwest. 1998. G. A. Petrides. Houghton Mifflin Co. Boston.

This Peterson guide contains illustrations, photos, range maps, and a detailed text for easy tree identification. The improved expanded 1998 edition includes identification charts and deals only with trees.

The Audubon Society Field Guide to North American Trees: Eastern Region. 1980. E. L. Little. Alfred Knopf, New York.

Easy to use key and informative text make this tree guide worthwhile. Includes photographs of leaves, bark, and some flowers and fruit.

A Field Guide to Medicinal Plants: Eastern and Central North America. 1990. S. Foster & J.A. Duke. Houghton Mifflin Company, Boston.

For those interested in herbal remedies and traditional uses of our local plants, this book has a wealth of information along these lines.

EdibleWild Plants. 1977. L.A. Peterson. Houghton Mifflin Company, Boston.
For those interested in finding and eating our local plants, this guide tells what to eat and what not to eat.Watch out for that Baneberry!

The Audubon Society Field Guide to North American Mushrooms. 1981. G.H. Lincoff. Alfred A. Knopf, New York.
Easy to use guide with nice photographs.

Mushrooms of North America. 1979. O.K. Miller. Chanticleer Press, New York.
Nice photographs, however most species have only scientific names listed.

Lichens of North America. 2001. I.R. Brodo, S.D. Sharnoff, & S. Sharnoff.Yale University Press, New Haven.
For those interested in the rich diversity of lichens in our area, this is the book for you. Beautiful photgraphs and a wealth of information about lichens. Be warned however, this book weighs in at over 6 pounds.

Classification of the Natural Communities of North Carolina (third approximation). 1990. M. P. Schafale & A. S. Weakley. North Carolina Natural Heritage Program, Division of Environment, Health, and Natural Resources. Raleigh, NC.
An impressive, technical description of the different habitats and plants found through the state, including the mountain communities.

BIRDS

National Geographic Field Guide to the Birds of North America. 2002. National Geographic Society, Washington, D.C.
Excellent illustrations, up-to-date information, and range maps opposite species descriptions make this guide a favorite.

A Field Guide to the Birds. 1980. R.T. Peterson. Houghton Mifflin Company, Boston.
Still the classic. The guide that started it all.

Birds of North America. 2000. K. Kaufman. Houghton Mifflin Co., Boston.
For those who prefer photographs for identification, this guide is for you. Well designed with easy to use color guides to track down bird groups. Small size is handy for the field.

The Sibley Field Guide to Birds of Eastern North America. 2003. D. A. Sibley. Knopf, New York.
This excellent guide is a scaled down version of The Sibley Guide to Birds. It is more field-friendly (smaller and lighter) with beautiful illustrations and color-coded maps opposite the species descriptions.

Smithsonian Handbooks: Birds of Eastern North America. 2001. F. Alsop. DK Pub Merchandise.
This bird guide uses enhanced photographs for identification. A single page is devoted to each species with range, vocalizations, and flight patterns. May be too large (3 pounds) to carry in the field but is a good information source.

A Field Guide to Warblers of North America. 1997. J.L. Dunn & K.L. Garrett. Houghton Mifflin Company, Boston.
For those birdwatchers that have a fondness for warblers (and what birdwatcher doesn't!) this guide is loaded with illustrations and information about these beautiful birds.

Birds of the Blue Ridge Mountains. 1992. M.B. Simpson. The University of North Carolina Press. Chapel Hill.
Although this book includes the Blue Ridge Parkway, Great Smoky Mountains and Shenandoah National Park, our area is well represented in this excellent "where to find the birds" book. Directions, maps, and probable birds that frequent the different locales are listed.

Birds of the Carolinas. 1980. E.F. Potter, R.P. Teulings, & J.F. Parnell. The University of North Carolina Press.
Although not useful as a field guide this reference book supplies information about statewide distribution in time and location for birds throughout the state.

Stokes Field Guide to Bird Songs, Eastern Region. 1997. E. Elliot, D. Stokes, & L. Stokes. Time Warner Audio Books, New York.
Three CD set that includes 372 species. Booklet and CD format make finding individual species easy and recordings are excellent. For those determined to learn bird songs, these CDs are a good starting point.

MAMMALS

Mammals of the Carolinas. 1985. W.D. Webster, J.F. Parnell, & W.C. Biggs, Jr. The University of North Carolina Press, Chapel Hill.
Excellent regional guide of our local mammals. Includes distribution maps, characteristics, and natural history information.

The Mammals of Virginia. 1998. D.W. Linzey. The McDonald & Woodward Publishing Company, Blacksburg, Virginia.
Although this impressive reference book focuses on Virginian mammals, it includes most of our local species. A lot of detail and information about each species, including skull drawings.

A Field Guide to the Mammals of America North of Mexico. 1998. W.H. Burt & R.P. Grossenheider. Houghton Mifflin Company, Boston.
This Peterson Field Guide includes illustrations, range maps, tracks, and a detailed text for each mammal species. Dental formulae and photographs of skulls add a nice touch.

The Audubon Society Field Guide to North American Mammals. 1996. J.O. Whitaker. Alfred A. Knopf, New York.
Excellent photographs and text make this guide well worth the price.

The Smithsonian Book of North American Mammals. 1999. Edited by D.E. Wilson & S. Ruff. Smithsonian Institution Press. Washington.
Excellent reference book for North American mammals with photos of each species.

Wild Mammals of North America, Biology, Management, and Economics. 1982. Edited by J.A. Chapman & G.A. Feldhamer. The Johns Hopkins University Press, Baltimore.
Highly detailed reference book with broad range of information about many mammal species.

AMPHIBIANS AND REPTILES

Amphibians and Reptiles of the Carolinas and Virginia. 1980. B.S. Martof, W.M. Palmer, J.R. Bailey, J.R. Harrison, and J. Dermid. University of North Carolina Press, Chapel Hill.
Excellent regional guide of our local herps. Includes distribution maps, characteristics, and natural history information.

A Field Guide to Reptiles & Amphibians, Eastern and Central North America. 1998. R. Conant & J.T. Collins. Houghton Mifflin Company, Boston.
Highly informative guide with photos, pictures, and range maps.

Salamanders of the United States and Canada. 1998. J.W. Petranka. Smithsonian Institution Press, Washington.
This is the salamander book. It may be too large to drag into the field, however it is a terrific reference book on all aspects of the biology of our salamander species.

Reptiles of North Carolina. 1995. W.M. Palmer & A.L. Braswell. The University of North Carolina Press, Chapel Hill.
Wealth of information about the reptiles of North Carolina. Includes useful county distribution maps for each species.

FISHES

Freshwater Fishes of the Carolinas, Virginia, Maryland, & Delaware. 1994. F.C. Rohde, R.G. Arndt, D.G. Lindquist, & J. Parnell. The University of North Carolina Press, Chapel Hill.
Very useful guide for our local fish. Includes family key, distribution maps, descriptions, habitat, and natural history information.

Freshwater Fishes. 1991. L.M. Page & B.M. Burr. Houghton Mifflin Company, Boston.
As this Peterson Field Guide includes all the freshwater fish of North America, it is more difficult to use than Rohde et.al. Nonetheless it supplies additional information and has good illustrations.

NOTE: Bold type is used to reference color plate pages.

Index

A

Abies fraseri 49, 53, 57
Accipiter
  cooperii 129
  striatus 129
Acer
  pennsylvanicum 15, 18, 25, 37, **85**
  rubrum 15, 37, 43, 47, 50, 53, 61, **85**, **100**
  saccharum 18
  spicatum 25, 50, **85**
Achillea millefolium **97**, 114
Actaea pachypoda 27, **79**, **99**
Actitis macularia 131
Adder's Tongue, Yellow 26
Adelges
  piceae 49
  tsugae 24
Adelgid
  Balsam Wooly 49
  Hemlock Wooly 24
Aegolius acadicus 130
Aesculus flava [octandra] 15, **85**, 22
Agastache scrophulariifolia 113
Agelaius phoeniceus 123, 132
Agkistrodon contortrix 147
Agrostis perennans 109
Aix sponsa 132
Alder
  Green 110, 131, 174
  Tag 33, **98**, 169, 171
Alexander
  Golden 27, **86**
  Heart-leaved 27
Alleghanian Orogeny 5
Alleghany County 9

Allium
  tricoccum 26, **75**, **101**
Alnus
  crispa 110
  serrulata 33, **98**
Alumroot 55, 58, **82**
Ambloplites rupestris 162
Ambrosia artemisiifolia **98**, 117
Ambystoma maculatum **104**, 155
Ambystomatidae 155
Ameiurus nebulosus 161
Amelanchier arborea 14, 15, 23, 47, 53, 56, 58, 61, **83**, **99**
Amianthium muscaetoxicum 38, **72**
Amphibians 150
Amphibolite 7, 8, 9, 180
Anas
  discors 132
  platyrhynchos 132
Anemone quinquefolia 27, **79**
Anemone, Wood 27, **79**
Angelica, Filmy 32, **86**, 110
Angelica triquinata 28, **86**, 110
Anole, Carolina 149
Anolis carolinensis 149
Anthocyanins 18
Aplectrum hyemale 29, **77**
Appalachian Trail 34, 51, 110, 173, 174
Aquila chrysaetos 131
Aquilegia canadensis 55, **79**
Aralia
  nudicaulis 38
  racemosa 38, **86**
  spinosa 39, **100**
Arbutus, Trailing 44, **89**
Archilochus colubris 124
Arctium minus 114
Ardea
  alba 132
  herodias 132
Arisaema triphyllum 27, **72**, **98**
Aristolochia macrophylla 25, **77**
Aronia melanocarpa 53
Arrowhead 63

Aruncus dioicus **83**
Asclepias
  exaltata **90**, **100**, 115
  syriaca **90**, 115
Ash
  Mountain 16, 18, 34, 50, 53, 54,
    58, **100**, 164, 165, 168, 173
  White 23, 167
Ashe County 3, **71**
Ashe Plateau 179
Aspen, Bigtooth 53, 165, 179
Asplenium
  montanum 55, **102**
  trichomanes 55, **102**
Aster
  acuminatus 51
  cordifolius **97**, 117
  curtisii 40, **97**
  divaricatus 51, **97**
  lateriflorus 118
  novae-angliae 117
  pilosus **97**, 117
  puniceus **97**, 117
Aster
  Calico 118
  Curtis' 40, **97**
  Heart-leaved 32, **97**, 117
  New England 117
  Purple-stemmed **97**, 117
  White Heath **97**, 117
  White Wood 16, 32, 40, **97**
  Whorled Wood 51
Asteraceae 16
Athyrium filix-femina 51
Atlantic Ocean 3, 6, 11
Aureolaria laevigata **92**
Avens, Spreading 58, **84**
Avery County 3, **70**, **71**
Aythya
  affinis 132
  collaris 132
Azalea
  Flame 15, 38, 62, **88**, 110, 172, 174
  Swamp 33, 61, 62

B

Babel Tower 59, 171
Baeolophus bicolor 129
Balm
  Bee 31, 34, **91**, 124
  Horse 31
Baneberry, White 16, 27, 28, **79**, **99**
Banner Elk 11, 12, 13, 132
Basalt 6, 7
Bass
  Largemouth 162
  Rock 162
  Smallmouth 162
Bass Lake 132, 137, 166
Basswood, American 18, 23, 164,
  171, 179
Bat
  Big Brown 144
  Virginia Big Eared 144, 166
Battus philenor 25, **108**
Beacon Heights 53, 59, 164
Bear, Black 141, 170
Bearberry 50, 165, 168, 173
Beaver, American 60, 137, 166, 177,
  178, 181
Beaver bog 60
Bedstraws 114
Bee Tree Creek 165
Beech, American 19, 22, 34, **98**, 110,
  167, 174, 177
Beech Creek Bog 61
Beech Drops 22
Beech Mountain 10
Beetle
  Locust Borer 46
  Red Milkweed **108**, 115
  Southern Pine Borer 42
Bellflower, Tall 32, **94**
Bellwort
  Large-flowered 26, 27, **73**
  Mountain 39, **73**
Bergamot
  Purple **91**
  Wild 39, **91**

Betula
  alleghaniensis 15, 50, 58
  lenta 18
Big Hump Mountain 174
Big Laurel Branch Wilderness 182
Big Lost Cove Cliffs 131, 169
Big Yellow Mountain 10, **70**, 175
Bindweed, Hedge 116
Birch
  Sweet 18, 22, 37, 164, 166, 171
  Yellow 1, 15, 18, 22, 24, **32**, 34,
    35, 50, 57, 164, 165, 167, 175,
    177, 178
Black Racer 146
Black Redhorse 160
Black Rock Cave 144
Black Rock Trail 168
Blackberry 16, 47
  Allegheny 111, 174
  Smooth 50, 173
  Tall 116
Blackbird, Red-winged 123, 132, 181
Blarina brevicauda 139
Bleeding Heart, Wild 57, **81**
Bloodroot 17, 26, **81**, 171
Blowing Rock 9
Blowing Rock gneiss 9
Blue Ridge Escarpment 9, 10, 169
Blue Ridge Mountains 3, 10, 11, 166,
    169, 181
Blue Ridge Parkway 1, 3, 9, 22, 27,
    41, 53, 56, 59, 129, 132, 135,
    163, 167
Blue Ridge Province 5, 9
Blueberry 58, 164, 165, 168, 169
  Early Lowbush 44
  Highbush 44, 50, 52, 110, 165, 174
  Northern Highbush 44
Bluebird, Eastern 122, 176
Bluegill 162
Bluet
  Mountain 58
  Roan Mountain 110

Thyme-leaved 28, 51, **93**, 109, 173
Bluff Mountain Preserve 63, 179, 180
Bobcat 142
Bobwhite, Northern 122
Bombycilla cedrorum 124
Bonasa umbellus 125
Boneset **95**, 118
Boone Fork 164
Boone Fork Bog 61, 62
Boone Fork Bowl 167
Boone Fork Creek 165, 167
Boone Fork Loop Trail 165
Botrychium dissectum 30, **102**
Boulderfield Forest 33
Bowman's Root 28
Boykinia aconitifolia 28
Branta canadensis 132
Brassica nigra 114
Bubo virginianus 129, 140
Bucephala albeola 132
Buckeye, Yellow 15, 16, 17, 22, 33,
    34, 35, **85**, 164, 167, 178
Bufflehead 132
Bufo americana **107**, 156
Bullfrog 156
Bullhead, Brown 161
Bulrushes 62
Bunchflower, Broad-leaved 32
Bunting
  Indigo 47, 123, 124, **131**, 133
  Snow 123
Burdock, Common 16, 114, 115
Burke County 3
Buteo
  jamaicensis 121
  platypterus 129
Butorides virescens 132
Buttercup, Creeping 113
Butterfly
  Monarch **108**, 115
  Pipevine Swallowtail 25

C

Cabin Trail 172
Caldwell County 3
Calloway Peak 48, 166, 168
Calloway Trail 35
Calycanthus floridus **80**
Calystegia sepium 116
Campanula
   americana 31, **94**
   divaricata 40, **94**
Campostoma anomalum 159
Cancer Root, One-flowered 22, **92**
Canis
   latrans 142
   lupus 142
Caprimulgidae 122
Carboniferous period 5
Cardamine clematitis 51
Cardinal Flower 28, **94**, 170
Cardinal, Northern 123, 133
Cardinalis cardinalis 123
Carduelis
   pinus 133
   tristis 123
Carex 58, 62
   brunnescens 109
   debilis 109
   pensylvanica 109
Carphophis amoenus 146
Carpinus caroliniana 33
Carpodacus
   mexicanus 122
   purpureus 133
Carver's Gap 51, 110, 173
Carya
   cordiformis 37
   glabra 37
   ovata 37
   tomentosa 37
Castor canadensis 137
Catawba River Basin 3

Catbird, Gray 47, 123, 130, 131
Catbrier 40, 47
Caterpillar
   Eastern Tent 47
   Monarch **108**
   Pipevine Swallowtail **108**
Catfish 160
   Channel 161
   Flathead 161
Cathartes aura 121
Catharus
   fuscescens 128
   guttatus 128, 130
   minimus 128
   ustulatus 128
Catostomidae 160
Catostomus commersoni 160
Cattail, Common 62
Caulophyllum thalictroides 17, **80**
Cedar
   Ground 31, **102**
   Running 31
Centrarchidae 162
Certhia americana 128
Cervus elaphus 143
Ceryle alcyon 131
Chaetura pelagica 122
Chelone
   glabra 32
   lyonii 51, **91**
Chelydra serpentina 148
Cherokee National Forest 168, 173, 182
Cherry
   Bird 47
   Black 15, 19, 23, 24, 47, 164, 166, 167, 177, 178
   Fire 15, 17, 46, 50, 53, **84**
   Pin 46
Chestnut, American 36, 165, 169, 179
Chestnut blight 36
Chickadee
   Black-capped 130
   Carolina 129, 133
Chickweed, Giant **78**

Chicory **95**, 114
Chimaphila maculata 39, **87**, **102**
Chimneys, The 170
Chipmunk, Eastern 134, 170
Chlorophyll 18
Chokeberry, Black 53, 165
Chordeiles minor 122
Chrysanthemum leucanthemum 15,
    96, 112
Chub
    Creek 159, 160
    River 159, 160
Chuck-will's-widow 122
Cichorium intybus **95**, 114
Cimicifuga racemosa 28, 34, **79**
Cinquefoil 109, 174
    Common **84**, 113
    Three-toothed 58, 109, 175
Circaea alpina 51
Circium vulgare **95**, 114
Circuta maculata 28
Cladonia 58
Claytonia 17, 50
    caroliniana **78**
    virginica 50, **78**
Clematis virginiana **79**, **99**, 115
Clemmys muhlenbergi 148
Clethra acuminata 25, 53
Clethrionomys gapperi 136
Climate 11
Climax forests 21
Clinostomus funduloides 159
Clintonia
    borealis 17, 51, **74**
    umbellulata 17, **74**
Cloudland Trail 174
Clubmoss 53
    Bog 62
    Shining 31, **103**
Coccothraustes vespertinus 133
Cohosh, Blue 17, 28, **80**, 167
Colaptes auratus 123
Colinus virginianus 122
Collinsonia canadensis 31
Coluber constrictor 146

Columbine, Wild 55, **79**
Condylura cristata 139
Cone Manor House 166
Coneflower, Green-headed 32, **95**
Conglomerate 7
Conley Cove Trail 41, 171
Conopholis americana 37, **92**
Contopus virens 127
Convallaria montana 26, **74**
Copperhead 147
Coreopsis, Greater 32
Coreopsis major 31
Cormorant, Double-crested 166
Cornus 16
    alternifolia 25, **87**, **100**
    florida 24, **100**
Corvus
    brachyrhynchos 123
    corax 130
Corydalis, Pale 17, 57, 58, **81**, 170
Corydalis sempervirens 57, **81**
Corynorhinus townsendii virginianus
    144
Cottidae 161
Cottontail
    Appalachian 140
    Eastern 47, 140
    New England 140
Cottus
    bairdi 161
    carolinae 161
Cove Forest 21, **65**, 164, 165, 167,
    171, 177, 178
Cow Wheat 39, 53, **93**
Cowbane 28
Cowbird, Brown-headed 123
Coyote 142
Cragway 53, 59, 131
Cragway Trail 50, 167
Cranberry 61, **100**
Cranberry Gneiss 7
Crataegus **99**
Creeper, Brown 130, 173, 177
Creeper, Virginia 40
Cress, Bitter 51

Crossbill
  Red 130, 168
  White-winged 130
Crotalus horridus 147
Crow, American 123
Crowfoot, Kidney-leaved 113
Cuckoo
  Black-billed 176
  Yellow-billed 176
Curculio rectus 37
Cuscuta gronovii 29
Cyanocitta cristata 128
Cymophyllus fraseri 35, 72
Cyprinella galactura 159
Cyprinidae 159
Cypripedium acaule 29, 75
Cyptobranchus alleganiensis 152
Cystopteris protrusa 30, 34

D

Dace
  Blacknose 159
  Longnose 159
  Mountain Redbelly 159
  Rosyside 159
Daisy, Ox-eye 15, **96**, 112
*Danaus plexippus **108**, 115*
Daniel Boone Scout Trail 34, 50, 51, 167, 168
Danthonia compressa 58, 109
Darter 161
  Greenfin 161
  Greenside 161
  Kanawha 161
*Daucus carota **87**, 114*
Deer, White-tailed 47, 143, 144, 170
Deerberry 44, **89**
Dendroctonus frontalis 42
Dendroica
  caerulescens 125
  castanea 133
  coronata 133
  discolor 133
  fusca 126

magnolia 130, 133
palmarum 133
pensylvanica 123
petechia 123
striata 133
tigrina 133
virens 126
Dennstaedtia punctilobula 109
*Dentaria laciniata 27, **82***
Deschampsia flexuosa 109
Desmognathus 150
  *fuscus **105**, 152*
  marmoratus 151
  *monticola **104***
  *ochrophaeus **104**, 152*
  *orestes **104**, 152*
  *quadramaculatus **105**, 151*
  *wrightii **105**, 153*
Devil's Walking Stick 39, **100**
Dewberry, Swamp 116
Diadophis punctatus 146
Dianthus ameria 114
Dicentra
  *canadensis 27, **81***
  *cucullaria 17, **81***
  *eximia 57, **81***
Didelphis virginiana 141
*Diphylleia cymosa 29, **80**, 99*
*Disporum lanuginosum 26, **74**, 98*
Dodder 29
Doe River 173
Doe River Gorge Scenic Area 182
Dog Hobble 33, **89**
Dogberry 33
Dogwood
  Alternate-leaved 25, **87**, **100**
  Flowering 24, **100**
Dolostone 7
Dove, Mourning 123, 133
Dry Ridge Forest 42, **66**, 171, 179
Dryocopus pileatus 127
Dryopteris
  campyloptera 51
  intermedia 30
  marginalis 30

Duck
Ring-necked 132
Wood 132, 166, 178, 181
Dumetella carolinensis 123
Dutchman's Breeches 17, 27, **81**, 167
Dutchman's Pipe 25, **77**
Dwarf American Beech Forest **65**

E

Eagle, Golden 131
Eastern Continental Divide 3
Eastern Deciduous Forest 1
Ecological Communities 20
Eft, Red 155
Egret, Great 132, 181
Elaisomes 17
Elaphe obsoleta 146
Elder
Common **93**, 116, 171
Red-berried 50, 54, **94**, **101**, 116, 173
Elk 111, 143, 144, 175
Elk Knob 9, 179
Elk River 3, 8, 24, 152, 177
Elk River Falls **71**, 178
Elk Valley Biological Station 177
Elk Valley Preserve 60, 62, **67**, 119, 137, 177
Empidonax
alnorum 110, 131
minimus 123
trailii 132
virescens 127
Enchanter's Nightshade, Small 28, 51
Engine Gap 174
Epifagus virginiana 22
Epigaea repens 44, **89**
Eptesicus fuscus 144
Equisetum arvense 63
Erechtites hieracifolia **95**, 118
Eremophila alpestris 123
Ericaceae 43, 52, 58
Erigeron
annuus 112

canadensis 118
philadelphicus **97**, 112
pulchellus 112
Erythronium
americanum **73**
umbilicatum 26
Etheostoma
blennioides 161
chlorobranchium 161
kanawhae 161
Euchaetias egle **108**, 115
Eumeces
fasciatus 149
inexpectatus 149
Eupatorium
fistulosum **95**, 118
perfoliatum **95**, 118
purpureum 32
rugosum 16, 47, **95**, 118
Eurosta solidaginis **108**, 117
Eurycea 150
bislineata 154
wilderae **105**, 154
Evening Primrose, Common **86**, 118

F

Fagus grandifolia **98**, 110
Falco
peregrinus 130
sparverius 121
Falcon, Peregrine 130, 131, 169
Farmland **68**
Feldspar 7, 8
Fern
Brittle 34
Christmas 30
Cinnamon 61
Cut-leaved Grape **102**
Fragile 30
Grape 30
Hay-scented 30, 109
Marginal Shield 30
Rock Cap 30, 55

Royal 61
Southern Lady 30, 51
Fetterbush, Mountain 43, **89**, 165
Finch
House 122, 133
Purple 133
Fir, Fraser 49, 53, 57, 168, 173
Fish 158
Flat Rock 163, 164
Trail 27
Flat Top Mountain 166
Flatrock 59
Fleabane
Common **97**, 112
Daisy 112, 118
Flicker, Northern 123, 124
Flint Mill Scenic Area 182
Flowering 14
Fly Poison 38, 39, **72**, 163
Flycatcher
Acadian 127, 131, 171
Alder 110, 131, 174
Great Crested 127
Least 123, 176, 181
Willow 132, 176, 181
Foamflower 28, **82**, 167
Forget-me-not 28, **91**
Fox
Gray 141, 170
Red 141, 142, 170
Foxglove, Appalachian False 40, **92**
Fragaria virginiana **83**, 109, 113
Fraser, John 49
Fraxinus americana 23
French Broad River 3
Frog 156
Green 157
Pickerel 157
Wood **107**, 155, 156, 177
Fruiting 14, 16

G

Gabbro 7
Galax 44, **89**, 163, 165, 171

aphylla 38, 44, 53
urceolata 38, 44, 53, **89**
Galearis spectabilis **29**, **76**
Galium 114
Gaultheria procumbens 44, 53, **89**
Gavia immer 132
Gaylussacia baccata 44, 52, 56
Gentian
Appalachian 110
Bottle 32, **90**, 110
Stiff 32
Gentiana
austromontana 110
clausa **90**, 110
quinquefolia 32
Geology 5
Geothlypis trichas 123, 132
Geranium maculatum **85**, 114
Geranium, Wild **85**, 114
Gerardia laevigata 40
Geum radiatum 58, **84**
Gill-over the-ground 113
Gillenia trifoliata 28, **83**
Ginger, Heartleaf 40, **77**, 171
Gingercake Mountain 170
Ginseng 39
Glaciers 2
Glaucomys
sabrinus 135
volans 135
Glechoma hederacea 113
Gnatcatcher, Blue-gray 123, 124
Gneiss 7, 8
Goat's Beard **83**
Goldenrod 116
Broad-leaved 117
Cluster 51
Curtis' 16, 40, **96**, 117
Elm-leaved 117
Erect 117
Gray **117**
Late 117
Mountain 117
Rough-leaved 62, 117
Tall 117

Zigzag 32
Goldenrod Fly 117
Goldenrod Fly Gall **108**
Goldfinch, American 123, 133, 181
Goodyera pubescens 29, **102**
Goose, Canada 132
Gooseberry
 Roundleaf 33, 54
 Skunk 33
Grackle, Common 123
Gragg Prong Creek 169
Grandfather Mountain 3, 8, 10, 11,
 12, 13, 32, 34, 45, 48, 50, 52, 53,
 56, 57, 59, **65**, **66**, **68**, 130, 131,
 144, 147, 154, 164, 165, 166,
 168
Grandfather Mountain Formation 8
Grandfather Mountain Incorporated
 167
Grandfather Mountain Window 6, 9
Grandfather Ranger District 168
Grandfather Trail 51, 167
Granite 6, 7, 8
Granitic gneiss 9
Grape
 Fox 47
 Summer 40
Grass
 Bent 109, 174
 Hair 109
 Mountain Oat 58, 175
 Oat 109, 174
Grassy Balds 3, 48, **67**, 109, 110, 172,
 173, 174, 175
Grassy Ridge 174
Grassy Ridge Bald 174
Gray, Asa 54, 110, 172
Grebe, Pied-billed 132, 166
Greenbrier 40
Grosbeak
 Evening 133
 Rose-breasted 127, 133
Groundhog 135
Grouse, Ruffed 125
Gum, Black 18, 43, 169, 171

Gyrinophilus 150
 porphyriticus **105**, 154

H

Hamamelis virginiana 19, **83**
Hanging Rock 10
Hardhack 61
Harebell, Southern 40, **94**
Harper Creek 169, 170
Hawk
 Broad-winged 129, 165
 Cooper's 129
 Red-tailed 121
 Sharp-shinned 129
Hawksbill 8, 10, 59, 129, 170, 171
Hawkweed
 Field 113
 Panicled 40
Hawthorne 34, **99**
Heal-all **91**, 113
Heath 52, **66**, 164, 168, 173
Heath Balds 15, 173, 174
Hedeoma pulegioides 113
Helenium autumnale **96**, 118
Helianthus
 decapetalous 118
 giganteus **96**, 118
Hellbender 152
Hellebore
 False 34
 Small-flowered 34
Heller's Blazing Star 58, **96**, 166,
 168, 180
Helmitheros vermivorus 125
Hemlock
 Carolina 43, 56, **101**, 171
 Eastern 24, 32, 43, 61, **101**, 127,
 164, 166, 167, 169, 171, 177
 Water 28
Hemlock Hill 177
Hemlock Scale, Elongate 24
Henbit 113
Heracleum

lanatum 113
maximum **87**, 113
Heron
    Great Blue 132, 178
    Green 132, 181
Heuchera villosa 55
Hexastylis
    arifolia 40
    heterophylla 40
    shuttleworthii 40, **77**
    virginica 40
Hickory
    Bitternut 37
    Mockernut 37
    Pignut 37, 166, 169
    Shagbark 37
Hieracium
    caespitosum 113
    paniculatum 40
    pilosella 113
    pratense 113
    venosum 39, **102**
High Elevation Deciduous Forest 34,
    65
Hirundo rustica 121
Hobblebush 16, 24, 50, **93**, **101**, 168
Hogsucker, Northern 160
Holly
    American 25
    Mountain 15, 17, 24, 25, 50, 53,
        61, 62, 168, 177
Honeysuckle, Clammy 62
Hornbeam, American 33, 178
Horse Nettle **91**, **101**
Horsetail, Field 63
Horseweed 118
Houstonia
    montana 58, 110
    purpurea 38, **93**
    serpyllifolia 51, **93**, 109
Houstonia, Large 38
Huckleberry, Black 44, 52, 56, 164,
    171
Hudsonia montana 57
Hummingbird, Ruby-throated 124

Hump Mountain 10, 34, **70**, 174
Hydrangea arborescens 16, **83**
Hydrangea, Wild 16, 24, **83**
Hydrophyllum
    canadense 28
    virginianum 28, **90**
Hyla
    chrysoscelis 157
    crucifer **107**, 157
Hylidae 157
Hylocichla mustelina 128
Hylocomium splendens 50
Hypentelium nigricans 160
Hypericum
    densiflorum 57
    graveolens 51
    mitchellianum 51
Hyphantria cunea 47
Hyssop, Purple Giant 113

I

Ice storms 12
Ictaluridae 160
Ictalurus punctatus 161
Icterus galbula 131
Igneous rocks 6
Ilex
    montana 50, 53
    opaca 25
    verticillata 61
Impatiens
    capensis 31, **85**
    pallida 31, **85**
Indian Cucumber Root 17, 26, 39, **75**,
    163, 171
Indian Physic 28, **83**
Indian Pipe 28, **87**
Insectivora 138
Invershiel Bog 60, 61, 62, **67**
Ipomoea purpurea 116
Iris 17
    cristata 27, **75**
    verna 53, **75**

Iris
Crested Dwarf 27, **75**, 167, 171
Dwarf 53, **75**
Ironweed, New York **95**, 118
Ivy
Ground 113
Poison 40, 115

J

Jack-in-the-Pulpit 27, 28, 38, **72**, **98**
Jane Bald 110, 174
Jay, Blue 128
Jewelweed 124
Pale 31, **85**
Spotted 31, **85**
Jimsonweed 113
Joe-Pye Weed
Hollow 32, 118
Purple 32
Julian Price Park 164, 165
Junco, Dark-eyed 123, 125, 130, 131,
173
Junco hyemalis 125
Juncus 62

K

Kalmia latifolia 15, 52, 56, 62, **88**
Kestrel, American 121
Killdeer 176
Kingbird, Eastern 122, 176
Kingfisher, Belted 131, 181
Kinglet
Golden-crowned 130, 173, 177
Ruby-crowned 133
Kistler Memorial Highway 170, 172
Knotweed 114

L

Lactuca canadensis 118
Ladies' Tresses, Nodding **77**, 119
Lady's Slipper, Pink 29, **75**
Lamium amplexaule 113
Lampropeltis triangulum 147
Laportea canadensis 28, **77**

Lark, Horned 123
Lasallia papulosa 58
Leaf color 18
Leaf dropping 14
Leafing 14, 17
Leek, Wild 26, **75**, **101**
Lees-McRae College 177
Leiophyllum buxifolium 56, **88**
Lepomis
auritus 162
macrochirus 162
Lettuce
Mountain 28, 167
Wild 118
Leucothoe
axillaris 33
fontanesiana 33, **89**
recurva 43, **89**
Liatris helleri 58, **96**
Lilium
grayi **73**, 110
michauxii 39
superbum 31, 39, **73**
Lily
Bluebead 17, 26, 27, 38, **74**, 163,
166, 171
Carolina 39
Clinton's 51
Gray's **73**, 110, 174, 175
Speckled Wood 26, 27, **74**
Trout 26, **73**
Turk's Cap 32, 39, **73**
Lily of the Valley 26, 27, **74**, 163
Limestone 7
Limnothylpis swainsonii 126
Linville Falls 9, 170
Linville Gorge 2, 3, 8, 10, 13, 15, 27,
32, 36, 41, 43, 44, 45, 56, 57, 59,
60, **65**, **66**, **69**, 129, 131, 147,
149, 170, 171, 172
Linville Mountain 170
Linville River 3, 9, 32, **69**, 170
Lion's Foot 40
Liriodendron tulipifera 18, 23, 47, **80**
Listera smallii 29

Little Hump Mountain 174, 176
Little Lost Cove Cliff Trail 45, 149
Little Lost Cove Cliffs 59, 169
Lizard, Eastern Fence 149
Lizards 149
Lobelia
  cardinalis 28, **94**
  inflata 119
  siphilitica **94**, 119
Lobelia, Great Blue **94**, 119
Locust, Black 17, 46, 47, **84**
Long Hope Valley 180
Loon, Common 132, 166
Loosestrife, Whorled 38, **89**, 171
Lophodytes cucullatus 132
Lost Cove Creek 22, 28, 45, 169, 170
Lousewort, Common **92**
Loxia
  curvirostra 130
  leucoptera 130
Luther Rock 179
Lutra canadensis 138
Luxilus coccogenis 159
Lycopodium 30, 44, 53
  complanatum 31
  inundatum 62
  lucidulum 31, **103**
  tristachyum 31, **102**
Lygaeus kalmii 115
Lynx rufus 142
Lyonia ligustrina 52, 56, 61
Lysimachia quadrifolia 39, **89**

M

MacRae Peak **68**, 168
Madtom, Margined 161
Magnolia
  acuminata 23
  fraseri 15, 53, **80**
  tripetala 23
Magnolia
  Cucumber 15, 17, 18, 23, 171
  Fraser 15, 17, 19, 23, 24, 37, 53,
    80, 164, 165, 166, 169, 171, 177

  Southern 23
  Umbrella 23
Maianthemum canadense 26, 51, **74**
Malacosoma americanum 47
Male-berry 52, 56, 61, 171
Mallard 132
Mammal-bird fruits 17
Mandarin, Yellow 26, **74**, **98**, 167
Maple
  Mountain 25, 50, **85**
  Red 15, 17, 18, 22, 24, 43, 47, 50,
    53, 61, **85**, **100**, 164, 165, 166,
    169, 171, 177, 179
  Striped 15, 18, 25, 37, **85**, 164, 166
  Sugar 18, 22, 24, 34, 35, 164, 175,
    177
Marble 8
Marmota monax 135
Martof, Bernard 151
Mayapple 26, 34, **80**, 113
Mayflower, Canada 26, 27, 51, **74**,
  167
McDowell County 3
Meadowlark, Eastern 122, 176
Meadowsweet, Narrow-leaved 61, 62
Medeola virginiana 17, **75**
Megacyllene robiniae 46
Melampyrum lineare 53, **93**
Melanerpes carolinus 127
Melanthium hybridum 32
Meleagris gallopavo 122
Melospiza
  georgiana 133
  melodia 122, 132
Menziesia pilosa 52, 58, 110
Mephitis mephitis 140
Merganser
  Hooded 132
  Red-breasted 132
Mergus serrator 132
Mesozoic Era 6
Metabasalt 8
Metaconglomerate 8
Metamorphic rocks 7
Metaquartz arenite 7, 8

Metarhyolite 8
Metasandstone 7, 8, 56, 164
Michaux, Andre 49, 57, 172
Micropterus
   dolomieu 162
   salmoides 162
Microtus pennsylvanicus 136
Milkweed
   Common **90**, 115
   Poke **90, 100**, 115
Milkweed Bug, Small Eastern 115
Mill Pond 132, 137
Mimus polyglottis 122
Mink 138, 181
Minnie-Bush 52, 110, 168
Minnow, Bluntnose 159
Mississippi River 3
Mitchell County 3
Mitchell, Elisha 172
Mitchella repens 17, 39, **93**, **101**
Mitella diphylla 28, **83**
Miterwort 28, **83**
Mixed Oak Forest 20, 36, **65**, 163,
   164, 166, 167, 169, 171, 179,
   180
Mniotilta varia 128
Mockingbird, Northern 122
Mole
   Eastern 139
   Hairy-tailed 139
   Star-nosed 139
Molothrus ater 123
Monarda
   didyma 31, **91**
   fistulosa 31, **91**
   media 31, **91**
Monotropa
   hypopithys **88**
   uniflora 28, **87**
Morning Glory, Common 116
Moses Cone Estate 41, 132, 137
Moses Cone Manor 166
Moss
   Haircap 62, **103**, 109
   Knight's Plume 50

Mountain Fern 50
   Sphagnum 61, **103**
Mount Jefferson 9, 179
Mount Mitchell 48, 174
Mount Rogers 48
Mountain Bog 60, **67**, 171, 180
Mountain breeze 13
Mountain Laurel 15, 38, 43, 52, 56,
   62, **88**, 164, 165, 166, 169, 171,
   172, 179
Mountain Lion 143, 170
Mouse
   Deer 136
   White-footed 136
Mouse Ear 113
Moxostoma duquesnei 160
Mudstone 7
Mullein, Woolly **92**, 114, 115
Mullerian Mimicry 155
Muscovite mica 8
Muskrat 137, 181
Mustard, Black 114
Mustela
   frenata 142
   nivalis 142
   vison 138
Mustelidae 138
Myiarchus crinitus 127
Myosotis scorpioides 28, **91**
Myotis
   lucifugus 144
   septentrionalis 144
Myotis
   Little Brown 144
   Northern 144
Myrtle, Sand 56, 58, **88**, 165, 168,
   171

N

Nature Conservancy 167, 175, 176,
   180
Neotoma magister 136
Nerodia sipedon 145
Nettle
   Horse 113

Wood 28, 35, **77**
New River 3, **71**, 132, 162, 179, 180, 181
New River Basin 3
New River State Park 181
Newt, Eastern **104**, 155, 177
Nighthawk, Common 122
Nightshade, Deadly 113
Ninebark 33, **83**, 171
Nocomis micropogon 159
North Carolina Natural Heritage Program 20
North Carolina Wildlife Resources Commission 180
North Toe River 3
Northern Hardwood Forest 21, 167, 173, 174
Notophthalmus viridescens **104**, 155
Notropus 160
  leuciodus 159
  photogenis 159
  scabriceps 159
Noturus insignis 161
Nuthatch
  Red-breasted 130, 133, 173, 177
  White-breasted 133
Nuwati Trail 167
Nyssa sylvatica 43

O

Oak
  Black 36
  Chestnut 1, 19, 36, 42, 56, 164, 166, 169, 171, 179
  Northern Red 18, 24, 34, 36, 47, 163, 164, 166, 169, 171, 175, 179
  Scarlet 18, 42, 169, 171
  White 37, 43, 166, 171
Oak-Chestnut Forest 36
Oaks 16
Odocoilius virginianus 143
Oenothera biennis **86**, 118
Old Field **67**, 177
Old growth forest 2

Old Man's Beard 115
Oncorhynchus mykiss 158
Ondatra zibethicus 137
Opossum, Virginia 141
Orchid
  Green Fringed 29, **76**
  Green Wood 29
  Large Purple Fringed 29, **76**
  Large Round-leaved 29
Orchis
  Cranefly 29, **76**
  Showy 29, **76**
Orchis spectabilis 29, **76**
Oriole
  Baltimore 131, 176, 181
  Orchard 176
Orobanche uniflora 22, **92**
Osmorhiza claytonii 27, **87**
Osmunda
  cinnamomea 61
  regalis 61
Osprey 181
Otter, River 138, 181
Otus asio 129
Ovenbird 124, 167
Overmountain Victory Trail 176
Owl
  Barred 129
  Eastern Screech 129
  Great Horned 129, 140
  Northern Saw-Whet 130, 166
Oxalis montana 51, **84**
Oxydendron arboreum 18, 43, 56

P

Paddy Mountain 179
Paleozoic Era 5
Panax quinquefolius 39
Parascalops breweri 139
Parsnip, Cow **87**, 113
Parthenocissus quinquefolia 40
Partridge Berry 17, 39, **93**, **101**
Parula americana 126
Parulidae 120
Passerculus sandwichensis 133

Passeriformes 120
Passerina cyanea 123
Pedicularis canadensis **92**
Pennyroyal, American 113
Penstemon smallii **91**
Penstemon, Small's 39, 41, **91**
Pepperbush 25, 53
Percidae 161
Permian period 5
Peromyscus
   leucopus 136
   maniculatus 136
Phacelia fimbriata 26, **90**
Phacelia, Fringed 26, **90,** 167
Phenology 14
Pheucticus ludovicianus 127
Phlox
   carolina **90**
   ovata 114
   paniculata 114
   stolonifera 114
Phlox
   Carolina **90**
   Creeping 114
   Garden 114
   Mountain 114
Phoebe, Eastern 131, 171, 181
Phoenix Mountain 179
Phoxinus oreas 159
Phyllite 7, 8
Physocarpus opulifolius 33, **83**
Phytolacca americana **78, 99,** 116
Picea rubens 49, 53, 57, 61
Picoides
   pubescens 127
   villosus 127
Piedmont Province 5, 9, 10
Pilewort **95,** 118
Pimephales notatus 159
Pine
   Ground 31, 44
   Pitch 42, 56, 61, 164, 169, 171
   Running 31
   Table Mountain 56, 59, **66,** 169, 171

Virginia 42, 171
   White 19, 37, 42, 61, 166, 169, 171
Pineola Bog 60, 62
Pinesap **88**
Pink
   Deptford 114
   Fire 39, 41, **78,** 170, 171
Pink Shell **88**
Pinnacle Rocks 129, 172
Pinus
   pungens 56
   rigida 42, 56, 61
   strobus 29, 42, 61
   virginianus 42
Pioneer Forest 46, 177
Pipilo erythrophthalmus 123
Pipistrelle, Eastern 144
Pipistrellus subflavus 144
Piranga olivacea 127
Pisgah National Forest 3, 22, 41, 45,
   59, **66, 68,** 131, 141, 149, 165,
   167, 168, 169, 170
Plantain
   Downy Rattlesnake 29, **102**
Plantain, Robin's **97,** 112
Plantanthera
   clavellata 29
   grandiflora 29, **76**
   lacera 29, **76**
   orbiculata 29
Platanus occidentalis 33
Plectrophenax nivalis 123
Plethodon 150, 151, 153
   cinereus **106,** 153
   glutinosus **106,** 153
   jordani **106,** 152
   richmondi 153
   welleri **106,** 153
   yonahlossee **106,** 153
Plethodontidae 150
Podilymbus podiceps 132
Podophyllum peltatum 26, 34, **80,**
   113

Poecile
  atricapillus 130
  carolinensis 129
Pokeweed 17, **78**, **99**, 116
Polioptila caerulea **123**, 124
Polygonatum biflorum 17, **74**, **98**
Polygonum 114
Polypodium virginianum 34, 55
Polypody, Rock 30, 34, 55
Polystichum acrostichoides 30
Polytrichum commune 62, **103**, 109
Pond Mountain Wilderness 182
Pooecetes gramineus 123
Populus grandidentata 53
Possumhaw 17, 61, **93**
Potentilla
  canadensis **84**, 109, 113
  tridentata 58, 109
Precambrian 5
Prenanthes
  roanensis 109
  serpentaria 40
Price Lake 132, 166
Price Park, Julian 62, 164, 165
Procyon lotor 138
Profile Trail 8, 32, 34, 35, 51, 167, 168
Provinces 5
Prunella vulgaris **91**, 113
Prunus
  pennsylvanica 18, 46, 50, 53, **84**
  serotina 15, 23, 47
Pseudacris crucifer **107**, 157
Pseudotriton 150
  ruber **107**, 154
Ptilium crista-castrensis 50
Puma concolor 143
Punctatum 56, **88**, 169, 171
Puttyroot 29, **77**
Pylodictus olivaris 161

Q

Quartz 7, 8
Queen Anne's Lace **87**, 114
Quercus 16
  alba 43
  coccinea 18, 42
  montana 56
  prinus 56
  rubra 18, 24, 47
  velutina 36
Quiscalus quiscula 123

R

Raccoon 138, 142
Ragweed
  Common **98**, 117
Ragwort
  Golden 34, 62, 109, 112
  Robbin's 109
  Small's **96**, 112
Rain shadow 13
Rainfall 12
Raisin, Northern Wild 61
Ramp 27, **75**, **101**
Rana
  catesbiana 156
  clamitans 157
  palustris 157
  sylvatica **107**, 155, 156
Ranunculaceae 113
Ranunculus
  abortivus 113
  repens 113
Raspberry
  Black 116
  Flowering **84**, **100**, 116
Rattlesnake Root, Roan Mountain 109
Rattlesnake, Timber 147
Rattlesnake Weed 39, **102**
Raven, Common 130, 165
Redstart, American 126
Reed, Bur 62
Refugium 2
Regina septemvittata 146
Regulus
  calendula 133
  satrapa 130

Resident birds 121
Rhinichthys
    atratulus 159
    cataractae 159
Rhododendron
    calendulaceum 38, 62, **88**, 110
    catawbiense 15, 43, 50, 52, 56, **88**,
        110
    maximum 15, 38, 62, **88**
    minus 56, **88**
    vaseyi **88**
    viscosum 61
Rhododendron Gardens 54, 173, 174
Rhododendron Heath **70**
Rhododendron
    Catawba 15, 43, 50, 52, 54, 56, 58,
        88, 110, 164, 165, 166, 167, 168,
        171, 173, 174, 179
    Rosebay 15, 24, 32, 34, 43, 62, **88**,
        164, 165, 166, 177, 179
Rhyolite 7
Ribes
    cynosbati 33
    glandulosum 33
    rotundifolia 54
Rich Mountain 9, 166
Ridge and Valley Province 5
Riparian Forest 171, 177, 178
Roan High Bluff 51, 173, 174
Roan High Knob 48
Roan Massif 109, 110
Roan Mountain 3, 15, 34, 48, 50, 51,
    54, **67**, **69**, **70**, 110, 130, 147, 172
Robin, American 122, 123, 131
Robinia pseudoacacia 17, 46, **84**
Rock Tripe
    Folded 58
    Smooth 55, 58, **103**
Rocks
    Amphibolite 7, 9
    Amphibolitic metagabbro 7
    Basalt 6
    Conglomerate 7
    Dolostone 7
    Epidote-biotite schist 7

Feldspar 7
Garnet 9
Gneiss 7
Granite 6
Hornblende 9
Igneous 6
Limestone 7
Marble 8
Metaconglomerate 8
Metamorphic 7
Metaquartz arenite 7, 8
Metarhyolite 8
Metasandstone 7
Mica 7
Mudstone 7
Muscovite mica 8
Phyllite 7, 8
Quartz 7, 8
Rhyolite 7
Sandstone 7
Schist 7
Sedimentary 7
Shale 7
Siltstone 7
Rocky Outcrop 55, **66**, 168, 171, 180
Rogers Ridge Scenic Area 182
Rosa
    multiflora **99**, 116
    palustris 61
Rosaceae 113
Rose
    Multiflora **99**, 116
    Swamp 61, 62
Rosy Twisted Stalk 26, 27, **74**
Rough Ridge 53, 164, 165
Round Bald 110, 174
Rubus 16, 47
    allegheniensis 111
    argutus 116
    canadensis 50
    flagellaris 116
    hispidus 116
    occidentalis 116
    odoratus **84**, **100**, 116
Rudbeckia laciniata 31, **95**

Rue
  Mountain Meadow 28, 51, **78**, 173
  Tassel 34, 109
Rushes 62

S

Sagittaria latifolia 63
Salamander 150
  Blackbelly **105**, 151
  Blue Ridge Dusky **104**, 152
  Blue Ridge Two-lined **105**, 154
  Jordan's **106**, 151, 152
  Mole 155
  Northern Dusky **105**, 152
  Pigmy **105**, 153, 154
  Ravine 153
  Red **107**, 154
  Redback **106**, 151, 153
  Seal **104**, 151, 152
  Shovel-nosed 151
  Slimy **106**, 151, 153
  Spotted **104**, 155, 177
  Spring **105**, 154
  Weller's **106**, 151, 153, 166, 168
  Yonahlossee **106**, 153
Salix sericea 61
Salmo trutta 158
Salmonidae 158
Salvelinus fontinalis 158
Sambucus 16
  canadensis **93**, 116
  pubens 50, 54, **94**, **101**, 116
  racemosa 50, 54, 116
Sandpiper
  Solitary 131
  Spotted 131, 181
Sandstone 7, 8
Sanguinaria canadensis 17, **81**
Sapsucker, Yellow-bellied 127
Sarsaparilla, Wild 17, 163
Sassafras 18, 43, 53, **81**, 165, 169
Sassafras albidum 18, 43, 53, **81**
Saxifraga michauxii 51, 57, **82**

Saxifrage
  Brook 28
  Michaux's 51, 57, 58, **82**, 173
Sayornis phoebe 131
Scalopus aquaticus 139
Scatterhoard 37
Scaup, Lesser 132
Sceloporus undulatus 149
Schist 7, 8
Scincella lateralis 149
Scirpus 62
Sciurus carolinensis 134
Scolopax minor 125
Sculpin
  Banded 161
  Mottled 161
Scutellaria integrifolia 113
Seasonality 14
Sedge, Fraser's 35, **72**
Sedimentary rocks 7
Sedum
  telephioides 58, **82**
  ternatum 27, **82**
Seiurus
  aurocapillus 124
  motacilla 131
  noveboracensis 133
Selaginella tortipila 56
Semotilus atromaculatus 159
Senecio
  anonymus **96**, 112
  aureus 62, 109, 112
  schweinitzianus 109
  smallii 112
Serviceberry 16, 17, 47, 53, 56, 58,
    61, **83**, **99**, 164, 165, 171
Setophaga ruticilla 126
Shale 7
Shiner
  New River 159, 160
  Silver 159, 160
  Tennessee 159, 160
  Warpaint 159
  Whitetail 159
Ship Rock 22, 53, 56, 59, 129, 131,

164, 165
Shortoff Mountain 170
Shrew 138
  Northern Short-tailed 139
  Pygmy 139
Sialia sialis 122
Silene virginica 39, **78**
Siltstone 7
Silverrod 117
Siskin, Pine 133
Sitta
  canadensis 128
  carolinensis 128
Sitting Bear Mountain 170
Skink
  Five-lined 149
  Ground 149
  Southeastern five-lined 149
Skullcap, Hyssop 113
Skunk
  Eastern Spotted 140
  Striped 140
Slate 7
Slope effect 13
Smilacina racemosa 38, 47, **74, 98**
Smilax 47
Smoky Mountains 48
Snake 145
  Black Rat 146
  Eastern Garter 145
  Eastern Milk 147
  Eastern Ribbon 146
  Northern Water 145, 146, 147, 151
  Queen 146
  Redbelly 147
  Ringneck 146
  Worm 146
Snake Mountain 9, **65**
Snakeroot
  Black 28, 34, **79**, 167
  White 16, 32, 47, **95**, 118
Sneezeweed **96**, 118
Snow 12
Solanaceae 113
Solanum carolinense **91, 101**, 113

Solidago
  altissima 117
  bicolor 117
  canadensis 117
  curtisii 16, **96**, 117
  erecta 117
  flexicaulis 117
  gigantea 117
  glomerata 51
  nemoralis 117
  patula 62, 117
  roanensis 117
  rugosa 117
  ulmifolia 117
Solomon's Seal 27, 38, **74, 98**, 166
Solomon's Seal, False 17, 27, 47, **74,**
    98, 166, 171
Sonchus oleraceus 113
Songbirds 120
Sorbus americana 50, 53, 58, **100**
Sorex hoyi 139
Sorrel, Wood 34, 51, **84**
Sourwood 18, 43, 56, 169, 171
Southern Appalachian Fen 63
Southern Appalachian Highlands
    Conservancy 172, 175, 176
Sparganium americanum 63
Sparrow
  Chipping 122
  Field 122
  Savannah 133
  Song 122, 131, 132, 133, 176, 181
  Swamp 133
  Vesper 123
  White-throated 122
Sphagnum 61
Sphyrapicus nuchalis 127
Spiderwort 41, **72**
Spikemoss 164, 169
  Twisted-Hair 56, 57, 58
Spikenard 38, **86**
Spilogale putorius 140
Spiraea 62
  alba 61
  tomentosa 61

Spiranthes cernua **77**, 119
Spizella
  passerina 122
  pusilla 122
Spleenwort 178
  Ebony 178
  Maidenhair 55, **102**
  Mountain 55, **102**
Spring Beauty 17, 26, 34, 50, **78**, 175
  Carolina **78**
Spring Peeper **107**, 157
Spruce, Red 33, 49, 53, 54, 57, 61,
    164, 165, 168, 173
Spruce-Fir Forest 3, 48, **66**, **69**, 153,
    167, 168, 172, 173, 174
Squawroot 37, **92**, 163
Squirrel
  Grey 134, 170
  Northern Flying 135, 166
  Red 133, 134, 170
  Southern Flying 135
Squirrel Corn **81**, 167
St. John's-wort
  Blue Ridge 51
  Dense-flowered 57, 171
Starling, European 123
Stelgidopteryx serripennis 121
Stellaria pubera **78**
Stonecrop,
  Allegheny 58, **82**
  Wild 27
Stoneroller, Central 159
Storeria occipitomaculata 147
Strawberry, Wild 16, **83**, 109, 113,
    174, 175
Streptopus roseus 26, **74**
Strix varia 129
Sturnella magna 122
Sturnus vulgaris 123
Succession 2
Sucker, White 160
Sunfish, Redbreast 162
Sunflower
  Tall **96**, 118
  Thin-leaved 118

Swallow
  Barn 121, 123
  Northern Rough-winged 121
  Tree 121, 122, 176, 181
Sweet Cicely 27, **87**, 171
Sweet Shrub **80**
Sweetleaf 43, **90**
Swift, Chimney 122
Sycamore 33, 171, 176
Sylvilagus
  floridanus 140
  obscurus 140
  transitionalis 140
Symplocos tinctoria 43, **90**

T

Table Rock 8, 10, 44, 57, 59, 129,
    170, 171
Table Rock Trail 27
Tachycineta bicolor 121
Tamias striatus 134
Tamiasciurus hudsonicus 134
Tanager, Scarlet 127
Tanawha Trail 22, 56, 164, 167
Tantilla coronata 149
Tater Hill 179
Teal, Blue-winged 132
Tennessee 4, 182
Terrapene carolina 148
Tetraopes tetraophthalmus **108**, 115
Thalictrum clavatum 51, **78**
Thamnophis
  sauritus 146
  sirtalis 145
Thistle
  Bull **95**, 114
  Common Sow 113
Thrasher, Brown 123
Three-Top Mountain 9, 179, 180
Thrush
  Gray-cheeked 133
  Hermit 130, 133, 168
  Swainson's 133
  Wood 128

Thryothorus ludovicianus 123
Tiarella cordifolia 28, **82**
Tiger Moth, Milkweed **108**, 115
Tilia americana 23
Timber Ridge 45
Tipularia discolor 29, **76**
Titmouse, Tufted 129, 133
Toad, American **107**, 156, 177
Toadskin, Common 58
Tobacco, Indian 119
Toe River 173
Toecane Ranger District 173
Toothwort, Cutleaf 27, **82**
Towhee
   Eastern 47, 123, 124, 130, 131, 133
Toxicodendron radicans 40, 115
Toxostoma rufum 123
Tradescantia subaspera 41, **72**
Trailing Arbutus 171
Transients 121, 132
Trautvetteria carolinensis 110
Treefrog, Gray 157
Trillium 17
   erectum 26, **75**
   grandiflorum 27, **75**
   undulatum 26, **75**
Trillium
   Large-flowered 27, **75**
   Painted 26, **75**, 167
Tringa solitaria 131
Troglodytes
   aedon 122
   troglodytes 130
Trout
   Brook 158, 169
   Brown 158
   Rainbow 158
Trout Lake 166
Tsuga
   canadensis 19, 24, 43, 61, **101**
   caroliniana 43, 56, **101**
Tuliptree 16, 37, 47, **80**, 164, 166, 179
Turdus migratorius 122
Turkey Beard 44, 53, 57, **72**

Turkey, Wild 122
Turtle 148
   Bog 62, 148
   Eastern Box 148
   Snapping 148
Turtlehead
   Pink 28, 32, 51, **91**, 173
   White 32
Twayblade
   Appalachian 29
   Kidney-leaved 165
Typha latifolia 62
Tyrannus tyrannus 122

U

Umbilicaria
   caroliniana 58
   mammulata 55, **103**
Umbrella-Leaf 29, **80**, **99**, 167
Unaka Mountain Wilderness 182
Unaka Mountains 3, 5, 173
Unaka Ranger District 173
Urocyon cinereoargenteus 141
Ursus americanus 141
Uvularia
   grandiflora 26, **73**
   puberula 39, **73**

V

Vaccinium
   constablaei 44, 50, 52, 110
   corymbosum 44
   erythrocarpum 50
   macrocarpon 61, **100**
   pallidum 44
   stamineum 44, **89**
Valle Crucis Park 122, 176
Valley breeze 13
Veery 130, 131, 173
Veratrum
   parviflorum 34
   viride 34

Verbascum thapsus **92**, 114
Vermivora
   chrysoptera 123, 133
   peregrina 133
Vernonia noveboracensis **95**, 118
Viburnum
   acerifolium 38, **93**, **101**
   alnifolium 16, 50
   cassinoides 17, 61
   lantanoides 16, 50, **93**, **101**
   nudum 17, **93**
Viburnum, Maple-leaf 17, 38, **93**, **101**
Viola
   blanda 26
   canadensis 26, **86**
   hastata 26, **86**
   papilionacea 26
   rotundifolia 26, **86**
   sororia **86**
Violet 17, 26
   Canada 26, **86**
   Common Blue 26, **86**
   Halbard-leaf 26, **86**
   Round-leaved 26, **86**
   Sweet White 26
Vireo
   olivaceus 126
   philadelphicus 133
   solitarius 126
Vireo
   Blue-headed 126, 130, 173
   Philadelphia 133
   Red-eyed 126
   Solitary 126
   Warbling 181
Virgin's Bower **79**, **99**, 115
Vitis
   aestivalis 40
   labrusca 47
Vole
   Meadow 136
   Southern Red-backed 136
Vulpes vulpes 141
Vulture, Turkey 121

W

Wake Robin 26, 38, **75**, 166
Warbler 120
   Bay-breasted 133
   Black and White 128
   Black-throated Blue 125
   Black-throated Green 126, 167
   Blackburnian 126, 167
   Blackpoll 133
   Canada 125, 130, 131, 167
   Cape May 133
   Chestnut-sided 47, 123, 131
   Golden-winged 123, 133
   Hooded 125
   Magnolia 130, 133, 168
   Northern Parula 126
   Palm 133
   Prairie 133
   Swainson's 126
   Worm-eating 125, 126
   Yellow 123, 176
   Yellow-rumped 133
Watauga County 3, **68**
Watauga River 3, 176
Waterleaf 28, **90**
   Broad-leaved 28, 170
Waterthrush
   Louisiana 131
   Northern 133
Waxwing, Cedar 124, 131
Weasel
   Least 142
   Long-tailed 142, 170
Weather 11, 13
Webworm, Fall 47
Weevils, Black Oak Acorn 37
Weller, Worthington 153
Whip-poor-will 122
Whistle Pig 135
Whitetop Mountain 48
Wildcat Lake 132
Willow, Silky 61, 62
Wilson Creek 3, 22, 28, 41, **68**, 164,
   165, 168

Wilson Creek Area 168
Wilson Creek Gorge 149, 169
Wilsonia
  canadenis 125
  citrina 125
Wind 12
Winter Residents 121
Winterberry 61, 62
Wintergreen 44, 53, **89**, 165, 171
  Spotted 39, **87**, **102**
Wiseman's View 129, 170, 171
Witch Hazel 38, **83**, 164, 169
Witch's Hair 29
Wolf, Gray 142
Wood-Pewee, Eastern 127
Woodchuck 135
Woodcock, American 125
Woodfern
  Evergreen 30
  Fancy 30
  Mountain 51
Woodpecker
  Downy 127
  Hairy 127
  Pileated 127
  Red-bellied 127
Woodrat, Allegheny 136
Wren
  Carolina 123, 176
  House 122
  Winter 130, 173, 177

X

Xanthoriza simplicissima **79**
Xerophyllum asphodeloides 44, 53,
  57, **72**

Y

Yadkin River 3
Yancey County 9
Yarrow **97**, 114
Yellow Birch Forest **65**
Yellow Mountain 22, **65**, 109, 111
Yellow Mountain Gap 174

Yellow Poplar 23
Yellowroot 28, **79**, 170, 171
Yellowthroat, Common 123, 132, 176
Yonahlossee Road 153

Z

Zenaida macroura 123
Zizia
  aptera 27, **86**
  aurea 27
Zonotrichia albicollis 122